Carving Out the Commons

DIVERSE ECONOMIES AND LIVABLE WORLDS

Series Editors: J. K. Gibson-Graham, Maliha Safri, Kevin St. Martin, Stephen Healy

Carving Out the Commons: Tenant Organizing and Housing Cooperatives in Washington, D.C.
Amanda Huron

Building Dignified Worlds: Geographies of Collective Action
Gerda Roelvink

Carving Out the Commons

Tenant Organizing and Housing Cooperatives
in Washington, D.C.

Amanda Huron

DIVERSE ECONOMIES AND LIVABLE WORLDS

University of Minnesota Press
Minneapolis
London

Published by the University of Minnesota Press
111 Third Avenue South, Suite 290
Minneapolis, MN 55401–2520
http://www.upress.umn.edu

ISBN 978-1-5179-0196-7 (hc)
ISBN 978-1-5179-0197-4 (pb)

A Cataloging-in-Publication record for this book is available from the Library of Congress.

Printed on acid-free paper

The University of Minnesota is an equal-opportunity educator and employer.

Contents

Introduction

"We Shall Not Be Moved!"

It is Christmas Eve, 1977, and the mail carrier is making his rounds through a working-class apartment complex in Washington, D.C. He can't help but notice, after a while, that he's delivering the exact same letter to every tenant. And he becomes curious, even concerned, about the letter's contents. Soon he runs into Sherry, a single mother living with her twin eight-month-old babies in a one-bedroom apartment in the complex. He asks Sherry what's inside the envelope. As Sherry recounts, years later,

> So I said, well I'll open one. And I did, and I started crying.
> And he read it, and *he* started crying, because he had to deliver
> them all!

The letters were eviction notices: the tenants were being informed that they had to be out of their homes in ninety days. Their entire eight-building complex, home to nearly a hundred people, was being evicted to make way for a developer who planned to raze the modest three-story structures and build tall luxury apartment buildings in their place. Sherry was shocked: she didn't know what to do. She wanted to stay in the neighborhood, Glover Park, which was relatively safe and convenient. She had left her old neighborhood after her apartment had been broken into one too many times. Desperate, she tacked flyers to the trees on her block, offering a $50 reward to anyone who could help her find an affordable apartment nearby.

The problem facing Sherry and her fellow tenants was part of a larger trend. In the mid-1970s, Washington, D.C., and a handful of other U.S. cities were hit with a newly recognized phenomenon: gentrification. Middle-class residents and investment dollars were returning to certain centrally located, historic neighborhoods in cities like D.C., San Francisco, and Boston. With gentrification came the displacement of lower-income residents who could no longer afford the rising rents—or who were being evicted wholesale to make room for new development (Clay 1979; Hartman et al. 1982; Henig 1984; Zeitz 1979). In the mid-1970s, stories of displacement in D.C. filled the news. The *New York Times* told the story of a developer who bought up a string of thirteen row houses on a single block in Washington's Adams Morgan neighborhood, evicting all twenty-six black families who lived there. In 1978, the *Washington Post* reported, evictions in the city jumped nearly five times over the previous year (Gately 1978c; Reinhold 1977). Eviction was everywhere and people were scared.

But unbeknownst to Sherry, her neighbors had already started organizing. Ruth was another young woman who lived in the complex. When she received the eviction notice, she recalls feeling "devastated." At first, she said,

> I didn't know what to do. But then I talked to somebody, who suggested I try to organize a meeting. So I did, in my apartment, and a lot of people came. And while we were in the meeting, there was a knock on the door. And it was a server, who was hand delivering the same [eviction] notice. But this time, we were all together. [She pauses.] It was very interesting. That was the moment where we began to intuit that we were going to have to do this together.

For nearly two years, the tenants worked together—first, to stop the evictions, and then, to buy the apartment complex collectively themselves. In buying the complex, they had few models to imitate and were mostly making it up as they went along. They knew they wanted control over their own homes, and they wanted to remain in place. But they were disturbed by the thought of owning the buildings as condominiums, the very ownership form they saw devouring low-income homes all over the city. So when they finally purchased the buildings in 1979, they decided to use the limited-equity co-operative ownership structure. Under the limited-equity co-op model, members paid low amounts for a co-op share and paid low monthly co-op fees. If they ever moved out, they could sell their share for the same amount for which they bought it, plus a small amount of interest, in order to keep the unit affordable for the next low- or moderate-income person. In addition, they set aside about 20 percent of their units for people using federal housing vouchers to pay their co-op fees. "We incorporated," Sherry said later, "to preserve affordable housing in Glover Park. That was kind of our mission. Other than our co-op, I don't know of any affordable housing in Glover Park, and maybe not even in [our part of the city]." Just as important as the affordability, Ruth emphasizes, was the fact that co-op members had control over their space and could collectively determine how to run it.

What these tenants were doing in late 1970s Washington was creating a commons. They were taking a resource—housing—that had been used to extract profit for their landlord, and they were reshaping it as a resource that was collectively owned and controlled by the people who lived in it. The purpose of the apartment complex was no longer to serve as an investment vehicle for its owner but rather to house people who needed an affordable, stable place to live. And the tenants were doing this in a capitalist city beset with struggles over land and housing, a place filled with strangers, where tenants often did not know one another well and had little prior basis for collective action. They were practicing the urban commons.

Theorizing the Commons

My purpose in this book is to theorize the practice of the urban commons. Commons have been studied all over the world, but until recently, little has been done to theorize the urban commons—which is materially and theoretically distinct from other forms of the commons conceived more broadly. Very little, too, has been done to examine how people who participate in commons themselves understand the commons. As Bruun (2015) notes, much of the extant commons research theorizes the institutions people build for commoning without including the analysis of those people themselves. My goal here is to develop a theory of the urban commons based on the experience and analysis of people who are direct and daily participants in the urban commons.

The commons can be best understood as made up of three components: a resource, a community of people who rely on that resource, and a set of institutions devised by that community for regulating that resource (Kip et al. 2015). Critically, a commons works to directly support life—that is, a commons is grounds for the daily life of subsistence, not a vehicle for making a profit. Just as critically, a commons is managed (and, in many cases, owned, though, as we will see later, ownership can have several meanings) by the community that uses it. While a commons has often been imagined as a seemingly inert natural resource—for instance, a meadow in which livestock graze—it is better understood as a resource intertwined with social practice, a practice Linebaugh (2008) calls "commoning."

Over several decades of research, two lines of scholarship have developed that take the commons seriously as a way to collectively self-regulate the resources needed to live. The first approach is made up of scholars who are known broadly as institutionalists. The institutionalists generally come from the perspective of political science and economics, and focus on the commons as a workable property regime. They are interested, as their name implies, in how different kinds of institutions operate. Concerned with what they variably call "common property resources" and "common pool resources," institutionalist researchers have in thousands of studies documented cases of contemporary functioning commons around the world. The cases they study range from mountain meadow tenure systems in Switzerland to irrigation collectives in the Philippines (Ostrom 1990). Mainstream recognition of the importance of theorizing the commons as workable self-managed property regimes arrived in 2009, when political scientist Elinor Ostrom, the single most important intellectual figure in the common pool resources field, received the Nobel Prize in Economics for her work (Uchitelle 2009).

The second stream of commons thought is less concerned with the empirical details of commons management in particular locales, and is more concerned with what the commons means politically on a larger scale. This stream of thought, which is deeply enmeshed with global anticapitalist movements, is associated with the rallying cry, *reclaim the commons*. These scholars and activists can be referred to as the alterglobalizationists.[1] The commons, for this group, is constituted by a vast mesh of resources and goods that, it is argued, are collectively produced and should therefore be freely available to all who participate in society—and not just to those with the wealth to buy them (N. Klein 2001; Starhawk 2004). Alterglobalizationists are particularly concerned with the question of the enclosure of the commons—that is, with the privatization of lands and resources that had previously served to sustain the lives of poor communities.

The institutionalists and the alterglobalizationists share a belief in the ability of people to collectively self-manage the resources they need to survive. But for the most part, these two perspectives treat two different aspects of the commons—and have a different politics. The institutionalists want to understand how commons and common property resources are maintained over time: they tend to focus at the scale of the case study, doing richly empirical work, without looking critically at larger structures of power within which these cases are embedded. The alterglobalizationists are more concerned with the need to seize or reclaim commons and to protect existing commons from enclosure. They are concerned with larger-scale, systemic questions, and make an explicit critique of capitalism, but they tend not to examine the nitty-gritty details of everyday commoning. Little research brings together these two approaches. One of the goals of this book is to examine how a commons is both reclaimed *and* maintained over time, using the empirical approach of the institutionalists and the political perspective of the alterglobalizationists. I devote chapter 1 to an in-depth examination of these two perspectives on the commons, and how they can be brought together, using the theoretical framework of diverse economies—a framework that recognizes the wide array of economic practices and possibilities that exist within the seemingly monolithic capitalist world.

Examining the Urban

Until recently, most research into the commons has ignored the urban. The few works that reference both the institutionalist and the alterglobalizationist approaches to the commons tend to be ecological in focus, looking at natural resources and questions of sustainability (see for example Wall 2014a). Most commons documented in the world today are rural. Scholars estimate that about one third of the world's population—living almost entirely in the global South—depend directly on natural resources for subsistence. A large chunk of the world's population is made up of people who must work together to manage their resources for survival (Ricoveri 2013). But commoning also happens in the urban context, and as the urban experience increasingly defines life for millions of people, it is critical that the urban commons be recognized and theorized. Though urban space has been included in the definition of the "new" commons (Hess 2000), little work has been done to theorize a specifically urban commons. A number of researchers have written about commons that exist in cities (see for example Alonso 2015; Clapp and Meyer 2000; Kassa 2008; Mandizadza 2008). While this work provides good case studies of commons in cities in particular places, it does not theorize the urban commons more broadly, or ask why the term "urban commons" might be useful theoretically. The recent research that does push forward the theorization of the urban commons I present in chapter 2.

There are at least three points that make the urban commons theoretically and materially distinct from the commons theorized more broadly. First, cities are made up of a relatively densely populated diversity of people: they are made up of strangers. Because cities are densely populated and co-created by a diversity of people, they are necessarily sites of conflict (Sennett 1970). In a city, different ideas of the commons—ideas about who should manage which commons, and how—come into conflict. Commons, Harvey insists in his 2012 piece on the urban commons, are always contested. A theory of the urban commons would need to account for the fact that commoners in cities do not necessarily share the same cultural background and worldview, as they so often do in more rural parts of the world. Second, cities have developed historically as sites of capital accumulation. At its core, the city is the physical manifestation of a collectively generated surplus; cities came into being as places to store a society's wealth (Childe 1950; Harvey 2008). A theory of the urban commons, then, would have to take into account the particular role the city plays in producing and storing surplus. Third, the city has also been theorized as a site of state regulation and control (Scott 1998). The state often works in partnership with the owners of capital to create what Hackworth (2007) refers to as the "neoliberal city." Many theorists of the commons are critical of what they see as the heavy-handedness of the state, and see the commons as separate from the state. But a theory of the urban commons would need to reckon directly with the relationship between the commons and the state.

I should also note here that this book focuses not just on the urban context but the urban context of what is known as the "developed" Western world. This focus is intentional. Much of the research on the urban commons examines experiences in so-called less-developed countries, for example subsistence food cultivation in Accra, Ghana (Federici 2011), or commoning practices around lakes in Bangalore, India (Sundaresan 2011). As I discuss in chapter 1, commoning has tended to be seen as a precapitalist practice, something that happened before the onset of capitalism and that may continue to happen in places that are—rightly or wrongly—seen as still not fully integrated into the global capitalist economy. The commons, according to this view, is not something that could exist in the "developed" world. But I want to draw attention to the ways commoning happens even in places like the contemporary "Western" city as a way of underscoring that commoning can and does happen even in places that are seen as being completely enmeshed in capitalism.

It is important to note up front that the "urban commons" is not a perfectly clear-cut category. I want to push thinking in the direction of the urban commons, but I am not arguing that the urban is a completely new way of understanding the commons. Rather, the urban provides a prism through which to see the commons in a new light. Theorizing the specific qualities of the urban commons, I think, can help highlight some of the contradictions that bedevil the commons more broadly. In chapter 2, I develop these ideas more fully, theorizing the urban commons and its contradictions.

Limited-equity Cooperatives as an Urban Commons

Limited-equity housing cooperatives, which are the focus of this book, represent one form of the urban commons. A limited-equity co-op works as follows: people buy into the co-op—that is, purchase shares in the co-op—for low amounts. They make relatively low monthly payments, usually called carrying charges or co-op fees, over the course of the time they live there. If they move out, they get back their initial payment for their share, plus a small amount of money determined by a formula, sometimes tied to the rise in the Consumer Price Index. In addition, co-op members can usually will their shares to their heirs. In order to be considered for co-op membership, applicants typically must earn below a certain income. Limited-equity co-ops, or LECs, are part of a larger universe of housing, known as "resale-restricted housing," in which resale prices are kept low in order to preserve the affordability of the housing over the long term, for multiple generations of owners. The ownership structure removes the housing from the speculative real estate market: it is not a financial investment for making profit. And it is collective, democratic ownership: co-ops are run by boards elected by their membership (DeFilippis 2004; Saegert and Benitez 2005; Sazama 2000). While most LECs in Washington, D.C., hire outside management companies, the work of running the co-op is, for members, still a considerable investment of time. Washington has quite a number of limited-equity cooperatives, a result of the work of progressive political leaders, tenant organizers, lawyers, mission-driven developers and, above all, the work of tenants-turned-co-op-members themselves. As of 2012, I estimated that the city had slightly over 3,100 units of limited-equity cooperative housing, representing about 1 percent of the city's total housing stock.[2] Ruth, Sherry, and other tenants from the apartment complex I describe at the outset of this chapter were an important part of this organizing work. I tell the history of this organizing, and describe how the commons constituted by LECs was able to emerge in D.C., in chapter 3.

I follow Balmer and Bernet (2015) in defining limited-equity cooperatives as a commons because this form of housing fits the two main traits of the commons: collective self-organization and decommodification. First, LECs are collectively owned and managed by their members. LECs share the trait of collective self-organization with many other housing forms, like market-rate cooperatives and condominiums, homeowners associations, and gated communities, all of which have also been theorized as commons (Nelson 2005). But to conceive of the latter forms of housing as a commons is incorrect, because these are all commodified housing forms, designed to maximize profit for developers and owners. The second trait in defining the commons is that they are valued by their members for their everyday use rather than their potential exchange value on the market. A limited-equity co-op, unlike other forms of collective homeownership and management, is structured to remove the profit motive from housing. The value of the housing is in its daily use, not in its potential market exchange; it has been decommodified. LECs are never fully decommodifed—shares are still bought and sold—but the share prices in the D.C. case are so extremely low, compared to market prices, that it is safe to say they are virtually decommodified. More about how these co-ops work is detailed in chapter 3.

Limited-equity cooperatives also fit my definition of the *urban* commons. One, they are commons that exist in an environment of relatively intense pressures on land, manifested by the fact that they normally take the physical form of apartment buildings, a form designed to maximize efficiency of space usage. The greater pressure on land values in cities vis-à-vis nonurban areas translates into greater pressure on commons that exist in cities than those in rural areas. Two, LECs are commons that tend to be populated with members who do not necessarily have anything in common other than the fact that they all used to be renters in the same apartment building. Though they may share similar income levels, they do not enter the commons with a particular shared background or politics.

These are unintentional communities, and therefore may be more difficult to enact than a commons in a more rural area in which people presumably have more in common. Importantly, an LEC serves as a commons for its current members, but it also serves as an affordable housing stock for future, as-yet-unknown members. While in some LECs new members gain access to the housing through family and community ties, LEC membership is open to a wide array of strangers. Being open to incorporating strangers as members is part of the heterogeneity of the urban commons. Three, LECs must negotiate the requirements of the state, and in the urban context, the state may lay more heavily on the land and its people. Because LECs exist within a context of relatively intense land pressures, heterogeneity of membership, and relatively heavy state regulation, they form a distinctly urban commons.

A limited-equity housing cooperative represents just the sort of noncapitalist economic practice that feminist geographer Gibson-Graham (2006) theorizes. It is housing created to directly fulfill the need of its residents, and it is purchased and developed collectively. An LEC represents one of a myriad of diverse economic practices that thread through the capitalist city. As I discuss in detail in chapter 4, limited-equity co-ops provide their members with tangible benefits that ease the difficulty of living in a highly commodified city. Yet these co-ops still exist within the larger landscape of capitalist housing markets: for example, they must deal with profit-driven entities like banks. It is exciting to find diverse economic practices, like co-ops, that challenge capitalist ways of being. But—precisely because of capitalist pressures—it can be very hard for noncapitalist practices like these co-ops to get started and to survive over the long haul. Here is a real tension at the core of the diverse economies approach: it can be extremely difficult to operate noncapitalist enterprises in the midst of capitalism. Even as the purpose of the commons is to evade and even challenge capitalism, it must be made to work in the here and now, in the midst of capitalism. This is the challenge of the commons in the contemporary capitalist world, and this challenge is heightened in the contemporary capitalist city. In chapter 5, I address the challenges of maintaining an urban commons over time—and what happens when the commons collapses. Throughout chapters 3, 4, and 5, I link the particular qualities of the urban commons to the challenges—and necessity—of reclaiming and maintaining commons in cities.

Researching the Urban Commons

This book began as a research project into how members of D.C.'s limited-equity cooperatives understood their unusual form of ownership. I first became aware of D.C.'s rich history of limited-equity cooperatives in 2004, when I was working for an organization that advocated for affordable housing in D.C. At the time, the nonprofit community was divided on the degree to which affordable, publicly-subsidized forms of homeownership, like limited-equity co-ops, should be subject to resale restrictions. Some argued that such housing needed resale restrictions so that the housing would remain affordable to the next generation of buyers. Others argued that a critical function of homeownership was wealth building, and that to deny low-income homeowners the chance to build wealth through restricting the resale value of their housing was to keep them impoverished. Throughout these debates, I was struck by the fact that no one seemed to be asking the low-income homeowners themselves what they thought. I wanted to hear their analysis of their particular form of ownership. Did they think it was worth it? Why was the housing important to them, even if they couldn't sell it at market rate? Why did they choose to live in this unusual form of housing? When I began a doctoral program a few years later, these questions stayed with me. I designed a research project to get at the question of how limited-equity co-op members understood their ownership. It was only after I began talking to people, and hearing about their experiences, that I realized these co-ops formed a kind of commons. But it was not a typical commons, of the kinds I'd read about in historical England or the mountain meadows of Switzerland or the rural Philippines. It seemed to be something different: an urban commons.

I use a set of case studies as a lens for examining the experience of limited-equity co-ops in Washington, D.C., in order to theorize the urban commons more broadly. The case study method involves intensive focus on a small number of cases, and it is particularly good for understanding complex processes that a larger-scale study might miss. The case study has been the principal method used by institutionalists in their study of natural resources commons. Prominent institutionalists explain why the case study has been an important method in their research:

> Case study research has . . . been a significant source of contributions related to collective action for the management of common-

pool resources. By challenging the conventional wisdom related to property rights and possibilities for collective action, case studies reset the terms of the debate. Case studies contribute to theory building by directing attention to the complexity of relationships between social and ecological systems, and by facilitating efforts to disentangle these relationships. (Poteete, Janssen, and Ostrom 2010, 45)

While the case study method has its critics—what can an in-depth look at a small scale tell you about larger systems?—a researcher may, through examining how things actually work in everyday life, discover truths that disrupt established understandings of the way the world operates. For the institutionalists, performing detailed case studies of how people manage natural resources has allowed them to see that resources can be regulated by people without the institutions of private, individual, or state property. "Case studies left little doubt," Poteete, Janssen, and Ostrom continue, "that, contrary to theoretical expectations, collective action on the commons *is* possible and *not* merely a vestigial form" (2010, 46, emphasis in the original). The commons, they argue, is not a historic relic: they document its existence in the here and now. The case study approach seemed like a good way to study a contemporary urban commons.

In my research, I focused on ten cases of current and former limited-equity cooperatives in Washington, D.C., I selected a sample to encompass a diversity of co-op size, years in existence, demographics, and location in the city. Seven of the projects were ongoing LECs at the time of my research; one had converted to a market-rate condominium ownership structure in the early 2000s; one had converted to a market-rate cooperative structure in the 1990s; and one sat empty and boarded-up after having briefly converted to a market-rate condominium in the early 2000s. The projects ranged in size from four to ninety units. They were located in six of the city's eight wards. They were founded between the years of 1979 and 2004. They represented a range of demographics: a few were virtually entirely African American; several had high concentrations of immigrants from the Caribbean, Central America, and Africa; two had significant white populations. Some were mostly low-income and working-class, while others were home to moderate-income people as well, and one had significant numbers of middle-class residents. I reached out to four of the co-ops through my personal connections with co-op members that I had made through my previous professional work with limited-equity co-ops; I reached out to five more through recommendations made by a lawyer, a developer, and an organizer who had helped many LECs form. The tenth project was one where I lived for several years.

My primary methods were archival research, direct and participant observation, and in-depth interviews. Though I conducted a fair amount of archival work in historic databases of local newspapers, the principal source of my archival work was the Washington Innercity Self Help (W.I.S.H.) Archives, housed in the Washingtoniana Division of the Martin Luther King Jr. Memorial Library, the central public library for Washington, D.C. The W.I.S.H. organization had helped a number of D.C.'s limited-equity co-ops form throughout the 1980s and 1990s, and staff had kept meticulous records of their work (Huron 2016).[3] I learned critical historical information in this archives. I was also able to make direct observations of all of the co-ops I studied: I met with co-op members in co-op offices and in their units; I attended membership meetings in co-op community rooms; and members led me on tours of co-op buildings and grounds. I engaged in participant observation in the co-op in which I had lived, including a stint serving on the board. (I should note, however, that I have been careful not to over-represent my particularly in-depth experiences in this co-op in the research.) My interviews, however, made up the bulk of what I learned. I conducted fifty in-depth interviews: ten with professionals who helped found co-ops and forty with co-op members, including co-op leaders (defined as board presidents and tenants who had helped lead the original purchase of the building) and less involved members, averaging four members per co-op. I am immensely grateful to the many people who took time to speak with me, and to share their experiences and their analysis. The words of twenty-eight of these forty co-op members have made it into this book. Names of all interviewees, along with names of all ten housing cooperatives in my sample, have been changed to protect confidentiality. In addition to the ten co-ops I studied in-depth, I have also at times included reference to the experiences of a number of other D.C. LECs that were not included in my confidential sample; the names of these co-ops are usually revealed in the footnoted archival sources.

In surveying the institutionalist research on the commons, McCay and Jentoft conclude that descriptions of commons management regimes are often either too thin or oversimplified. Thin description does not provide enough information about how a commons is actually self-regulated.

Oversimplification may result in the commons being romanticized; a good narrative takes the place of more rigorous analysis. "Good story lines," they write, "are easily applied to many situations with the risk of misrepresenting the more complex and shifting social, cultural, and ecological relationships and processes at stake" (1998, 23). They call for using "thick description" in studying the commons: description that is rich, nuanced, and engages the complexity of the social and material relations at hand. Thick description was what I was after. And every time I found myself beginning to be romanced by a good story line of the commons, I'd run up against a contradiction that would burst my bubble and make me think harder.

Struggling for the Urban Commons

The political approach of the alterglobalizationists has been just as important to my methodology as the case study methods of the institutionalists. The commons are always contested, always a site of struggle; the alterglobalizationists' focus on capitalism is critical to understanding how commons can form, and how they collapse. In my research, I have worked to ground the cases of these co-ops in the larger historical context of Washington, D.C., to directly address the tensions between the commons and capitalism, and to theorize what these commons mean for a larger political project of creating new, more just worlds. Though this book focuses on limited-equity cooperatives in Washington, D.C., it is not just about these particular cases in this particular place. The book is, empirically, an in-depth look at a single set of experiences in a single city. Theoretically, though, the book operates at a larger scale. The larger questions my research raises—Why is an urban commons necessary? What are the particular challenges of reclaiming and maintaining the urban commons? How can a practice of the urban commons be sustained and expanded?—are questions that, I hope, will be of interest to scholars and activists theorizing and practicing the urban commons in a wide range of practices—housing, food production, work, education, leisure, and more—in places around the world. I want people to use this book to understand the commoning all around them, and I hope this book prompts people to ask new questions about how that commoning takes place.

Researchers don't just describe what is happening in the world; we can also help call new worlds into being, through naming what we see happening around us, and placing it in a larger context. Gibson-Graham discusses the role of the diverse economies researcher not just in terms of scholar-activism, but in terms of helping create new worlds through how we make meaning. "This vision of the performativity of knowledge," she argues,

> its implication in what it purports to describe, its productive power of "making," has placed new responsibility on the shoulders of scholars—to recognize their constitutive role in the worlds that exist, and their power to bring new worlds into being. Not single-handedly, of course, but alongside other world-makers, both inside and outside the academy. (Gibson-Graham 2008, 614)

I take this to mean that, as a researcher who is committed to not just studying diverse economic practices, but helping them come into being, what is critical is changing ideas about how these co-ops—these economic practices—are understood, and to show their importance in the city. Gibson-Graham again:

> [W]e confront a choice: to continue to marginalize (by ignoring or disparaging) the plethora of hidden and alternative economic activities that contribute to social well-being and environmental regeneration, or to make them the focus of our research and teaching in order to make them more "real," more credible, more viable as objects of policy and activism, more present as everyday realities that touch all our lives and dynamically shape our futures. This is the performative ontological project of "diverse economies." (2008, 618)

I am committed here to focusing on the "alternative economic activities" of LECs in order to make them, as Gibson-Graham writes, "more present as everyday realities." That said, my deep interest in this form of housing—and in the urban commons broadly—is exactly what drives my skepticism about it. I have zero interest in promoting an idea that does not work in practice. Practicing the commons is not easy—especially for those of us reared in capitalism. Whether it works is, in every case, up for grabs. I think it can work, and I demonstrate the intricacies of its workings throughout this book. But I also devote time to looking closely at the failure, cooptation and reenclosure of the commons—important questions to address head on if we wish to truly build a better world.

In the spring of 1978, Ruth and her fellow tenants threw a block party on the streets bordering their apartment complex. They had organized the party to gain neighborhood support for their effort to stave off eviction, and ultimately to purchase the buildings collectively themselves. *The Washington Post* covered the party, and Ruth was captured in a reporter's photograph. She is speaking to a crowd, with banners strung up behind her: "Moratorium on evictions!" reads one; "We shall not be moved!" reads another. But as Ruth told the *Post* reporter, the block party was organized not just to publicize the plight of this one group of tenants. It was also an effort to show solidarity with the many other tenants across the city who were, at that time in the late 1970s, facing eviction (J. Eisen 1978).

Ultimately, Ruth, Sherry, and their fellow tenants were able to purchase their complex, creating the Aspen Cooperative. Nearly forty years later, the Aspen Cooperative was still going strong, providing a modest, affordable place to live, in a peaceful, convenient neighborhood, for nearly a hundred people. In taking over their housing and reforming it to meet their life needs, the tenants were reclaiming the urban commons. But simultaneously, they were also helping other tenants around the city take action at their buildings, too. The Aspen Co-op hosted countless delegations of tenants groups—from D.C. and beyond—who wanted to learn how they had been able to purchase their housing. Their struggle helped create structural change, as well. Their work helped inform a city law that was finalized in 1980, giving tenants the opportunity to purchase their homes should their landlord put them up for sale, thus giving tenants associations across the city the ability to take control over their housing. In creating a commons at one scale, then, the co-op members were also helping create the structural change to enable the expansion of the commons at a broader scale.

The practice of the urban commons, I find, is a dialectical one, toggling between reclamation and expansion. And it is a practice that is learned through doing. In chapter 6, I theorize several key facets of the practice of the urban commons, emphasizing that the urban commons is above all a pragmatic practice. And finally, in the book's conclusion, I ask whether commoning can be taught and learned—and how, as a city, as a society, we can do this in the here and now.

What Is the Commons?

Merging Two Perspectives

Doris lives in the Magnolia Cooperative, east of Washington's Anacostia River, an area that for decades has been economically severed from the rest of the city. An African American in her fifties, Doris shares a four-bedroom apartment with her husband and three of their five adult children. She grew up in public housing in D.C., and in the 1990s, she was living with her family in the Benning Terrace public housing project. Throughout the time Doris and her family lived there, Benning Terrace was notorious for its drug-trade-related violence. Over the span of just four years in the 1990s, dozens of people were murdered in the streets that ran through the housing complex (Gillis and Miller 1997). "Oh my god," Doris recalls, "the killing and the fighting—it was just non-stop." She was desperate to get herself and her children out.

Doris found some peace in her new home, a complex made up of ninety townhouse-style units, each with its own small yard. One of the things she has appreciated about the Magnolia is its house rules, which regulate behavior of members. One of these rules is a curfew: members can't make noise outside their units after 10:00 P.M. in the winter and after 11:00 P.M. in the summer. This is critical for Doris because she has to wake up very early to get to work: at the time we spoke, in 2010, she had been working as a pharmacy technician for twenty-three years, at a drugstore across town. The curfew, she explains, regulates

> certain times that you can be out, the loud music, because you really want to give your neighbors that respect. . . . And we get up at 4:00. And when you're getting up at 4:00 in the morning, when you got people outside your window at 10:00, 11:00 at night, hollering, cursing, and all that, it ain't nice. And you really don't get much sleep. So a lot of the things [house rules], I'm pretty—I'm glad

we've got some of them. Not to say a lot of people are following them, but we do have them in place. And I'm really thankful for a lot of the things.

Coming up with rules to collectively self-govern—and then enforcing those rules—takes work. After she moved into the co-op, Doris served on the committee that revised the house rules. She is sometimes frustrated that some co-op members won't always follow the rules that she and her fellow members put many hours into crafting. But overall, she is happy with where she lives. Doris's co-op fees are quite low—at the time we spoke, in 2010, she was paying $609 for her four-bedroom unit. The location, she tells me, is good: the co-op is just a few blocks from a subway station. And she can plant flowers in her little yard without worrying about people running through the flowerbeds—again, because of the house rules she helped write.

Doris is a member of a commons. Her housing is not part of D.C.'s red-hot real estate market—it is an eddy of affordability and stability in a raging tide of high rents and anxiety. She has control over her space—she has helped create the structures that govern life in her co-op. Her housing is not perfect, but its affordability allows her family to live with a bit of breathing room, and the collective control of the space ensures a more livable environment than what she had experienced before—and what many low-income renters, regardless of whether their housing is publicly or privately owned, experience.

Understanding the Commons

My purpose in this chapter is to provide an overview of the commons in theory and practice, and ultimately to argue for understanding the commons as existing in dialectical tension with capital. First I introduce the idea of the commons, as it has been understood historically, and as it was (tragically) theorized by Garrett Hardin in 1968. I then delve into the two main strains of commons research that emerged in the 1980s, partly in response to Hardin. First, I discuss the institutionalist approach and next, the alterglobalizationist approach. I apply each approach to the case of Doris's co-op, and I discuss the gaps of each approach. Finally, I suggest how a diverse economies perspective can help bring these two approaches together in order to theorize the commons more richly, as a practice that takes place in tension with capital.

The commons is an idea that stretches back centuries and spans continents. One vein of scholarship examines the commons of the medieval English landscape. These were spaces—often "waste" spaces—used as a basis for subsistence by peasants who owned no land, through activities like pasturing animals and collecting fuel, food, and other materials necessary for life (Goldstein 2013; Linebaugh 2008; Neeson 1993; E. P. Thompson 1963). Many scholars who study these historical commons follow Marx (1973) in conceiving of the commons as precapitalist spaces. Capitalism could arise, in part, because of what Marx called "so-called primitive accumulation:" the series of enclosures that forced commoners off the lands they had used for survival. Because they no longer had a reliable means of subsistence, erstwhile commoners were forced to go to work in the burgeoning capitalist economy, thus providing the labor force necessary to further concentrate wealth in the hands of a few. The lands that had been enclosed were also put to work in a new way: no longer as a basis for direct subsistence, but to produce goods to sell on the market. With the revving of the engine of capitalism came exploration and conquest of distant lands, and the enclosure of the commons of other peoples. Cronon (2003), for instance, describes the commons of native peoples of the North American continent, how their management practices shaped the land, and the effects enclosure, perpetrated by newly arrived colonists, had on their lands. Many of these colonists, it should be noted, were English commoners who had been kicked off their own commons: dispossession runs in cycles. The enclosure of the land of the commons and the labor of the commoners, according to this analysis, was the basis for the development of capitalism. (I will return to this point a bit later in the chapter.)

Those were analyses of historic commons. But for years, the idea of a commons that might exist in modern times was shaped by ecologist Garret Hardin's 1968 essay, "The Tragedy of the Commons." In what became a seminal piece, Hardin argues that human overpopulation and the resulting overexploitation of natural resources leads inevitably to ecological disaster. To prove his point, he engages in a thought experiment: imagine, he says, a group of herdsmen who share a grazing area. Each man owns a herd of cattle, but none of them owns the land on which the cattle graze; it is a grazing commons. It is to the individual advantage of each herdsman,

Hardin argues, to continually add more cattle to his stock, even though the cumulative effect of each herdsman adding more cattle will eventually lead to depletion of the commons through overgrazing. The benefit of adding cattle accrues immediately to the individual owners of the herds, while the cost of degrading the pasture is borne in the long term by all the herdsmen as a whole (Hardin 1968). Under Hardin's logic, an individual herder who chooses not to add cattle out of concern for the long-term ecological consequences is a "sucker", since other herders will inevitably continue to profit by adding more cattle (Ostrom 1990). "Each man is locked into a system that compels him to increase his herd without limit—in a world that is limited," Hardin writes, in an oft-quoted passage. "Ruin is the destination toward which all men rush, each pursuing his own best interest in a society that believes in the freedom of the commons. Freedom in a commons brings ruin to all" (1968, 1244). For Hardin, individuals acting in their own rational self-interest will inevitably lead to the depletion of the commons. Hardin's idea that resources held in common would inevitably lead to tragic outcomes has been enormously influential, becoming "the dominant framework within which social scientists portray environmental and resource issues" (quoted in McCay and Acheson 1987, 1).

But that framework has begun to crack. Since the mid-1980s, two streams of thought have emerged that take the commons seriously. We can refer to these two groups of thinkers as the institutionalists, on the one hand, and the alterglobalizationists, on the other. Doris's experience of the commons—and the experience of all commoners—can be examined from these two different perspectives. Not all work on the commons can be neatly sorted as aligning with one or the other of these two perspectives. But overall, the gulf between the institutionalists and alterglobalizationists is striking. As Wall (2014a) has noted in a recent survey of the literature, scholars from these two traditions rarely communicate, or even reference each other's work, with very few exceptions.

The Institutionalist Perspective

The emergence of what I am calling the institutionalist perspective on the commons began in the 1980s. Institutionalists can trace their intellectual lineage to what is more precisely known as the new institutional economics. New institutional economics accepts the basic tenets of neoclassical economics—people are in competition for scarce resources—but disputes the neoclassical assumption that people are perfectly rational in making decisions. People can't be fully rational, the new institutionalists argue, because they don't have access to all the information they need to make decisions, and because their mental models—the ways they see the world—vary greatly, depending on culture. Because they are not perfectly rational beings, they need institutions to help regulate economic exchange. The institutionalists, as their name implies, are interested in the institutions—both formal and informal—that people create to help regulate economic exchange (Coase 1998; North 1992; Williamson 1998).

One of the ways in which new institutional economics has been applied is in the study of common pool resources. Common pool resources, scholars theorize, are natural resources that are both subtractable (one person's use of the resource subtracts from another person's ability to use it) and nonexcludable (it is difficult to keep people from using the resource). Examples include forests, fishing waters, and grazing lands (Ostrom 1990). The problem of potential overuse of subtractable, nonexcludable resources was, of course, the problem Garrett Hardin bemoaned. For Hardin, the only solution to the eventual degradation of the resource from overuse was either to privatize resources so that there was an economic incentive for resource owners to keep them healthy—or to have the state take over the resources and legislate how they could be used. But the institutionalists argue that there is a third way: collective governance by the people who actually use, and depend on, the resources (Feeny et al. 1990). The institutions people create to enable collective, sustainable governance of resources are referred to by institutionalists as common property regimes. Though the term "common property resources" conflates the nature of the resource (common pool) with the management regime (common property), the term "common property resources" has been most widely used in the literature. All three concepts—common pool resources, common property resources, and common property regimes—are known by the single acronym, CPR. Over the years, CPR research began to be more broadly theorized by institutionalists as research into, simply, the "commons."

By 1985, the work of the institutionalists had generated enough interest that the National Research Council, the U.S. Agency for International Development, the Ford Foundation, and the World Wildlife Fund decided to jointly fund the Conference on Common Property Resource Management. The 1985 conference, widely regarded as a turning point in the institutionalist work on the commons, laid out the stakes of the research. As Hess describes it, the conference "brought together a wide variety of scholars who rejected Hardin's formulaic, impressionistic narrative, who chose to look more closely and deeply into the problem of shared resources" (Hess 2000, 2–3). The opening sentences of the preface to the conference proceedings make clear the focus of the conference—and this line of research:

> Economic well-being throughout the world is directly related to the management and productivity of environmental systems. . . . [D]rawing on the adaptations of the past, as well as on contemporary scientific insight, management systems can be improved so that the resources basic to the availability of food, fuel, fodder, and shelter can be restored and exploited on a sustainable basis. (National Research Council 1986, vii)

These scholars were concerned with environmental degradation in many parts of the world, and they were particularly concerned with these problems in the developing world (in part because that was the interest of funders). What the institutionalists added to the growing chorus of concern about environmental devastation was the recognition that indigenous peoples had long-standing systems for managing their resources, that attention needed to be paid to those systems, and that, through scientific management, these systems could be improved. In 1988, they founded the International Association for the Study of Common Property Resources to further the understanding (and improvement) of commons management across the globe in a systematic way. (This group was later rechristened the International Association for the Study of the Commons.)

Managing the Commons

Institutionalists are interested in the nitty-gritty of how successful common property regimes work. From the beginning, Elinor Ostrom, who held a PhD in political science but called herself a political economist, was one of their leading figures (Aligica 2014; Pennington 2012; Wall 2014b). Her book, *Governing the Commons: The Evolution of Institutions for Collective Action*, has become a classic in the field of CPR research (Ostrom 1990). In the book, Ostrom draws on an array of case studies of collective self-management of natural resources around the world. She looks at communal tenure of mountain meadows and forests in Switzerland and Japan; irrigation systems in Spain, the Philippines, and Sri Lanka; fisheries in Turkey, Sri Lanka, and Nova Scotia; and water basins in Southern California. In this book Ostrom outlines the design principles of successful CPRs. Over time, Ostrom simplified the wording of these principles, but the basic meaning has remained intact. In a 2007 publication, she articulates them as follows:

1. Clearly defined boundaries should be in place.
2. Rules in use are well matched to local needs and conditions.
3. Individuals affected by these rules can usually participate in modifying the rules.
4. The right of community members to devise their own rules is respected by external authorities.
5. A system for self-monitoring members' behavior has been established.
6. A graduated system of sanctions is available.
7. Community members have access to low-cost conflict-resolution mechanisms.
8. Nested enterprises—that is, appropriation, provision, monitoring and sanctioning, conflict resolution, and other governance activities—are organized in a nested structure with multiple layers of activities. (Hess and Ostrom 2007a, 7)

A close look at these principles reveals much about the institutionalist understanding of the commons. A commons, first of all is bounded; it is not, as Hardin theorized, "open-access." As Ostrom has noted in *Governing the Commons* and elsewhere, this bounding is twofold: first, the physical terrain comprising the commons must be clear, so that people know when they are on or off the commons; and second, the membership of the commons is also bounded, so that people know who is or is not part of the commons community. The next three principles have to do with rules for governing the commons: the appropriateness of the rules, how they are devised and modified, and importantly, that they are respected by authorities external to the commons. The following three principles deal with behavior and conflict: successful commons have ways to monitor behavior, punish members when they break the rules, and resolve conflicts among members. Finally, more complex commons are nested within other decision-making structures, and the rules at each level must be followed in order for the commons to work. Overall, the thrust of the principles is on defining boundaries and rules, and dealing with conflict.

These principles have been used by scholars all over the world to analyze and evaluate the efficacy of common property resources management in cases ranging from Japan, the Andes, Turkey, Brazil, India, Morocco, Uganda, Nepal, Ecuador, and Bolivia to many other places around the globe (see for example Bromley 1992; Ghate, Jodha, and Mukhopadhyay 2008; Gibson, McKean, and Ostrom 2000). Elinor Ostrom had not been willing to argue, in 1990, that all eight of her principles must be followed for a CPR to be successful; her point was that it is possible, through careful study of cases, to devise a set of key characteristics of successful CPRs. But the principles have stood the test of time. As Brewer writes in her discussion of the lobster commons of Maine, Ostrom's eight principles have become a "canonical list of criteria" (2012, 386).

Since the early 2000s, institutionalists have become increasingly interested in what they sometimes term the "new commons," and they have been thinking about how Ostrom's principles could apply beyond the natural resources context. One is the commons variably understood as the "knowledge," "digital," or "information" commons (Hess and Ostrom 2007b). A tangible result of the institutionalist interest in the knowledge commons was the creation of the Digital Library of the Commons, an online, open-access compendium of research on the commons, hosted by the Workshop in Political Theory and Policy Analysis and the University of Indiana (see https://dlc.dlib.indiana.edu). A second, more recent, way to conceive of the commons is in terms of the "global" commons, which represents "a class of environmental problems that require international cooperation" (Bromley and Cochrane 1995, 3). Climate change is often mentioned as one of the most pressing questions of the global commons (Paavola 2012). The third new way scholars are thinking about the commons is in terms of what we might refer to as the "cultural" commons. Some examples come from a 2000 survey of the "new commons," which cited recent research that theorized a wide variety of shared resources as commons, including surfers' waves, budgets, public radio, highways, cultural treasures, traditional music, tourist landscapes, car sharing institutions, and, of course, the Internet (Hess 2000). Theorizing CPRs as humanmade—or, we might say, as socially produced—has been a big shift for the institutionalists. From their beginnings focusing solely on natural resources, the institutionalists have more recently been moving into a much wider range of commons study.

It is in all three of these ways of thinking about the new commons—the knowledge, global, and cultural commons—that the institutionalists, as we will see, begin to share interests with the alterglobalizationists. But though they may converge in terms of the types of commons they study, their basic approaches to theorizing these commons remain fundamentally different.

Applying the Institutionalist Approach

I want to ground the institutionalists' approach by thinking about how this group of scholars would address one manifestation of the commons: Doris's limited-equity cooperative, the Magnolia. Doris, recall, had participated on a committee that rewrote the co-op's house rules. Doris and I discussed the mechanics of how the new house rules were approved by the co-op membership, referred to as shareholders:

> DORIS: First we did it as our committee, and then we had to take it before the board of directors first, and then they went over it, then we presented it to the shareholders. That's how we had to do it . . . They had to be read out, and then you agreed, or you disagreed on whatever one, and that's how it was.
>
> AMANDA: And did the shareholders vote at that time?
>
> DORIS: Right, when we bring it to them. And you get a chance to vote on it, and you accept it, or you don't accept it.

The institutionalists would study the commons constituted by the Magnolia with nuance. They would want to know how the co-op's board of directors was elected, the different committees it oversaw, and how the board, committees, and members interacted in the collective governance process. They would want to understand the process of, for example, re-writing the co-op's house rules, a process in which Doris participated. If not everyone follows the house rules all the time, as Doris claims, institutionalists would want to know what the punishment was (though they would use the more technical term "sanction"). How do members monitor each other to make sure they are following the rules? How do co-op members manage conflict among themselves? To what degree is the commons constituted by this co-op "nested" within other institutions that operate at a larger scale, like the city government, which has helped subsidize the co-op? These are important questions that institutionalist researchers would pose, that would help enlarge the understanding of this form of collective governance. In my fieldwork with limited-equity co-ops, I follow the institutionalists in paying close attention to how co-op members collectively manage their particular resources. I am interested in what is failing, as well as what is working.

Gaps in the Institutionalist Approach

The institutionalist fieldwork is rich, thick with detail, and finely attuned to the particulars of each case. But something is missing here. Simply stated, this line of research is not terribly interested in the big picture. Very little attention is paid to the origins of a commons like Doris's, and the larger structures within which it necessarily exists. The commons described by the institutionalists—particularly the natural resources commons—seem to emerge from a historical mist: there was not a point in time in which they were created or reclaimed. This changes somewhat with discussion of the new commons. Some national governments, for instance, have recognized that commons exist—that people collectively self-regulate the resources upon which they depend—and these governments have come up with ways to "co-manage" resources drawing on the local knowledge of local appropriators (see for example Agrawal 2003). So some attention is paid to the need to "re-form" commons under the aegis of the state. But this is more a resurrecting of earlier commoning practices, this time with state intervention, than the wholesale reclaiming of a commons that had previously been enclosed. Institutionalists may study other, more recently formed commons—like software collectives or neighborhood watch patrols—but they do not appear to be interested in the moment of creation of that new way of governing resources. Rather, their focus is on the minutiae of management over time. The idea of seizing, or reclaiming, a commons is rarely taken up in this literature.

Institutionalists are not interested in the question of the reclamation of the commons, it appears, because they do not pose a distinction between capitalism and the commons. Capitalism is rarely discussed in the literature, and commons are not theorized in relationship to it. Ostrom specifically has been critiqued for her apparent lack of interest in inequality and power dynamics (Fine 2010). But it is the very distinction between capitalism and commons that is at the core of the alterglobalizationist approach.

The Alterglobalizationist Perspective

The alterglobalizationist perspective on the commons, like that of the institutionalists, emerged in the 1980s. The term "alterglobalization" was coined as a response to the term "antiglobalization," a word that has been used to describe a movement deeply critical of capitalist forms of globalization. Alterglobalization in contrast, emphasizes that the critique is not of the increasing interconnectedness of the world per se, but its capitalist forms, which lead inexorably, it is claimed, to deepening inequality, suffering, and environmental devastation. Alterglobalization appeared to be a better term than antiglobalization, given that activists were working to, as the international peasant activist network La Via Campesina noted in their slogan, "globalize the struggle and globalize hope" (quoted in Pleyers 2010, 6). The alterglobalizationist perspective, unlike the institutionalist perspective, is rooted as much in activism as in scholarship.

The 1980s witnessed two major shifts that helped form the alterglobalizationist perspective on the commons. On the one hand, communist states were collapsing throughout the decade, culminating in the demise of the Soviet Union. On the other hand, over the course of the 1980s, peoples across the world were engaged in a string of revolts, which had at their root the desire to keep hold of their common lands in the face of the imposition of structural adjustment policies and agricultural "reform." These revolts took place primarily in the global South, but also in global North cities like New York and Berlin, where people engaged in squatting as resistance to structural adjustment policies at the scale of the city (Caffentzis, 2004). The emergence of the Zapatistas onto the consciousness of the world was perhaps the most compelling of these uprisings. The Zapatistas had begun organizing in the Mexican state of Chiapas in the mid-1980s, questioning the injustices and mistreatment endured by the indigenous peoples of southern Mexico in the centuries since Spanish conquest. In 1992, the Mexican government had changed Article 27 of the Mexican Constitution, allowing for common lands (*ejidos*) to be subdivided into individually owned parcels and bought and sold. The change to Article 27, which would make it easier for Mexican land ownership to be integrated into the global economy, had been made in preparation for the implementation of the North American Free Trade Agreement, or NAFTA. NAFTA went into effect on January 1, 1994. It was on this day that the Zapatistas made their presence known, when they engaged in an armed uprising against the Mexican government specifically, and global capitalism broadly, demanding justice and democracy, land and freedom (H. Klein 2015). Commons scholar Peter Linebaugh argues that these twin historical moments—the disintegration of the Soviet Union and the appearance of the Zapatistas— "changed the atmosphere of scholarly investigation in America" (2014, 5). Suddenly, people had to think about what anticapitalist collectivism could look like without a strong central state; and simultaneously, they had an example, in the Zapatistas.

Part of the reason the Zapatistas were able to explode onto the global consciousness with such force was because they emerged just at the moment that the Internet was becoming a global tool of communication. The rise of the Internet and the World Wide Web, and the recognition of the role the Internet could play in facilitating a knowledge commons, are other reasons for the alterglobalizationists' increased interest in the commons. The Internet facilitated the awareness among disparate peoples all over the globe that they were engaged in similar struggles. The Internet, that is, produced a knowledge commons in a technical sense—as the institutionalists also recognized—but also helped produce a global commoner consciousness. The global alterglobalization movement erupted on the world scene in late 1999, with massive protests at the World Trade Organization meetings in Seattle—protests organized by a wide array of groups from all over the world, facilitated by the Internet.

Indian activist Vandana Shiva was one among thousands of participants in the Seattle protests. Her definition of the commons is perhaps one of the best for summing up the perspective of the alterglobalizationists. The commons, Shiva argues,

> implies a resource that is vital to our collective well-being and sustenance that is owned, managed and used by the community. A commons embodies social relations based on democratic participation, interdependence and cooperation. (Shiva 2013, vii)

For alterglobalizationists, the commons is necessary for subsistence, is managed collectively, and is embedded in social relations.

From the idea of the commons, some alterglobalizationist scholars have moved to theorizing "the common" more broadly. The common, Hardt and Negri (2009) argue, is both a source of wealth and the means of producing wealth; it is the basis of life. Hardt and Negri seize on the city (they prefer the term "metropolis") as the locus of the common. What Hardt and Negri want to do with identifying "the common" as opposed to "the commons" is point to something much broader than a particular, embedded, material thing, which is what "the commons" is often seen to be: for example, a particular field. But the commons, in the alterglobalizationist tradition, is vast, and Hardt and Negri want to underscore that. Says Linebaugh:

> Somehow that term, "the commons," comes to embrace the entire social product of human beings, the countries of the world, the substances of the earth, air, water, and fire, the biosphere, the electromagnetic spectrum, and outer space. (2014, 237)

This is envisioning the commons at a very large scale. Though Hardt and Negri may be making a particular philosophical point by speaking of "the common" rather than "the commons," alterglobalizationists generally seem to think in these broader terms. Wall (2014b) communicates it well: the institutionalists are concerned with the micro questions of the commons, and the anticapitalists (as he terms them) with the macro questions.

Reclaiming the Commons, Resisting Enclosure

While the institutionalists are focused on managing the commons, the alterglobalizationists are focused on reclaiming or creating commons, and they have a particular concern with enclosure. As Caffentzis explains, the origins of capitalism, according to Marx (1973) depended (at least in part) on the enclosure of the commons. "[I]n order for capitalism to exist there has to be a working class to exploit; and the main condition for there to be such a working class is that workers are separated from the means of subsistence" (Caffentzis 2004, 6). The commons are that means of subsistence: a place to forage for firewood, to graze your cow, to gather water or plant a few vegetables. Get pushed off the commons, and your only option for survival is getting a job, or turning to crime. This perspective, unlike that of the institutionalists, has roots that go far back in time: it is relentlessly historical. As noted earlier, commons and enclosures have been studied in particular detail in England, where written records going back centuries have provided the historical detail necessary to make the case (Linebaugh 2008; Marx 1973; Neeson 1993; E. P. Thompson 1963). But longstanding commons and their enclosure have also been studied in the Americas, Africa, and the South Pacific, among other parts of the world (Bennholdt-Thomsen and Mies 1999; Cronon 2003; Federici 2011).

An important piece of the alterglobalizationist perspective is in making explicit the relationship between the commons and the ability to refuse waged work. The commons were not necessarily super-abundant, but they did provide a means of subsistence. And for people who were able to live within the limits of what the commons provided, lives were freer. As Neeson argues in her study of English commoners:

> One consequence was that commoners who were able to live on a little were unlikely to develop expensive wants. As long as they had what they thought of as enough they had no need to spend time getting more. From this freedom came time to spend doing things other than work, as well as the ability to refuse work. (1993, 178)

Focusing on the need to reclaim commons in order to resist wage labor—and more broadly, to have more control over one's life—is key to alterglobalizationist thinking on the commons.

For alterglobalizationists—activists and scholars alike—the call to "reclaim the commons!" has resonated widely around the world (N. Klein 2001; Menzies 2014; Mies and Bennholdt-Thomsen 2001; Starhawk 2004). Like the institutionalists, alterglobalizationists have theorized the commons constituted by natural resources, knowledge commons, a variety of global commons, including for example the gene pool, and a wide range of cultural commons (Bollier 2002; Nonini 2007; Scharper and Cunningham 2007). But the key difference is that this research is grounded in the forces of enclosure: in protecting existing commons from enclosure and in reclaiming commons from previously enclosed environments. The dynamic relationship between commons and enclosure points to the social nature of the commons. The commons, alterglobalizationists argue, needs to be thought of as a social process, as an activity, not as a "resource." As Linebaugh emphasizes:

The activity of commoning is conducted *through* labor *with* other resources; it does not make a division between "labor" and "natural resources." On the contrary, it is labor which creates something as a resource, and it is by resources that the collectivity of labor comes to pass. As an action it is thus best understood as a verb rather than as a "common pool resource." (2014, 13, emphasis in the original)

The commons, that is, is an ongoing practice: it is labor and activity, not a seemingly inert resource that exists outside human social life.

One of the most important ways in which alterglobalizationists contribute to the discourse on the commons is through an explicitly feminist perspective. There are at least two critical components of a feminist perspective on the commons. I have noted that alterglobalizationists insist that the commons is a social process grounded in labor: a feminist perspective helps make this labor visible. Feminist theorists understand the commons as a place of social reproduction, where labor is often made invisible. Federici explains how this came to be:

[I]n pre-capitalist Europe women's subordination to men had been tempered by the fact that they had access to the commons and other communal assets, while in the new capitalist regime *women themselves became the commons*, as their work was defined as a natural resource, laying outside the sphere of market relations. (2004, 97, emphasis in the original)

Under newly emergent capitalism, Federici argues, women became for men a substitute for the lands lost to enclosure: their labor was seen as natural, available to all, and, critically, not seen as labor at all. It was "housework," something different from "real" work. This was, Federici argues, primitive accumulation at the scale of the body: women's working bodies were enclosed and domesticated into the "private" sphere (in this case the sphere of the home). Bennholdt-Thomsen and Mies make a similar point. "In a way," they argue, "women are treated like commons and commons are treated like women, and the link is the modern notion of nature" (1999, 159). Seeing women as commons—and seeing how women's labor has been obscured and naturalized—helps us see that the work of the commons has likewise been naturalized and ignored.

Second, a feminist perspective helps us see that the commons are not necessarily spaces of liberation. Commons, bound in tradition, can in fact be deeply oppressive. Just because people are collectively self-regulating a resource to sustain life does not make that social action an egalitarian movement. In just one example: the squatted buildings of contemporary Europe, which have been theorized as commons, include fascist squats and squats that retain elements of patriarchy (Azozomox 2014; Squatting Europe Kollective, Cattaneo, and Martinez 2014). Women in some commons may have fewer rights to the commons than do men (Wall 2014a). A feminist perspective would emphasize that a call to reclaim the commons is not a call to return to some sort of mythical precapitalist society, but to create a new society, based in the commons and truly emancipatory.

Applying the Alterglobalizationist Approach

Let's think now about how the alterglobalizationists would approach studying Doris's co-op. They would be interested in how her commons was reclaimed: in the intense organizing, stretching over many years, that was required to create the Magnolia. They would also be focused on the larger political and economic context in which the commons—and its members—exist. Doris comes from relative poverty, having grown up in public housing and lived in it as an adult before moving into her co-op. It is not that she hasn't worked: for twenty-three years she has worked as a pharmacy technician, a position that in 2014 paid an average wage of $14 an hour, or just under $30,000 annually (Bureau of Labor Statistics 2015). But in 2014, she would need to earn over $28 an hour, or *twice* the average wage for the profession, to afford just a typical *two*-bedroom apartment in Washington, D.C. (National Low Income Housing Coalition 2014). And when Doris moved into her co-op, she and her husband were raising five children, so they needed more than two bedrooms. Even though she has affordable housing, Doris has to work hard, commuting long hours, to get by. She was involved, for a time, in the formal structures of co-op life. But after serving as a board member and as a member of the committee that rewrote the house rules, she got tired. It was a lot of work. Many of Doris's fellow commons members are in a similar situation: they work very hard in order to survive and are not well-compensated for their waged labor. They are often exhausted, and this can cut down on their ability to participate in the life of the commons.

It is the larger structures that the commons are supposed to help mitigate *against*—the capitalist prerogatives of life—that can, paradoxically, make managing the commons so hard. Without attending to the effects larger economic and political structures have on management of the commons, commoning, in the long run, may not be possible. An alterglobalizationist might say to an institutionalist: your detailed case studies of how individual commons operate over time are impressive. But without paying attention to the forces of capitalism, your research is moot.

Gaps in the Alterglobalizationist Approach

But what is missing in the alterglobalizationist approach is that, for the most part, these scholars don't delve into the details of how commons operate in contemporary life. They theorize broadly about the need to reclaim the commons and resist enclosure. A certain subset of scholars looks in detail at how commons have been managed in precapitalist history. But there is an urgent need to study how contemporary commons actually operate and to study them through this political framework. Some alterglobalizationist scholars have theorized what Eizenberg calls "actually existing commons"—Eizenberg, for one, does look closely at the commons constituted by community gardens in New York City (2011). But others are critical of the tendency in the alterglobalization stream of commons theorization to be concerned more with the commons in a formal theoretical sense, and less in the material way the commons can be used to support everyday existence. As Federici writes of Hardt and Negri's theory of the common:

> [W]ith its emphasis on knowledge and information, this theory skirts the question of the reproduction of everyday life. This, however, is true of the discourse on the commons as a whole, which is mostly concerned with the formal preconditions for the existence of commons and less with the material requirements for the construction of a commons-based economy enabling us to resist dependence on wage labor and subordination to capitalist relations. (2012, 4)

Federici is critiquing Hardt and Negri specifically, but her critique holds for alterglobalizationist scholars broadly. She wants more attention paid to how anticapitalist commons actually function. She knows the argument for reclaiming commons and resisting enclosure very well: what she is calling for, I think, is an investigation of how a commons actually operates on the ground.

A second gap in the alterglobalizationist approach is that they tend not to deal straightforwardly with the problem of exclusion and access in the commons. The institutionalists are clear that commons are closed systems, open only to members. The alterglobalizationists are not as consistent. Some acknowledge that commons are bounded, with precise membership; Armiero, for instance, theorizes the fishing waters of nineteenth century Naples as an "urban sea commons" in which members regulated their commons intensely, and sometimes violently, shooting at boats that weren't supposed to be in their waters (Armiero 2011). This was a social space from which some were excluded. But other alterglobalizationists insist otherwise: "In the commons," Shiva writes, for example, "no one can be excluded" (2013, x). Commons that are theorized at a very large scale are seen as open to all. Many alterglobalizationist scholars seem leery of insisting that the commons are open only to members, even as the few commons they actually empirically investigate are clearly closed communities: New York City community gardens, for example, tend to be padlocked, and only garden members have the keys (Eizenberg 2011). But often, when alterglobalizationists—be they activists or academics—talk about the commons, they are talking about something that is, or they think should be, freely available to all, regardless of ability to contribute to its functioning. This is a major issue that muddies alterglobalizationist thought on the commons, and it can have serious ramifications for the commons in practice. There is a romanticization of the commons that shines through the alterglobalizationist literature, which, though it may be appealing, is not helpful in terms of actually figuring out how to live in opposition to capitalist practices.

Joining Two Perspectives

Institutionalists and alterglobalizationists seem to have a similar working definition of the commons. For both sets of scholars, a commons is made up of three parts, as noted in the Introduction: (1) a resource of some kind, (2) institutions for governing that resource, and (3) the communities of people, sometimes referred to as commoners, who create those institutions of governance (Kip et al. 2015). Despite their seeming agreement on definitions, these scholars have tended not to talk to each other. Caffentzis argues that, while the institutionalists make many distinctions between types of common property regimes, the one distinction they don't make is between "those regimes antagonistic to and subversive of capitalist accumulation and those regimes that are compatible with and potentiating of capitalist accumulation" (2004, 22). He draws the distinction here between commodity-producing commons, which he claims the CPR scholars examine, and subsistence-producing commons, a distinction Bennholdt-Thomsen and Mies (1999) also make. The institutionalists, he argues, are interested in management and good institutional design; anticapitalists are interested in the commons as part of a larger rejection of capitalism in a globalizing world. Because institutionalists have no critique of capitalism (and in fact, he argues, work to open up commons to capitalist extraction), there can be no common ground between them and those critical of capitalism.

I am sympathetic to Caffentzis's analysis, but I think that something can be learned from the institutionalists. For one, a number of institutionalists are quite concerned with the problem of enclosure, and though they may not frame this concern as part of a larger concern about capitalism, they do recognize it is a problem, particularly with regards to natural resources and the knowledge commons (Hess and Ostrom 2007a; McCay 2012). This concern points to some common ground between the two perspectives. But perhaps more importantly, the institutionalists have devised methods for studying the commons from which alterglobalizationists can learn. These methods are often grounded in case studies of specific places, and include direct observation of how commons function; interviews with commons members, including leaders, to understand how they engage in self-governance; historical research that explains how the management of the commons has evolved; and quantitative analysis of relevant data (Poteete et al. 2010). Alterglobalizationists, too, can use these methods.

Alterglobalizationist scholars have recognized that their on-the-ground study of existing commons is thin. They call for more and better study of the commons—and that this study be from a perspective that is critical of capitalism, and that poses the commons as a grounds for life outside of capitalism. In speaking to fellow scholars and activists, Caffentzis emphasizes the need for:

us . . . to become more precise as to what kinds of commons will increase the power of workers against capital. . . . This precision will require our development of traditions and methods of counter-research that would increase knowledge of alternative commons solutions, but would not lead to the subversion or repression of the commons and commoners in question. . . . It is time, as Fanon urged us, to invent, in this case, a methodology that can measure the compatibility of a commons with capital. (2004, 26–27)

My guess is that in calling for a new critical "counter-research" into the commons, Caffentzis is calling for research into how anticapitalist commons actually function in relationship to capitalism. Wall (2014a) also calls for new research into the commons. He recognizes the different approaches to studying the commons, and he believes that the best approach may be to combine perspectives. Wall, who identifies as a Marxist, is interested specifically in studying historical ecological commons. But his call for making use of a plurality of approaches is relevant for any commons scholars. The question is whether one believes some of the specific methods of institutionalists, as described above, can be wedded to a perspective critical of capitalism. I think that they can, through the theoretical framework of diverse economies.

Theorizing Commons through Diverse Economies

The diverse economies theoretical framework has evolved from a frustration with the way many Marxists have theorized capitalism: as a unified, singular, and totalizing force, one that must be fully destroyed before any new alternatives can be built (Gibson-Graham 1996). A diverse economies perspective, as I understand it, is made up of four key elements, each of which I will discuss here briefly in turn.

First, diverse economies theorists have a critique of what they call "capitalocentrism." In *The End of Capitalism (as we knew it): A Feminist Critique of Political Economy*, J. K. Gibson-Graham explains capitalocentrism as follows:

When we say that most economic discourse is "capitalocentric," we mean that other forms of economy (not to mention noneconomic aspects of social life) are often understood primarily with reference to capitalism: as being fundamentally the same as (or modeled upon) capitalism, or as being deficient or substandard imitations; as being opposite to capitalism; as being the complement of capitalism; as existing in capitalism's space or orbit. (1996, 6)

A capitalocentric approach, Gibson-Graham argues, obscures ways of seeing, understanding, and living in the world that are not in relation to capitalism. It theorizes any noncapitalist practices as about-to-be-commodified—or, thinking in terms of the commons, about-to-be-enclosed—by the all-consuming monster of capitalism. And, critically, it can lead to an impoverished imagination about what is, and what could be. Derickson explains:

> Capitalocentrism not only helps to maintain the hegemony of capitalism, but is politically disabling as well. Because capitalocentrism theorizes capitalism as a coherent, ever-present system, its demise requires total systemic overhaul. Instead, [Gibson-Graham] argue for a conception of the socio-economic-political world as multiple and heterogeneous, in which capitalist social relations exist, but are just one of many different types of existing and meaningful economic relationships. (2009, 11)

Questioning the very idea of what "capitalism" is, Gibson-Graham, Derickson, and others argue, allows for the opening up of new imaginations about what can be, and what already exists all around us in the here and now.

The second key piece of diverse economies theory is rethinking what constitutes "the economy" more broadly. In her 2006 follow-up work, *A Postcapitalist Politics*, Gibson-Graham develops her thought further, calling for rethinking what becomes reified as "the economy" as, rather, "an ethical space of decision" (86). The economy, for her, is an eminently social field in which people must constantly make joint decisions and experiment with as-yet untested economic ways of being. As she writes:

> If we wish to emphasize the *becoming* of new and as yet unthought ways of economic being, we might focus on the multiple possibilities that emerge from the inessential commonality of negotiating our own implication in the existence of others. An ethical praxis of being-in-common could involve cultivating an awareness of:

- what is *necessary* to personal and social survival;
- how social *surplus* is appropriated and distributed;
- whether and how social surplus is to be produced and *consumed*; and
- how a *commons* is produced and sustained. (2006, 88, emphasis in original)

Gibson-Graham is hardly alone in her desire to rethink what constitutes "the economy." Pavlovskaya writes of the "multiple economies" of post-Soviet Moscow, detailing the ways in which households engaged in multiple economic practices to make do in the rapidly changing time of the 1990s. Recognizing the wide range of household economic practices, she argues, is crucial for understanding not only how everyday life functioned at the micro-scale, but also for understanding macro-scale economic transitions (Pavlovskaya 2004). Graeber goes further, arguing against the very idea of a thing called "the economy," a thing separate from moral and political life. As he writes, "Economics assumes a division between different spheres of human behavior that among [many peoples] simply does not exist" (2011, 33). For Graeber, this separating of the "economic" from the moral and political has had profound consequences. Mitchell argues that "the economy," as a concept, is of relatively recent vintage. While "economy," he explains, had been long used to mean "the proper husbanding of material resources or to proper management," it was not until the mid-twentieth century that a world was brought into being "that for the first time could be measured and calculated as though it were a free-standing object, *the economy*" (2008, 1116, emphasis added). The economy was no longer a process, or a practice, but an object. The critique of the idea of "the economy" as free-standing object, unrelated to "culture" or "society," seems to me to be at the heart of the diverse economies project.

This brings us to the third key component of the diverse economies project: bringing to light the many different kinds of economic practices that exist all around, in the here and now.

Rather than theorize a single, stand-alone object of "the economy," Gibson-Graham encourages us to look at the world in new ways, in order to recognize a proliferation of economic practices, including, among many others, bartering, gift-giving, gleaning, and cooperative enterprise (2006). Uncovering and theorizing these practices can have important political ramifications. As St. Martin writes in his discussion of bringing a diverse economic theoretical framework to mapping a fishing commons:

[Counter-mapping] is not only an effective method for reclaiming material resources for those who have been dispossessed, but it works to counter particular forms of economic subjectivity and space . . . it inserts a noncapitalist presence into locations where only a capitalist potential had been identified. (2009, 494)

Counter-mapping, for St. Martin, is the practice of mapping data in a way that emphasizes noncapitalist relations, and it is one way to make noncapitalist economic practices like commoning visible. Other scholars have applied a diverse economic perspective to recognize and theorize a wide range of noncapitalist economic practices, including community-supported agriculture, worker-owned cooperatives, time banking, and many more (Cameron 2015; Healy 2015; Werner 2015).

The fourth element of the diverse economies framework is the necessary relationship between theory and political practice. The very idea for thinking in terms of diverse economies, Gibson-Graham writes, was inspired by collective organizing on the ground—the "exciting proliferation of economic experiments occurring worldwide in the current moment" (2008, 613). Over the years, Gibson-Graham and her collaborators in the Community Economies Research Collective have worked to identify, theorize, and promote a wide range of economic practices in many different parts of the world. In the 2015 volume *Making Other Worlds Possible: Performing Diverse Economies*, the editors explain what they are up to: "More than just an analytical frame, then, diverse economies suggests a research program that is always already an intentional intervention into making other worlds possible" (St. Martin, Roelvink, and Gibson-Graham 2015, 1). This research does not stand alone: it is part of a larger political project.

The diverse economies perspective, as outlined here, provides what I think is the best framework for theorizing the commons in the here and now. A diverse economic framework is grounded in close attention to what is actually taking place in terms of how people live their economic and more-than-economic lives. This careful attention to the details of daily life—which includes the ongoing management of the commons—is the focus of the institutionalist scholars. But a diverse economic framework is also concerned with larger questions of how commons arise, and how people work collectively to make better worlds in the midst of capitalism. This explicit engagement with capitalism—most often theorized in the creation or reclamation of commons—is the focus of the alterglobalizationist scholars. What a diverse economic perspective allows us to do is theorize both the creation and the ongoing maintenance of the commons. But most importantly, a diverse economic perspective allows for examining the dynamic, ongoing, dialectical relationship between commons and capital. The institutionalists, as I have noted, tend not to treat larger structures of capitalism and its effects on commons and commoners. The alterglobalizationists, for their part, have a tendency to see the commons as somehow outside of capitalism: whether historically or in the current moment. But commoning, as we will see throughout this book, is a practice that exists in a dialectical relationship with capitalism, often but not always in explicit opposition to it. The co-ops I study in this book are commons: noncapitalist economic structures that exist in the midst of a capitalist real estate market. Their members engage with, and against, capitalism in a variety of ways, as will be seen. And they are sites of experimentation, where members have been learning how to live in common, and where economic ways of being are, as Gibson-Graham writes, "new and as yet unthought."

In this chapter, I have outlined two different perspectives on the study of the commons: that of the institutionalists and that of the alterglobalizationists. It bears repeating that drawing such a sharp division between the two perspectives can be a bit misleading. There are institutionalists, for instance, who are concerned with questions of justice and livelihood in their work (see McCay 2012). And there are alterglobalizationists who look in some detail at how commons operate over time (see Noterman 2015). But broadly speaking, the two approaches intersect little. The institutionalists focus on how commons are managed over time; they don't have a specific politics that is critical of capitalism; they study actually existing commons at small scales and in fine detail. The alterglobalizationists focus on the need to reclaim commons and resist enclosure; they are explicitly critical of capitalism; they theorize broadly about the potential of the commons for helping to create new worlds. It is my belief that the framework of diverse economies can help bring these two approaches together in order to theorize the commons more richly. My hope is that, through bringing together these two approaches, I can add to the understanding of how commons are formed and maintained, and how they succeed and fail. Most importantly, I am interested in teasing apart the dialectical relationship between the commons and capital: in understanding the commons, and commoning, in relation to capital. I think this relationship can be best examined in the heightened capitalist conditions of the contemporary city. It is to the particular question of the urban commons, therefore, that I now turn.

2
_____

The Urban Commons

Contradictions of Community, Capital, and the State

Commons exist in a dialectical relationship with capital. Contemporary commons are both created—some might say reclaimed—and maintained over time in the context of capitalism. This is true of commons generally. But it is perhaps truer—and it is certainly more obvious—in the urban context. It is more obvious because of three key characteristics of the urban: the urban is a site of a densely populated, heterogeneous population; it is a site of capital accumulation, not subsistence; and it is a site of state regulation and surveillance. As I will discuss, all three of these factors should make it harder to develop and maintain commons in cities. As the world continues to urbanize, it is critical to ask whether an urban commons is possible. Close examination of the urban commons can shed light on the theory and practice of the commons more broadly.

In this chapter, I theorize the urban commons. I start by laying out how I understand the urban. Next, I bring the urban together with the commons, reviewing key recent literature in the urban commons. I then discuss what I see as the key contradictions of the urban commons. Finally, I theorize how we might work through the contradictions of the urban commons, bringing a feminist perspective to bear.

Conceptualizing the Urban

The study of the urban commons can be situated in the somewhat amorphous field known as "urban studies." But what is "the urban" in urban studies or the urban commons or urban anything else? It is a question that gnaws at scholars who study cities. The question of what is meant by "urban," for geographers and others who think about place, is analogous to the question of what is meant by "black" or "white," for those who think about race. Upon close inspection (and in fact the inspection needn't be all that close), categories begin to break down. But the job of scientists is, in part, to categorize in order to generalize, and the job of social scientists is, in part, to categorize people and their creations, so as to generalize. Black is this, white means that. By identifying a place or process as urban, we think we know some particular things about how it operates. But definitions are tricky.

One thing, perhaps, is clear: "the urban" is distinct from "the city." It is important to recognize the distinction between the city as a place and the urban as a process. In his now-classic 1938 essay, "Urbanism as a Way of Life," Wirth makes the key point that the physical form of the city cannot be equated with the idea of the urban. "As long as we identify urbanism with the physical entity of the city," he writes, "viewing it merely as rigidly delimited in space, and proceed as if urban attributes abruptly ceased to be manifested beyond an invisible boundary line, we are not likely to arrive at any adequate conception of urbanism as a mode of life" (Wirth 1938, 4). For Wirth, it is not the morphology of the city that is important—whether you are inside or outside the limits of a "city" as demarcated on a map. What is important is the urban way of life. As Wirth writes, "while the city is the characteristic locus of urbanism, the urban mode of life is not confined to cities" (1). The urban way of life "has drawn the most remote parts of the world into its orbit and woven diverse areas, people and activities into a cosmos" (2). The urban, for Wirth, is enmeshed with global processes that stretch far beyond the boundaries of any particular city.

So "the city" as a place is different from "the urban" as a process. But still: what *of* the urban? What do we mean when we describe something this way? Ananya Roy does well in reminding us, "The effort to conceptualize the urban is of course an integral part of the practice—and existential crisis—of urban studies" (2016, 6). There should always be some skepticism around strict definitions, and it is a good thing to be continually nagged a bit by an existential crisis of knowledge: it means we might be open to a new idea or to seeing things in a new light. What is significant, for Roy, is the ongoing *effort* to conceptualize the urban, as part of an ongoing practice of urban studies. It is in that spirit of ongoing effort that I next outline what I argue are the three key components of the urban—in order to then, in the following section, build on these components to theorize the urban commons.

Urban Populations: Big, Dense, and Diverse

First, the urban is constituted by a relatively large, densely clustered, and heterogeneous population. As Wirth writes, again, "For sociological purposes, a city may be defined as a relatively large, dense, and permanent settlement of socially heterogeneous individuals" (8). These three factors are, of course, all relative—relative, necessarily, to the areas that are considered "nonurban." If this logic sounds circular, it is because Wirth refuses to deal in absolutes. But his larger point is that living in relatively large, dense, and heterogeneous settlements creates a new kind of life. The large numbers of people living together in a city means that an urbanite can't know everyone else with whom she lives: unlike rural or village life, she only has a personal relationship with a tiny percentage of the people she sees every day. For Simmel, writing in his (1950 [1903]) essay "The Metropolis and Mental Life," the impossibility in a city of having full relationships with everyone with whom one comes into contact can create a blasé attitude. Most urban social relations, for Simmel, are superficial, anonymous, and transitory. Of course, there are many cases of tight-knit community being formed in the midst of a city: Gans's (1962) study of Italian Americans' community life in Boston's West End neighborhood, and Borchert's (1980) study of African American life in the alley communities of Washington, D.C., are just two examples. But overall, the anonymity of living with many others—the experience of being surrounded by strangers in daily life—seems to be a key element of the urban experience. And these strangers live tightly clustered together: density of people—and all their activities—is a critical component of urban life. Archaeologist V. Gordon Childe theorizes the transition from small, kin-based societies to large-scale urban societies as an "urban revolution," and outlines ten key characteristics of the world's earliest cities: the first characteristic of the early city, for Childe, was that the size and density of its population was significantly greater than that of other settlements (1950). Urban populations are also more diverse than nonurban communities: people move to cities from other places, bringing their disparate cultures with them (Wirth 1938). This heterogeneity may mean there is greater potential for conflict in cities—but there also may be more opportunity to learn to live together with a wide variety of people (Sennett 1970).

The qualities of size and density of population are echoed in how states define urban places for their own internal purposes. In some countries, population size alone determines whether an area is considered urban: in desolate Greenland, for example, any locality of more than 200 residents is considered urban, while in packed Palestine, an area must have 10,000 residents in order to be considered urban. In other countries, "urban" is defined by population size considered together with density: in Canada, places that have at least 1,000 dwellers, living at a density of 400 or more people per square kilometer, are considered urban, while in the United States, there must be at least 2,500 people, living at a density of 1,000 people per square mile (United Nations 2014, 4).

The quality of diversity refers not just to the different kinds of people living in cities, but also to the different kinds of work they do to survive. The manner in and degree to which inhabitants are integrated into "the economy" constitute an important part of national definitions of the urban. For instance, in Zambia, settlements of at least 5,000 people are considered urban if at least half of the inhabitants depend on "non-agricultural activities." Many other countries—including India, Cambodia, Botswana, Chile, Kazakhstan, and the Netherlands—define urban at least partly in terms of the percentage of the workforce that is employed in nonagricultural work. The urban then, is here defined in contrast to the agricultural. Increasingly, nations are defining the urban by the percentage of inhabitants commuting to waged work. For example, the Organisation for Economic Co-operation and Development, an international group, in a (2012) report, identifies urban areas as "functional economic units"—meaning geographic areas that are tied together through patterns of commuting to waged employment. If at least 15 percent of the population of a given area commutes to a city center, that area is considered urban. The commuting threshold is higher for U.S. (25 percent) and Canadian (50 percent) definitions of urban areas, but tying the definition of the urban to commuting patterns—commuting, that is, to waged labor—still holds. Wachsmuth (2014) argues that commuting patterns are splintering, and that commuting patterns no longer provide a good way to define a metro area. But the fact remains that this is how many policymakers define the urban: the extent to which the surrounding population is integrated into the labor market, and therefore into larger economic structures outside of a subsistence way of life.

The City as a Site of Capital Accumulation

This brings us to the second key characteristic of the urban: the city as a site of capital accumulation. In his essay, Wirth also theorizes the urban in terms of capitalism. Cities developed in the context of what he calls the "money economy." In the city, he argues, the "purchasability of services and things has displaced personal relations as the basis of association" (1938, 17). The city, for Wirth, is a place where you must use money to buy what you need. It is not a place of subsistence. "On the whole," he writes, "the city discourages an economic life in which the individual in time of crisis has a basis of subsistence to fall back upon, and it discourages self-employment" (1938, 21–22). For Childe, the second key characteristic of the urban is that a significant percentage of the population, which traditionally included craftsmen, priests, and merchants, was engaged in non-subsistence activity. And Childe's third key characteristic of a city was that the "primary producers" paid taxes or tithes to "an imaginary deity or a divine king who thus concentrated the surplus" (1950, 11). The city as a place of concentrated wealth—surplus—is critical for Childe. His remaining key traits of cities relate to how that surplus gets used: for the construction of grand public buildings; for the support of all those nonsubsistence workers, who formed a "ruling class," and who created systems of recording and writing in order to administer the surplus; for the support of artists; and for the purchase of goods that could not be found locally.

Marxist theorists of the city later zeroed in on the city's central role in producing, appropriating, and concentrating surplus wealth (Harvey 1973). Echoing Wirth's 1938 argument, they emphasize that the urban is less a particular place and more a process, made up of social relations. Lefebvre's approach is that the essential aspect of the urban is centrality: the city brings together things, people, and processes. In *The Urban Revolution*, originally published in 1970, he suggests:

> The city brings together whatever is engendered somewhere else, by nature or labor: fruits and objects, products and producers, works and creations, activities and situations. What does the city create? Nothing. It centralizes creation. And yet it creates everything. Nothing exists without exchange, without union, without proximity, that is, without relationships. . . . The urban is, therefore,

pure form: a place of encounter, assembly, simultaneity. This
form has no specific content, but is a center of attraction and life.
(Lefebvre 2003 [1970], 117–118)

In his 1968 essay "La droit à la ville," Lefebvre argues that the right to the
city is the right to this centralization of creation that makes up the city.
Though the concept of "centrality" can be maddeningly vague, there is
something powerful about the idea of the right not just to *exist* at the center as defined by spatial coordinates, but the right to centrality in terms of
decision-making powers. Harvey puts it this way: "Since the urban process
is a major channel of surplus use, establishing democratic management
over its urban deployment constitutes the right to the city" (2008, 37). The
city represents the site of capital accumulation, and the urban can be defined, in part, as the process of centralization of surplus wealth.

Brenner and Schmid argue that urban processes have extended out to
encompass the entire globe, leaving no place outside the realm of the urban.
Today, they claim,

it is no longer plausible to characterise the differences between
densely agglomerated zones and the less densely settled zones of
a region, a nation territory, a continent, or the globe through the
inherited urban/rural (or urban/non-urban) distinction. Today,
the urban represents an increasingly worldwide condition in which
political-economic relations are enmeshed. (Brenner and Schmid
2011, 12)

This condition they name as planetary urbanization, or planetary urbanism. The urban as a process of capital accumulation and relations, for
Brenner and Schmid, has extended throughout the globe.

Not everyone agrees with the analysis that equates urban processes
with capitalism. Roy and Ong argue that, in fact, the way capitalism plays
out in a plethora of cities around the world—not just the Western, and
European, cities that have received the most scholarly attention—is not
always so all-encompassing (2011). Ong explains:

This reliance on frameworks that depend on global generalization
has shaped metropolitan studies to such an extent that empirical
heterogeneity, flux, and uncertainty tend to be subsumed under a

minimal set of explanatory conditions. . . . The overall effect . . . is to put the variation in and particularly of urban development, as well as metropolitan life, everywhere at the mercy of a universal- izing force called globalization. The assumption is that there is a single system of capitalist domination, and a set of unified effects of regular causal factors that can foment nearly identical problems and responses in different global sites. (2011, 5–6)

In fact, Ong argues, it is more complicated. The Marxist approach to under- standing cities, in privileging capitalism as the only mechanism at work, risks overlooking all sorts of ways that cities, and people living in cities, actually work. By paying close attention to how non-Western cities—in the case of her book with Roy, Asian cities—work, we can see how the urban actually operates at the scale of the everyday, rather than attempting to cre- ate an abstract unifying theory of "the urban." It is to this methodology—of close attention to the particulars of how things actually work in cities— that I will return.

The City as a Site of State Regulation

Just as the urban may be understood as a concentrated process of sur- plus and exchange, it may also be understood as a concentrated process of statecraft. The earliest urban settlements, as Childe (1950) notes, were places of surplus—but the surplus was invariably controlled by a divine king or some other ruler, personified antecedents to "the state" as such. Scott argues that states have encouraged permanent settlements as a way to control their populations. As he writes of Southeast Asia:

The precolonial state was thus vitally interested in the sedentariza- tion of its population—in the creation of permanent, fixed settle- ments. The greater the concentration of people, providing they produced an economic surplus, the greater the ease of appropriat- ing grain, labor, and military service. (1998, 185)

Permanent, fixed settlements marked the beginning of the urban condition—and for Scott, in many ways the beginning of a less free exis- tence. The urban, Roy notes, is "a state designation, an administrative cate- gory that creates distinctive governed populations" (2016, 9). Scott, Colin

Ward, Jane Jacobs, and others critical of modernist city planning decry the overly heavy hand of the state on the modern city, a place in which much of life is organized in a top-down fashion, in such a way as to impede the development of social networks and community (Jacobs 1961; Scott 1998; Ward 1982).

The city has also been theorized as a place of intensive surveillance by the state, usually taking the form of police surveillance. Mike Davis (1990) has described this for Los Angeles. Davis argues that Los Angeles police surveillance of the urban population has reached new heights—literally, in the case of its massive helicopter force that peers down on Angelenos from above. For Davis, the L.A. Police Department understands "good citizens" as people who are off the public streets, ensconced in private spaces of consumption, and "bad citizens" as people on the streets, presumably up to no good. Mitchell theorizes how the state has used its power to enact and enforce all sorts of laws against existing in public urban space: laws against sitting on sidewalks, sleeping in public, and laws regulating or prohibiting begging (D. Mitchell 2003). For both Davis and Mitchell, the concentration of humanity in urban spaces—the density inherent to urban life—presents real challenges to state control and can therefore lead to a ratcheting up of policing efforts. Of course, policing is not just a state function; private security firms play their role in the city, too, though typically these have been theorized in relationship to the private, often gated, communities they serve (see for example Low 2003). But private firms often work in conjunction with the state.

The relationship between public and private policing bodies, in fact, is one of many examples of the thin border between the "state" and "capital" in producing urban space. Urban renewal, which destroyed thousands of mostly African American neighborhoods in the United States throughout the 1950s and 1960s, is another example of a public-private partnership with massive consequences for urban life (Fullilove 2004). Business improvement districts, in which neighborhood businesses pool funds to pay for services not provided by the city—including, sometimes, policing—are a contemporary example of the thin line between capital and the state (Morçöl et al. 2008). If the city is to be understood as a site of capital accumulation, it must also be understood as a site of state regulation. The urban is the product of ongoing collaboration, and tension, between the state and capital.

Theorizing the Urban Commons

To summarize, I am understanding "the urban" as marked by three charac-teristics: large, diverse, and dense populations of people; centralization of surplus wealth; and regulation and surveillance by the state. I now move to thinking through what is particular about the urban commons. The ques-tion of the urban commons has been a relatively recent one, for both the institutionalists and the alterglobalizationists. As of 2000, according to one survey of new commons research among institutionalists, the study of the urban commons was "still quite undeveloped" (Hess 2000, 12). Over the next decade, a number of researchers wrote about commons that existed in cities, ranging from work on the urban sea commons of Naples, urban brownfields commons, and urban commons in Ethiopia and South Africa (Armiero 2011; Clapp and Meyer 2000; Kassa 2008; Mandizadza 2008). While this work provides good case studies of commons in cities in particu-lar places, it does not theorize the urban commons more broadly, or ask why the term "urban commons" might be useful. Pointing to this lack, a num-ber of scholars have called for more attention to and better theorization of the urban commons (Blomley 2008; Bravo and De Moor 2008; Foster 2011; McShane 2010). In the introduction to their (2015) edited volume, *Urban Commons: Moving Beyond State and Market*, Kip et al. point out that until recently, much of the nascent research on the urban commons was research into commons that happened to be located within the spatial confines of a city—not research that theorized the urban as a process. Similarly, Korn-berger and Borch, in the introduction to their edited volume, *Urban Com-mons: Rethinking the City*, lament that what they call the "objectified notion of the commons"—the commons as a static object, not as a web of social relations—"has been translated uncritically into urban studies" (2015, 5).

But this has begun to change, with scholars increasingly attending to what may be theoretically and materially distinct about the urban com-mons. Some scholars have focused on the ways in which the urban com-mons is unique because of the diverse, constantly changing nature of urban life. Kip et al. argue that, since two of the defining characteristics of the urban are diversity and change, a key component of urban common-ing is figuring out how to create commoning institutions in the context of diversity and change. Elsewhere, Kip builds on this idea to emphasize that one of the main challenges of the urban commons is in negotiating "boundaries and solidarities" of commoning, given the difference inherent in the urban experience (2015, 53).

Scholars have also honed in on the particular relationship of the urban to capital, and what that relationship means for theorizing the urban commons. Kornberger and Borch understand the urban commons as a particular experience because, they argue, it is the urban itself that generates the commons. To make this point, they turn to pioneering urbanist Ebenezer Howard. For Howard (1965 [1898]), city land had value not because of the intrinsic worth of the buildings and soil, but because of the density of people and activities that took place there. Urban value was predicated on location, an inherently relational phenomenon. The more people that lived in a place and the more they did there, the higher the value of the place. For Howard, the question was how everyday urban dwellers could access this value that they had helped create, rather than letting it continue to flow to the owners of property as what he termed the "unearned increment." This key insight of Howard's—that the wealth generated through the city belongs by right to those who make up the city—anticipates Harvey (2012) and Hardt and Negri (2009), among other theorists. Howard's theory of value, Kornberger and Borch argue, is a theory of the urban commons: "value is the corollary of proximity and density which are both *relational* concepts" (2015, 7, emphasis in the original). Or, as Hardt and Negri note, the metropolis does not just create the common; it also *is* the common. The city, they write, "is the source of the common and the receptacle into which it flows" (2009, 154). The challenge, for Kip, is to expand the urban commons "in order to match and outdo capitalist urbanization"—a tall order indeed, though one well worth pursuing (2015, 53).

Some scholars have also examined the particular relationship between the state and the commons, and how this relationship is highlighted in the urban context. Jerram focuses on spaces created by the state, like public restrooms, that became places for gay male mingling and sex in London and Berlin in the 1930s. He theorizes these spaces as a kind of urban commons, and he suggests that a distinctive feature of the urban commons might be that they are "exploitable in ways in which their creators never intended" (Jerram 2015, 54). His key point here is that gay men turned these spaces into a commons "*in practice*" (54, his emphasis) through using them for meeting and sex. The state did not intend to create an urban gay sex commons through building public restrooms: the state built public restrooms in order to address the needs of people living in a densely populated area.

Commoners—gay men—made a commons of the restrooms through their own particular, sexual practices.

If the urban is in part defined by heightened regulation by the state, then urban commoners would have to reckon with this regulation—and, perhaps, with evading it. As Gidwani and Baviskar argue in their piece on the urban commons, the commons should be understood

> as a dynamic and collective resource—a variegated form of social wealth—governed by emergent custom and constantly negotiating, rebuffing, and evading the fixity of law. . . . In a sense, commons thrive and survive by dancing in and out of the State's gaze, by escaping its notice, because notice invariably brings with it the desire to transform commons into state property or capitalist commodity. (2011, 42)

In the city, such evasion may prove more difficult—and the urban commons may therefore, as Gidwani and Baviskar warn, be more subject to cooptation by the market and/or the state. (I return to the question of cooptation in chapter 5.)

Thinking through the idea of the urban commons throws into high relief several key contradictions that, I think, bedevil the theory of the commons more broadly. Each contradiction maps onto one of the distinctive qualities of the urban, as outlined above. First, there is the contradiction of access and exclusion in the urban commons, which is related to the density and diversity of urban places. The second contradiction is the relationship between the urban commons and the market, or, put more broadly, capitalism. The third contradiction is the relationship between the urban commons and the state, or what is considered "public." All three contradictions overlap, but I will address each in turn here, drawing on recent literature on the urban commons.

Access and Exclusion

As discussed, the commons is often theorized as open access—as open to all. This is certainly how Hardin theorized the commons in his 1968 piece, and it is how many alterglobalizationists theorize the commons, as well, as I noted in the last chapter. Other times, the commons is theorized as closed, open only to a group of defined members. This tends to be how the institutionalists understand the commons. When thinking about questions of exclusion and inclusion, it is critical to first understand the scale that is intended by the researcher. For some theorists, the scale of the commons is the scale of the entirety of human culture. Hardt and Negri (2009), in their theory of the common, provide an example of this very large-scale vision: the common is that which is collectively generated by humanity and is necessary for life. Similarly, Kornberger and Borch (2015) argue that the urban commons should be understood as that which all urban dwellers collectively generate: by living in the city and using the commons, urban dwellers help create the commons. The commons, they insist, is not a subtractive resource, or a zero-sum game. These broad understandings of the commons can be put to good work politically. For instance, understanding that the production of human knowledge is part of the commons, as Hardt and Negri insist, is a good basis for arguing against the privatization of scientific discoveries. Similarly, if one sees the city writ large as a commons, as a place of collectively generated surplus, as Kornberger and Borch do, along with Harvey (2012) and many others, one may then build an argument about the right for all city dwellers to share in this surplus. But thinking the commons at these larger scales can skirt the problems of the material needs of everyday life, as Federici (2011) has warned—which means skirting the problem of access and exclusion. Commons also exist in material ways at specific, smaller scales.

The question of access to and exclusion from the commons is thrown into high relief in the urban context because of the key characteristics of urban population: big, dense, and diverse. A relatively large number of humans living in a relatively small amount of space means that people are more often forced to either share or compete for resources. As Sundaresan communicates in his work on the urban commons of a lake in Bangalore, India, urban life is marked by "intense sharing of various kinds of resources that support individual and communal capacities" (2011, 14). Lee and Webster, in their study of the enclosure of the urban commons in China, argue that exclusion is "a more imminent necessity in the city where population is denser" (Lee and Webster 2006, 31). As noted in the previous chapter, much of the research on daily practices of the commons has been conducted in rural or maritime areas, where human populations are relatively sparse. But as of the early twenty-first century, most of the world's people live in cities (United Nations Population Fund 2007). How can so many people, packed so closely together, collectively self-regulate the resources they need for life? The diversity inherent in urban life also points to serious questions of exclusion and access. Cities are places where a wide variety of people live together, in contrast to a village in which people may share more in terms of background and values. Institutionalists have argued that sociocultural diversity has negative effects on people's ability to collectively self-govern commons; this is typically attributed to lower levels of trust among people who are more dissimilar (Ruttan 2006). If that is the case, then it should be difficult to common in the urban context. In a city, different ideas of the commons—ideas about who should manage which commons, and how—come into conflict. As discussed, community gardens have been theorized as a form of commons in the city (Foster 2011; Linn 2007). Yet in New York City's Lower East Side in the 1980s, community gardens were seen as taking up land that could be used for a different form of commons: affordable housing (Schmelzkopf 1995). Commons, Harvey insists, are always contested. "One commons," he writes, ". . . may need to be protected at the expense of another" (2011, 102). In a city, the potential conflict among commons becomes obvious. Conflict within and among commons is an important practical and theoretical task to consider; with the city as our focus, this task is unavoidable.

Housing is a particularly interesting place to study inclusion and exclusion in the commons because housing is apparently so obviously exclusionary: you are either in (you have a key to your apartment), or you are out (no key). Yet some interesting recent research theorizes certain housing arrangements as an urban commons, dealing with the question of exclusion in creative ways. Bruun, for instance, theorizes the cooperative housing of Copenhagen as an urban commons. This is housing that, similar to LECs in the United States, provides affordable, stable living quarters to its dwellers. About one third of all housing in Copenhagen is made up of cooperative units. During the housing boom of the early 2000s—before the global financial crisis of 2008—many of these co-ops decided to raise the price of their shares, so that members could sell their units at a profit. The decision to raise the share prices—which would render much of these residences unaffordable to the next generation—was denounced by many Danes. The public outcry around this decision, Bruun argues, indicates that the co-op members should not be seen as the only legitimate owners of the housing. "Rather," she argues,

> housing cooperatives can be seen as an urban commons shared by the whole of Danish society, and cooperative members as

caretakers or stewards of the commons, which they depend on as their homes but hold only temporarily. (2015, 154)

Understanding the (urban, housing) commons this way, for Bruun, makes a difference when dealing with questions of apparent exclusivity. Her theory opens up the idea that a commons can exist at a specific material scale, meeting the immediate needs of its current membership; but it can also exist at a larger, societal scale, serving as a sort of promise to other would-be-commoners that they, too, will ultimately benefit. Han and Imamasa make a similar point in their (2015) study of a housing commons in South Korea. This housing, made up of a set of collective apartments in Seoul, is known as *Bin-Zib*, which means "empty house" or "guest's house." This "urban commoning movement," as the authors call it, was founded in the early 2000s in response to Seoul's severe crisis of affordable housing. The term *Bin-Zib*, the authors relate, "was coined to represent the community's radical openness and unconditional hospitality" (2015, 91). *Bin-Zib* members, no matter how long they live in the housing, consider themselves to be merely guests, who at some point will move on, opening the housing to others. Over the years, as individual houses have filled up, members have pooled funds to create new houses, thus expanding the *Bin-Zib* network and, at least to a certain extent, mitigating exclusion through expanding the commons. (I will return to this idea in chapter 6.)

A theory and practice of the urban commons must work through the contradiction of the need to bound resources and membership. Though the question of access and exclusion may be more obvious in cities than in smaller, less densely populated, less diverse places, it holds for commons theory and practice more broadly. Yet the seeming contradiction of access and exclusion raises questions: could density, diversity, and working with as-yet-unknown strangers, help create stronger commons? And could re-thinking access in terms of a longer temporal scale, of multiple generations of commoners, help reframe the problem of "exclusion"? These propositions can be well tested in the urban context.

Capital and the Urban Commons

In a fundamental way, the "urban commons" appears to be a contradiction in terms. The contradiction arises because, historically, the city has been the place commoners have been pushed *into* when they have been forced off their common lands through acts of enclosure and expropriation. As noted earlier, Marx (1973) describes the process of enclosure as "so-called primitive accumulation." The violent taking of land and resources through colonization, enslavement, and other means was, Marx argues, what lay the groundwork for the development of capitalism: this theft provided the original, wildly uneven store of wealth from which capitalism could evolve. Primitive accumulation, for Marx, was twofold. One, it included the accumulation of land and resources that could be put to work to generate profit: for instance, the fencing in of common lands in order to create enormous sheep farms to produce wool on a commercial scale. And two, it included the accumulation of a desperate labor force: people who, because their subsistence lands had been taken from them, were forced to search for waged work in order not to starve. As Goldstein puts it, summarizing Perelman's theory of enclosure, "primitive accumulation [was] a concerted and generalized assault against self-provisioning, with the express intent of pushing a newly 'freed' laboring population into the wage market" (2013, 358).

Much of this waged work historically has been in cities. In eighteenth century England, this waged work was found first in factories that had been built along streams in order to harness water power. But with the advent of the steam engine, proximity to waterways was no longer necessary, and factories became clustered in towns and cities. Marx gives an historical example:

In the eighteenth century the Gaels were both driven from the land and forbidden to emigrate, with a view to driving them forcibly to Glasgow and other manufacturing towns. (1973, 890–91)

Marx argues that primitive accumulation created the conditions for capitalism. Harvey argues that the process was not just a one-time jump-start for capital: rather, the process is ongoing, taking the form of what he calls accumulation by dispossession, in which lands and resources are continually enclosed, and people are continually thrown into waged labor. Today, Harvey points out, it is peasants in Mexico and India who, because of NAFTA and WTO rules, are thrown off their lands and forced to look for work in cities (2003). Mike Davis (2006) makes a similar point, arguing that World Bank and IMF policies have forced many rural denizens of the Global South into cities, even as the cities themselves have ceased to provide much in the way of employment opportunities. In her close examination of the lives of Zapatista women, Hilary Klein describes the dynamic at play in contemporary Chiapas. She quotes one Zapatista woman's analysis of how the Mexican government is undermining the ability of indigenous peoples to sustain themselves on the land:

> Through their capitalist projects, they're privatizing the land, the mountain springs and the waterfalls, medicinal plants, oils, and the mines. They want to hand over our country's riches and our sovereignty. Privatizing the land means we will have to compete on the free market with big companies, but not only that. We will also be expelled from our own land by industrialization in order to provide cheap labor for the *maquilas* [sweatshops]. (2015, 92, italics and translation in the original)

Though *maquilas* are not always located in cities per se, they are part of the larger trend of urbanization in northern Mexico. Privatization, or enclosure, forces commoners off the land and into waged labor.

The town, Linebaugh points out in his essay on the urban commons, was the original enclosed space. He notes how John Horne Tooke, who he describes as the "imprisoned radical and etymologist of the 1790s," understood the etymology of the word "town:" it "derived from the Anglo-Saxon meaning inclosed, encompassed, or shut in" (Linebaugh 2014, 25). The city is where capital is accumulated: this is the original site of wage labor, the place where people were forced into wage relations and became dependent on the wage and no longer able to support themselves directly through subsistence life on the commons. It is where people flock to when they can no longer make a living in the countryside. It is a place not of subsistence, but of exchange. The city, Linebaugh argues, appears to be the opposite of the commons. So how can the city also be a place of commons formation?

A theory and practice of the urban commons needs to reckon with the historic, and contemporary, fact of the city as the site of capital accumulation and wage relations: a place largely of surplus, consumption and exchange, not of subsistence. To use the phrase "urban commons" without recognizing this history obscures the theoretical contradictions of the urban commons. If, as noted earlier, urban areas are defined in part by the ways in which people who live within them are connected to waged labor, then how can the commons—a site for resisting waged labor—exist in the urban context? Yet this second contradiction, like the first, raises a question: if the city is made up of people thrown off the commons, is it also the opportunity for these thrown-together people to create new forms of commoning?

The Commons versus the State

If urban commons are marked in part by greater state regulation, then how do urban commons interact with the state? How is "the public" differentiated from "the commons," and why does it matter? Kratzwald, in theorizing the urban commons, makes a two-part argument. First, she argues that the idea of the "commons" predates the idea of "the public." A main function of the modern state, she argues, has been to guarantee the functioning of capitalism, and "[f]rom the beginning," she asserts, "the state has existed in conflict with the idea of the commons" (2015, 32). But she still thinks it is possible to "employ the concept of the commons in defense of urban public space, and thereby to shift the term 'public' in an emancipatory direction" (31). Similarly, Bruun draws upon Carol Rose's (1994) distinction among two types of public property to distinguish between the public and the commons. Rose distinguishes between public property owned and managed by a government body, and, as Bruun describes it, "public property collectively 'owned' by society at large with claims that are independent of and superior to government" (2015, 165). For Bruun, the latter represents the commons. Neither scholar is quite ready to reject "the public" as a concept; both seem to think that the theory and practice of the commons can be used to push the idea of the public, as Kratzwald puts it, in an "emancipatory direction."

Another tension can be found in the critique that the commons can be used to absolve the state of its responsibility to care for its citizens. Rightwing champions of the commons, of which there are plenty, delight in the commons precisely because of its potential for replacing the public and the state with voluntary collective activity (see for example Aligica 2014). In examining urban commons in Australia, McShane warns that the resurgence of the commons could also serve to sneak in the "Trojan horse" of a regressive anti-state agenda. To embrace the collective self-provisioning of the commons can be, in a sense, to tell the state it isn't necessary (McShane 2010). Movements of self-provisioning—that reject state care in favor of a self-help, do-it-yourself approach—are often critiqued for letting the state off the hook. In an analysis of self-help housing in New York City and

Berlin in the 1980s, Katz and Mayer argue that self-help movements help members gain autonomy while providing a democratic challenge to state bureaucracy and meeting their own material needs. But these movements are also quite convenient, they say, for a neoliberal state. As they write:

> From the point of view of the state, self-help represents not only a partial solution to fiscal crisis tendencies—through the use of state clients' non-monetized labour—but also a new structure for reshaping and disciplining the normative orientations of citizens. That is, self-help is represented as a form of social self-maintenance and self-policing. (1985, 17)

Katz and Mayer are examining movements of collective self-help in the 1980s: tenant takeovers of buildings abandoned by landlords in New York City and squatters movements in what was then West Berlin. What tenants and squatters in New York City and West Berlin were doing, I would argue, was seizing and maintaining a commons. In doing so, they provided for themselves, in more or less democratic ways. But in putting their energies toward providing for themselves rather than toward petitioning the state for better housing, they essentially gave up on the possibility of a welfare state and shouldered more responsibilities themselves. They gained a great deal from this, materially and socially (Kolodny and Gellerman 1973; Leavitt and Saegert 1990). But in embracing the commons and rejecting the state, they are taking a tremendous risk: that they will be able to care for themselves collectively in the long term, without the state's assistance (never mind the challenges faced by future generations in this regard). Lutz finds the same tension at work in his study of homeless tent cities in the United States. These tent cities, which he theorizes as an urban commons, have in some cases been legalized, which has allowed cities to more effectively police the tent city inhabitants—and at a much cheaper price than jailing them. "Therefore," Lutz argues, echoing Caffentzis (2010), "the tent commons provide a useful fix for multiple crises in an existing homeless management system whose aim is to deal with this potentially troublesome population" (2015, 107). This tension between committing to collective self-provisioning and/or placing demands on the state is difficult to tease out and resolve.

Finally, this third contradiction, of the relationship between the commons and the state, raises another question: is there a way the state could support a commons? Could a commons exist, that is, not in opposition to the state, but supported by it? The urban provides a rich environment for testing this.

A Feminist Perspective

Given the contradictions I am arguing are inherent in the urban commons, how can the urban commons be useful, theoretically and materially? A feminist perspective—on urban studies broadly, and on the urban commons specifically—can help begin to work through these contradictions.

A feminist approach to urban studies provides the groundwork for studying the urban commons. A feminist approach requires attending to the everyday quality of urbanism: to understanding how people make their lives in cities, day in and day out. Derickson, in her (2015) critique of contemporary urban studies scholarship, builds on Chakrabarty's (2000) distinction between History 1 ("histories posited by capital") and History 2 ("histories that exist outside of capital's life-process"). Derickson sees the study of cities divided into two broad camps: Urbanization 1, made up of scholars who theorize cities and urbanization processes "from above," and Urbanization 2, made up of scholars who theorize the city "from below," attending to the specific experiences of urban dwellers. (More properly, she points out, the latter should be understood as "Urbanization 2s," because of the multiple ways of seeing and creating the city from below.) The Urbanization 1 tradition, Derickson believes, doesn't do enough to explore actually existing conditions of people making lives in cities. Peake (2016) agrees, critiquing the "grand theory" line of scholarship for not having any agents, any people *doing stuff* in cities. Though Peake is specifically critiquing Brenner's (2014) edited volume *Implosions/Explosions: Towards a Study of Planetary Urbanism* (incidentally or not, of the book's twenty-one authors, just one is a woman), she is concerned more broadly about the trend in urban studies of talking about cities without talking to people who live in cities—and she is worried about the clout such (mostly male) theorizing appears to hold.[1] In the tradition of Urbanization 2s, Derickson argues, "academic inquiry should be in deep, sustained conversation with those making the city" (2015, 651). Derickson draws here on Gibson-Graham (1996) to critique the "capitalocentric" logic of the Urbanization 1 approach. "Urbanization 2, then," Derickson writes, "is an epistemological posture that aims to produce knowledge about life in cities and the processes of urbanization that are not understood in relation to trajectories of capitalist urbanization" (2015, 653). Or, she clarifies later, the point is to understand urban life and urbanization not *solely* in relation to capitalist urbanization.

Derickson's case for Urbanization 2s echoes Sheppard et al.'s case for subaltern urbanism. As these authors explain:

> By subaltern urbanism, we mean some of the approaches to the study of cities that privilege everyday lived urban life over research strategies that view cities from a distance, explicitly or implicitly working to disrupt mainstream global urbanism by attending to the tactics of survival and subversion resorted to by subaltern or subordinated populations. (Sheppard, Leitner, and Maringanti 2013, 897)

Subaltern urbanism, for Sheppard et al., contrasts with the "global urbanism" theorized by scholars like Brenner, Schmid, and Merrifield (Brenner 2014; Brenner and Schmid 2011; Merrifield 2014). But a feminist perspective is not just about confining one's lens to the local and the everyday. As Derickson emphasizes, the most promising work in the Urbanization 2 tradition comes when theorists "train their focus on the inbetween spaces of everyday life as it shapes and is shaped by power structures, social relations, political economic processes, and geopolitical orders that are expressed at more-than-local scales" (2015, 654). This, to my mind, is a critical piece of her argument: a feminist perspective is not just understanding processes "from below," but is also interested in the relationship between the everyday and larger structures of capital and the state.

A feminist approach to the urban commons would entail close examination of the ways people reclaim and maintain commons in the urban context—which necessarily means attending both to particular experiences and larger forces. Urban commoning is the messy, everyday, necessarily compromised work of trying to build networks of survival in the midst of the high-pressure centrality of the urban. Urban commoning is not pure. It should in no way be romanticized. It is often, as will be seen in future chapters, an act of desperation, and as noted here, it is marked by contradiction.

But a feminist perspective can help work through the contradictions of the urban commons. A feminist perspective, for instance, may shed light on the questions of access and exclusion. Commoning can be exclusionary. When openings arise in limited-equity cooperatives, for example, members may prioritize making apartments available to family and friends. These networks of family and friends often overlap with networks of care for children, the elderly, and the sick and disabled. Sustaining such networks has shown to be of particular value for poor and working-class women (Hansen 2005). Prioritizing such networks, as we will see in later chapters, may help safeguard the life of the commons. On the other hand, keeping the commons radically open to future, as-yet-unknown members may also be a feminist move. This, too, we will learn more about in chapters to come.

A feminist perspective also shows us that, though a site of capital accumulation, the city can also be a site of subsistence. A grounding in diverse economies helps see all the ways people survive in cities, without access to waged labor. Though the city is the site of capital accumulation, it is not wholly a capitalist machine. Subsistence living can and does happen in cities, in all sorts of ways, and women are often the ones innovating urban subsistence. For instance, Federici describes women taking over land to plant food in African cities: in Accra, Ghana, such urban gardens supply the city with 90 percent of its vegetables; in Kinshasa, Democratic Republic of Congo, manioc is planted everywhere, and goats graze in public space (2011). She theorizes these spaces as forms of urban commons. Squatting housing is another form of subsistence living that takes place in cities across the globe (Neuwirth 2005; Squatting Europe Kollective et al. 2014). Some co-op members, as we will see, rely on their housing commons for at least partial subsistence in the midst of a high-cost city that would otherwise seem to demand full participation in waged labor.

A feminist perspective also reveals that, while the urban is certainly marked by regulation and surveillance by the state, it can also be a space of freedom. The city, Elizabeth Wilson suggests, "might be a place of liberation for women. The city offers women freedom" (1991, 7). She contrasts this freedom with the patriarchy of the small town and traditional community. Peake and Rieker note that the city can be a place of "economic independence and an array of freedoms," for many, including for women (2013, 6). The city may also be a space of freedom for people whose sexualities have been seen as deviant in the small towns, suburbs, or rural areas in which they were raised. San Francisco provides the classic U.S. example, but cities around the world have provided this freedom (Castells 1983). In the U.S. context in general and the Washington, D.C., context in particular, the city has also been theorized as a site of (at least partial) black freedom from the racist violence of the rural South (Masur 2010; Wilkerson 2010). As the medieval adage goes, "city air makes people free" (Bookchin 1974, 1). While many of the traditional commons throughout history have been imprinted with patriarchal society, an urban commons may offer up a more egalitarian way to structure life. A feminist perspective brings a particular emphasis on freedom.

The urban commons is materially and theoretically distinct from the commons as understood more broadly: the urban commons is marked by its density and diversity, and its close relationship with capital and the state. The urban commons, above all, is marked by contradiction. Though the contradictions of the urban commons can be found in many types of commons, the contradictions are more obvious, and are of greater urgency, in the urban context. Working through these contradictions opens up some opportunities for understanding how commons operate, both in the urban context and more broadly.

One opportunity is in understanding how commons are formed, or reclaimed. Cities, as discussed here, have arisen as sites of wealth accumulation, as places poor people have been pushed into when they have been pushed off the commons. Any commons that exists in the urban context necessarily had to have been reclaimed from a capitalist web of social relations. In cities, therefore, we have the opportunity to understand how commons arise. Approaching this question historically—trying to determine how urban commons have been seized—I think is an enormous opportunity for understanding commons more broadly. We can easily investigate this question in cities, because *all* commons in cities are necessarily the result of some sort of collective action of seizure. Studying how commons have arisen—or been created, or been seized—in the past, can help us learn how we can continue to seize, or create, and expand commons today.

A second opportunity is in understanding how commons are maintained over time. The institutionalists have done a good job at documenting how commons have been maintained—but since they have little critique of capitalism, it is hard for a lot of that work to be useful to a political project. A place packed with strangers, and facing ongoing financial pressures on land, provides an excellent laboratory for testing how commoners can maintain collective resources over time.

Finally, in cities, we have the opportunity to practice commoning. That is, we have the opportunity to practice how to collectively regulate resources among diverse people. There are many opportunities in the city, because of its density and diversity, to practice commoning. In the next several chapters, I explore how a commons has been created in Washington, D.C.; I emphasize what that commons provides for its members; and I discuss how members have maintained commons over time—and in some cases failed to maintain them. Ultimately, I return to the question of practicing the urban commons.

3

Forged in Crisis

Claiming a Home in the City

Addisu immigrated to Washington, D.C., from Ethiopia in the early 1980s, part of a growing stream of immigrants to D.C. from that East African nation, torn by famine and war. When he first arrived, he landed in a two-bedroom apartment in a rough neighborhood, living with four or five other people. When a neighbor broke in and stole all his things, Addisu moved in with his brother, who was living in a one-bedroom apartment in a run-down building in D.C.'s Columbia Heights neighborhood. When, in the late 1980s, their fifteen-unit building was put up for sale, Addisu was one of the tenants who helped organize to collectively buy it and turn it into a limited-equity cooperative. He found the purchase process thrilling:

> So we organized, we created a committee for management, and we are having fun, really, amazingly! I mean we don't have any money, so collectively, we can decide on $300,000—we borrow $300,000 I think, from the cooperative bank, under the city. So it was a process. In fact, we had a good advantage. One thing, we had good people there . . . There were—Mr. [Gonzalez], he doesn't speak English, but I think he passed through a lot, I think. And he has a daughter who lived in a separate apartment. There is Mr. [Suarez], another Spanish person. The Ethiopians, there were three or four people, and there were African-Americans. So it is a good combination.

This commons was reclaimed by a diversity of strangers, many of whom did not even speak the same language. Addisu continues:

> So there were many people that relate. [Working on the process of co-op formation] brings you together as a unit, fifteen families, as

a unit, it brings you. You discuss, you share their problems. This is the innermost thing. So it brings you as a collective, and it gives you confidence too, really, to decide on things.

Together, the tenants made many decisions, highlighted in papers documenting their purchase process. They determined how much their carrying charges would be and what kinds of renovations they would undertake. They wrote bylaws and house rules. They interviewed three different management companies, discussed the role of a management company vis-à-vis the co-op board, and finally selected a management company to hire. It was a lot of work, and tenants were deeply committed to it: on average, nine tenants, out of the fifteen total households, attended each of the many meetings leading up to their purchase of the building in 1991. It was through claiming the resource, and devising institutions to govern it, that they built a community and a commons. They named their new home the Walnut Cooperative.

People like Addisu and his fellow tenants create a commons through coming together to claim ownership of the conditions needed for life and its reproduction (De Angelis and Harvie 2014). But how is a commons reclaimed from a city, where space is already enclosed, and people don't necessarily have the shared background thought necessary for building commons?

As I have noted, the institutionalist literature has very little to say about the act of reclaiming the commons. As outlined in chapter 1, I suspect this is for two reasons. First, these theorists have tended to be interested in ongoing commons, and in understanding how long-term commons have existed over time, rather than how they are reclaimed or created in the first place. And second, they do not seem particularly interested in the politics of reclaiming space; while no doubt many of them are politically supportive of commons efforts, they tend to couch their work in economistic, rather than political, terms. As Kratzwald argues in her piece on the urban commons, a key weakness of Ostrom and her school of research is that they

> examined [commons institutions] during or after their establishment. What preceded the establishment, the conflicts and power relations that led to their formation, is not present. All of the struggles for commons in the course of the enforcement of capital-

ism, as described in detail by Linebaugh or Polanyi, do not play a role in institutional research. (2015, 35)

It is precisely the struggles for commons in, as Kratzwald writes, "the course of the enforcement of capitalism," that I explore in this chapter.

The time of reclaiming the commons is of a particular nature: exciting, intense, and suffused with energy. The idea that a group of people—often, people who have had little power over their work and home lives—can collectively take over space and make it their own is powerful enough to buoy them through months, even years, of hard work. The reclamation of a commons is necessarily a political act: it is a taking of power, and it can be deeply thrilling for participants. Blomley describes the intense activities that surrounded attempts to reclaim the commons in the form of the takeover of an abandoned building in downtown Vancouver. People cleaned up the building, painted it, designed and hung posters declaring their collective right to the building, and attempted to occupy the interior of the building itself (Blomley 2008). In Harlem, New York, and Echo Park-Silverlake, Los Angeles, tenants worked very hard to found their limited-equity co-ops. They held countless meetings with fellow tenants, negotiated with their respective city governments, and worked to fix up their buildings and devise their own management structures (Heskin 1991; Leavitt and Saegert 1990). Because the phase of commons creation has such clear and tangible goals, it tends to be deeply meaningful for participants. More generally, the rousing call to "reclaim the commons!" (cf N. Klein 2001) resonates with people who yearn for collective control over common resources.

In this chapter, I tell the story of how a commons has been created in Washington, D.C. This story is important for three reasons. One, this story illuminates the specific history of a commons created in a contemporary urban context. Historian Leif Jerram (2015) critiques much commons scholarship for having an overly romanticized historical vision of the commons. I want to take this critique seriously by investigating exactly how it was that a commons emerged in the particular place of Washington, D.C., and the particular time of the 1970s and 1980s—because the creation of a commons is not guaranteed but is contingent on historical forces at work. Understanding the particulars of this experience can help enlarge the imagination for how commons might be created in other times and other contexts. Two, this story is important because it makes clear the role the state can play in opening up the possibility for a commons. The commons constituted by D.C. LECs could not have been created were it not for the legal protections and financial assistance that the city, under pressure from tenant organizers, agreed to provide. Commons theorists—both of the institutionalist and alterglobalizationist bent—often have an intense critique of the state. But the experience of D.C. LECs is that the state has played a crucial role in enabling the creation of these commons. Finally, this story is important because it underscores that urban commons are often created in times of crisis. The urban commons, I am ultimately arguing, should be understood more as a pragmatic practice in the face of crisis than as a utopian project, dreamed up in a time of leisure.

I begin this chapter by examining the tenant activism that led to the creation of the city policies that have allowed for, and supported, the founding of LECs. I discuss the particular relationship between race, the commons, and the concept of homeownership, and then turn to the reclamation stories of several of the co-ops I examined in my research. I end by exploring the question of the commons in relation to capitalism. This chapter focuses closely on the Washington, D.C., experience. But the experiences of D.C. tenants in many ways mirrors experiences in other cities, in the United States and around the world, where tenants have fought for—and won—the ability to wrest their housing from the market and control it themselves.

Creating Structures to Allow for Commons Creation: The Role of the State

Many theorists of the commons—from the right and the left—are skeptical of the state, seeing it as oppressive and/or inefficient (Aligica 2014; De Angelis 2003; Lutz 2015; Pennington 2012). But my research shows that the state can play a critical role in allowing a commons to flourish. This may be particularly the case in an urban context. Wall insists, following Ostrom, that commons must be generated by commoners: "A government," he writes, "cannot proclaim a commons from the top down. If commons are to have a real existence, they need to be built on the ground by citizens who cooperate and learn" (2014a, 125). But, Wall goes on to say, governments can introduce legislation that supports commons. Similarly, Blomley (2008) suggests that the state may play a critical role in creating structures to support commons in cities. In the contemporary urban context, such state support is critical—perhaps even necessary—for long-term commons. Because of the capitalist pressures threading through the city, reclaiming a commons of any significant scale and duration requires some amount of structural policy change. This is important: as the alter-globalizationists insist, commons don't just arise: they must be created. But structural change, enabled by the state, won't happen without political will. The nature and extent of this political will depends on the specific historical circumstances of the place the commons is to be reclaimed. We can use the case of Washington, D.C., to see how, with state support, a commons has been able to emerge. I argue that the confluence of two specific historical circumstances in D.C. in the mid-1970s allowed for the generation of the political will to change local policy structures to allow for the reclamation of the commons. (For further elucidation of the argument laid out below, see Huron 2014.)

The first historical circumstance was the return, in the 1970s, of (partial) democracy to the nation's capital. In 1973, District residents finally received the right to vote for their own local self-representation. This victory was the culmination of a long civil rights battle, going back more than a century.

The struggle for the vote in D.C., as elsewhere, had long been racialized. The city of Washington was created at the end of the eighteenth century to serve as the capital of the new nation of the United States. From its early years, white male property owners—later, white men who paid a school tax—were the only ones with the right to vote. Slavery was legal in the capital, and slaves outnumbered free blacks by large margins. But slavery was outlawed in the city in April 1862, about nine months prior to the Emancipation Proclamation (Masur 2010). And over the course of the Civil War, thousands of African Americans streamed into the nation's capital, fleeing slavery and brutality in the South. Since Washington was the headquarters of the Union army, it was seen as a safer place to be black—especially to be an escaped slave from the Confederate south (Green 1967). In 1867, Radical Republicans in Congress voted to give black men the right to vote in the nation's capital, over the strenuous objections of the city's local (white, male) electorate—three years before the ratification of the Fifteenth Amendment granted black men the right to vote nationally (Masur 2010).

But in the 1870s, as Washington's African American population continued to swell, the city's white elite made a bold decision: they agreed to give up voting rights for *all* Washingtonians rather than risk allowing black men to continue to vote. The white elite was frightened of growing black political power, and they also worried about the economic future of a city that at the time was in debt due to a rash of post-Civil War construction. As historian Kate Masur argues, white city leaders blamed the city's growing debt load on black enfranchisement. African American men (along with many white men) had voted for a municipal bond to support continued infrastructure improvements in the city, which added to the city's debt (2010).

In 1874, Congress took away the right to vote in the city, and for the next one hundred years, Washington residents could not elect their own mayor and city council. Instead, the city was run by a three-man commission appointed by the U.S. President and by Congressional committees—the chairs of which were often notoriously racist. In the 1930s, the House Subcommittee on District Appropriations was chaired by a racist from Mississippi, Ross Collins; Theodore Bilbo, a Klansman from Mississippi, led the Senate committee on the District in the 1940s; and John McMillan, the segregationist Democratic Congressman from South Carolina, chaired the House committee on the District for decades, beginning in the 1940s (Jaffe and Sherwood 1994). In 1957, Washington became the first major U.S. city to become majority African American, and many District residents equated their Congressional overseers, like McMillan, with plantation bosses (Smith 1974). For years, McMillan refused to let Congress consider Home Rule legislation for the District—legislation that would give city residents the right to vote for their own local leaders. But the passage of the 1965 Voting Rights Act opened up new opportunities for creative organizing for voting rights in D.C. In 1972, civil rights organizers from Washington organized among newly enfranchised black South Carolinians to vote John McMillan out of office, thus clearing the way for new leadership in the House committee that oversaw the city, and allowing for the passage of the Home Rule Act in 1973 (Fauntroy 2003).

Finally, this majority-black city could elect its own mayor and its own city council, and enact its own laws. These laws were (and are, as of this writing) still subject to approval by Congress, and District residents still didn't (and still don't, as of this writing) have any voting representation in Congress. But nonetheless, the opportunity to create new city policy—potentially, more than just new city policy—was thrilling. By the early 1970s, the city was about 70 percent African American, and many of the people elected to office were progressive African Americans, seasoned in the civil rights movement. The city's newly gained black political power, overlaid onto its longstanding black cultural and educational institutions, made it a compelling place for black political and cultural life. Over the course of the 1970s, the nation's capital became known as "Chocolate City" (Hopkinson 2012; J. Williams 1980).

But the second historical circumstance of the mid-1970s threatened to change the kinds of people who called Chocolate City home. Just at the moment that Home Rule was becoming a reality, the city was hit with a wave of gentrification and displacement of low-income people. In the early 1970s, as noted in this book's introduction, gentrification began hitting a few U.S. cities. Gentrification—the return of capital and the "gentry" to disinvested urban neighborhoods—was documented closely in 1970s lower Manhattan (Zukin 1982), and it was also affecting Boston, San Francisco, Washington, and a few other cities (U.S. Department of Housing and Urban Development 1974). The process described by gentrification was not new in the District of Columbia. In the 1930s through the 1960s, for example, the Georgetown neighborhood lost most of its large black population due to periodic influxes of young whites who could afford higher rents and home prices (Lesko, Babb, and Gibbs 1991). When, in the 1970s, other D.C. neighborhoods began to experience rising housing costs, influxes of young whites, and displacement of blacks, they were said to be experiencing "Georgetownization" (Mansfield 1977). But the new term "gentrification" was important, because it described a broader phenomenon beyond just the experience of a particular neighborhood. In D.C., home sales prices in central neighborhoods increased by 96.6 percent between 1975 and 1978—nearly doubling in just three years (Paige and Reuss 1983). Centrally located neighborhoods like Adams Morgan, Mt. Pleasant, and Capitol Hill were the subject of scholarly research examining the "back-to-the-city" movement (Gale 1976, 1977; Henig 1982). Local leaders expressed concern that the "back-to-the-city" movement had pushed the price of housing beyond the reach of the poor (*Washington Post* 1978).

In sum, just as this majority-black city was gaining the right to govern itself, low-income people, mostly African American, were threatened with displacement from the city. In response, tenants organized. The City-Wide Housing Coalition was formed in 1973 to lobby the newly elected city council for rent control and to organize and educate tenants across neighborhood lines (Reed 1981). In 1974 the Adams Morgan Organization and the Capitol East Housing Coalition, two neighborhood-based groups, teamed up to organize the day-long public forum, "Blockbusting—1974 Style," in which speakers addressed the threats to low-income renters. From this forum emerged an Anti-Speculation Task Force, which lobbied the city council to enact legislation discouraging real estate speculation (Paige and Reuss 1983; Wells 2015). The Southern Columbia Heights Tenants Union worked to organize area tenants and also pushed for changes in city law to protect poor tenants (Institute for Community Economics 1982). These groups protested in the streets and squatted in vacant buildings to pressure their newly elected leaders to focus on the housing crisis (Reed 1981).

When the city's first elected mayor and city council members of the twentieth century took their seats in January 1975, they responded to the city's housing crisis—and the pressure brought about by tenant organizing—by immediately passing a series of laws to counter displacement. In 1975, the city passed its first local rent control program (Turner 1998). The next year, in response to massive numbers of condominium conversions, legislators passed the Condominium Act of 1976, which required that developers receive permission from the mayor in order to proceed with condominium conversion plans, and also required, among other things, that over half of the heads of household of a rental building agree to a condo conversion (Diner 1983). Several times over the course of the late 1970s, the council passed temporary moratoria on condo conversion in order to buy time to figure out how to help the thousands of tenants who would potentially be affected by conversions (Camp 1978; Gallaher 2016). Another policy was the city's Real Property Transfer Excise Tax, which went into effect in July of 1978, and was aimed at stemming the flipping of residential properties. The tax was imposed on home sellers who held property for short periods of time and then resold it for gains above a certain percentage of the price for which they bought. Essentially, the shorter the period of time the investor held the property, the higher the tax on the property (J. E. Davis 2006a). Known as the "anti-speculation tax," it ultimately failed in its aims, but the tax was representative of the creativity that went into the attempt to craft policy that could counter displacement (Wells 2015).

Another creative piece of policy was a provision of the Rental Housing Act of 1977, which gave tenants the opportunity to purchase their homes should their landlords choose to sell. It was an unusual law, giving tenants an unusual degree of protection. But the law did not clearly outline how tenants could invoke their rights, and activists wanted more (Gallaher

2016; *Washington Post* 1975). One way to stem the tides of displacement, organizers believed, was to pressure the city to pass a stronger tenant purchase law, and to demand city financing to help low-income tenants purchase their homes. In late 1978 activists wrote mayor-elect Marion Barry demanding that he create a city office to help low-income tenants purchase their apartment buildings and convert them to cooperatives. "We need money to buy our buildings," insisted Evelyn Onwuachi, director of the City-Wide Housing Coalition, to achieve "tenant ownership and tenant-managed buildings" (Gately 1978c).

Activist pressure, which included the hard work of members of the Aspen Cooperative, discussed in the introduction, helped push the city council to pass the Tenant Opportunity to Purchase Act, known as TOPA, as part of the comprehensive Rental Housing Conversion and Sale Act of 1980. TOPA clarified tenants' right to purchase their homes and also gave them leverage if they wished to make other choices at the time their landlord sold. Under TOPA tenants could accept a buy-out to leave the building, negotiate to stay for an affordable or reduced rent, purchase their homes, assign their right to purchase to a third party, or negotiate for still other options (Gallaher 2016; O'Toole and Jones 2009). Significantly, however, the law required owners to give tenants the opportunity to purchase at a price and terms that represented a "bona fide offer of sale," which meant that tenants had to pay what were essentially market rates for their homes (Harrison Institute for Public Law 2006). Tenants may have gained the right to purchase their housing, but without the financial assistance Onwuachi insisted upon, low-income tenants had no way to exercise that right.

The city addressed this dilemma by providing low-cost financing to low-income tenant associations to help with purchases. In exchange for receiving this financing, typically a low- or zero-interest loan, cooperatives were required to remain limited-equity for the life of the loan. With this financing, even very-low-income tenants could purchase their homes. While condominium ownership would require individual residents to qualify for individual mortgages, the limited-equity cooperative structure enabled tenant households to participate in a collective, or "blanket," mortgage, and tenants typically were able to buy into the co-op for $800–$1,500. Though tenants could use TOPA to exercise a range of options, the law encouraged tenants to choose LECs by providing stronger negotiating rights for tenants who chose that option (R. Eisen, Looney, and Williams 1980).

By 1980—just five years after the city's first elected government in one hundred years had come to power—groundbreaking legislation had been passed that gave tenants the legal and financial framework for staying in place as their buildings were sold off. The city government—because of consistent pressure from tenant activists—had created a structure for enabling the creation of a commons.

Reclaiming Housing, Creating a Commons

When historian Peter Linebaugh began studying the Magna Carta, the English document first issued in 1215, he came to a key realization. The Magna Carta, originally known as the Charter of Liberties, is the well-known document that outlines such basic rights as *habeus corpus*, and which has formed the basis for many national constitutions, including that of the United States. But at the same time that the Charter of Liberties was issued, a second charter was issued, as well: the lesser-known Charter of the Forest. The Charter of the Forest outlines rights to subsistence in the forest, or common lands. Linebaugh's realization was that the two had to exist in tandem. "The message of the two charters . . ." Linebaugh writes, "is plain: political and legal rights can only exist on an economic foundation" (2008, 6). It is the commons, he argues, working directly from the Charter of the Forest, which provides the economic foundation for political rights. We can see the logic of the two charters playing out in Washington, D.C., in the late 1970s. Washingtonians had finally gained political rights, but they needed an economic foundation in order to exercise those rights. That economic foundation was provided, in small part, by a commons, in the form of the limited-equity co-op.

As described in the introduction, limited-equity co-ops are part of a larger universe of resale-restricted housing, which also includes community land trusts, that functions to keep land and housing off the speculative market, controlled by community members, and affordable in the long term (J. E. Davis 1993). In the United States, the contemporary community land trust model was born in the rural South of the 1960s. Civil rights activists, including members of the National Sharecroppers Fund and the Southwest Alabama Farmers' Cooperative Association, organized to purchase land in order to ensure that African American farmers could have control over the land they worked (J. E. Davis 2010a). From the inception of the community land trust movement, gaining collective, nonspeculative control over housing and land has often been framed as a civil rights issue (Community Economics 1992; Institute for Community Economics 1982). Similarly, some of the people who have helped form LECs in D.C. frame these cooperatives in terms of civil rights struggles. One longtime organizer of D.C. LECs explains:

> D.C. was a center of the civil rights movement. In fact, probably D.C. had—a large number of the folks who were in [the Student Nonviolent Coordinating Committee]—and when I think of the civil rights movement, that's what I think of [laughs]— live in D.C.! So I would expect that some of the principles that they were involved in organizing below the Mason-Dixon line, which includes here, but even further south, around voting rights, around voting, around cooperatives—you know one of the leaders—the founder—of SNCC, Ella Jo Baker, was a leader in cooperatives. And Ms. Fannie Lou Hamer, which was one of our civil rights leaders, or human rights leaders, was very much involved in cooperatives in Mississippi. So a lot of those folks were involved in collectivism.

For this organizer and others, community control over land was a critical piece of a larger civil rights struggle: land was the economic basis for life and for freedom from white supremacist control over black labor. In the urban context, control over land became control over housing.

D.C. tenants were so eager to purchase their buildings and convert them into cooperatives that, even before the final version of the TOPA law passed, they began organizing for collective ownership. Limited-equity cooperatives grew at a rapid clip in every quadrant of the city. From late 1979 to late 1980, low-income tenants created seventeen LECs comprising one thousand units; as of November 1980, twenty more tenant associations were in the process of negotiating to buy their buildings, for a total of two thousand more units (Bowman 1980). Tenants of the Jeffrey Terrace Apartments in the Southeast quadrant of the city purchased sixty-seven units in 1979 and named their new LEC "The People's Co-op." A group in the Northwest Shaw neighborhood bought a four-building complex, comprising fifty-one units, in 1980; some of the tenants had lived in the complex since the turn of the twentieth century, and they were, the tenant association president declared, "determined not to be displaced" (V. C. Thompson 1980). By 1981 about fifty buildings, containing nearly six thousand units, had been reclaimed from the investor-driven real estate market and converted into limited-equity co-ops (Hartman et al. 1982).

It was a heady time for LECs, and tenant leaders, most of whom were low-income African American women, received some glowing press coverage. In late 1980, *Washington Post* reporter LaBarbara Bowman described the experience of co-op formation in detail:

> Armed with only the law, these black women, many of whom have only high school educations, have found lawyers and organizations to help them unite tenants and arrange the complicated procedure of financing the acquisition and rehabilitation of the buildings. They have fought frustration, apathy and indifference among tenants who work as janitors, cooks, clerks, and others who either are retired or on public assistance—people who never have owned property and never dreamed that they ever could. They have spent long hours baking pies and cakes, frying chicken, cooking dinners, organizing cabarets and trips to raise money needed to help pay engineers and make down payments. And they have learned about their rights, contracts, and financing. While developers and more affluent tenants have converted more than 9,000 apartment units to condominiums, lower-income tenants are converting to cooperatives where individual tenants buy stock in their building, which entitles them to a unit. Their more affluent counterparts look forward to their buildings increasing dramatically in value to push up sales prices, but these poorer tenants have written bylaws to limit the appreciation on their properties. With appreciation curbed, sales prices will remain relatively low, and a core of housing will be preserved in the city for those earning less than $20,000 a year. (1980)

In a city where housing costs were spiraling ever upward and condominium conversion was rampant, the work of these tenants—mostly black, mostly women—was helping to keep housing within reach for low-income residents.

Blackness, Homeownership, and the Commons

Since the 1960s, cooperatives have gained something of a reputation, in the U.S. context, as the province of white alternative culture—and as projects that have emerged from countercultural desire rather than economic necessity. But the bulk of cooperative effort over the course of U.S. history has been made in an effort to address economic need through collective action (Curl, 2009). African Americans, excluded from other economic options, have played particularly important roles in developing cooperatives, as Nembhard (2014) details so well. Nembhard's work serves as a critical corrective to the lack of attention paid to U.S. black cooperativism. But the black experience of commoning more broadly has been grossly undertheorized, with a few exceptions. Linebaugh and Rediker (2013) have theorized the multiracial commons formed by European sailors and African slaves in wake of shipwrecks in the Americas of the sevententh century; Besson (2000) has theorized the "maroon commons" of escaped slaves in the Caribbean; and Borchert (1980) has described the alleyways that served as the center of much of the culture of poor black life in D.C. throughout the first half of the twentieth century as a kind of commons. While developing a theory of the black commons is not the goal of this book, I am hopeful that other scholars will take up the question of blackness and the commons, or do more to theorize race and the commons more broadly. Here, I briefly discuss the intersection of blackness, homeownership, and the commons, in the context of Washington D.C.

In D.C., as noted earlier, LECs have faced some opposition on the grounds that they do not allow their members to build significant wealth. Because most low-income people in the city in recent decades have been African American, this argument has been about race as much as class. Why support a homeownership structure for low-income people, the argument goes, if it does not allow them access to what is assumed to be the most important function of homeownership: wealth (on this debate, see Diamond 2009)? As one African American D.C. co-op expert told me, when he first learned about the LEC ownership structure years ago, he thought it sounded like something a bunch of white people thought up to keep black people poor. He is not alone in this perspective. (After witnessing the benefits of LECs, however, he later changed his mind, and became a proponent of the LEC ownership form.)

Home ownership in U.S. society is so bound up with the promise of future exchange value of one's home that it can be difficult to conceive of a form of ownership that is not commodified—or why this form of ownership might be valuable. But low-income tenants, faced with the imminent crisis of losing their homes, may have a different perspective on homeownership than do people examining the question from the comfort of a middle-class position. Previous research indicates that, at the time they gain control of their housing, LEC members are not typically thinking in terms of the future exchange value of their homes. As Kolodny and Gellerman found in an early study of LECs in New York City:

> Ownership in and of itself is not the major attraction of the conversion formula . . . . The tenants' main interest is in gaining control over their residential circumstances in order to improve them. (1973, ii)

Control over the conditions of their housing, for these new co-op members, was more important than traditional homeownership, which the authors equate with the right to sell on the market. Other research on New York City LECs suggests that, by taking over their buildings through purchasing them collectively, tenants are subverting the traditional ideology of homeownership. Tenants, Clark finds, use the ideology of homeownership to convince the city that they should be allowed to buy their buildings:

> Promoted as providing homeownership, cooperatives could be presented as socially and politically desirable, although the meaning of ownership in that context was very unlike its traditional meaning. Cooperative residents view ownership as a source of political legitimacy, secure tenure, collective control, and permanent low-income housing . . . They do not view it as a commodity from which they may profit or as a symbol of individuation. (1994, 947)

My research finds that LEC members understand ownership as Clark's respondents did. Contra Kolodny and Gellerman, ownership in fact *was* a main attraction for tenants who were looking to convert their buildings into LECs. But the purpose of ownership, for most of my respondents, was not to gain the ability to sell their unit on the market—which is how Kolodny and Gellerman seem to be conceiving of ownership. Tenants who worked very hard on collectively purchasing their buildings were not focused on turning their homes into commodities. Far from it: they were interested in transforming what had been the commodity of rental housing into a space over which they had control. But they were very interested in being owners, and felt like owners, even if ownership did not include the right to sell their unit on the market.

I was schooled in this distinction by Mary, whose analysis of the matter is typical. Mary is an African American woman in her fifties who helped found the Sycamore Cooperative, in the Brightwood neighborhood in the late 1980s, and moved out in 2000 to purchase her own rowhouse a few blocks away. When I ask Mary if she felt like an owner in the years she lived at the Sycamore, despite the co-op's limited-equity restrictions, her voice rises in pitch, and she sounds indignant that I have even asked the question:

> I most certainly *did!* I was happy! I was elated. And at work—I was proud. It was something to boast about. And I did. I was very proud of the fact that we as tenants took it on, and it was a lot of hard work, it was a lot of arguing, but we took it on, and we made a success out of it. So I was very proud, I was very proud of it, yes. Because I feel like it's—the idea of you owning a piece of it, it's not the same thing as purchasing a house or something like that, but at least you have some say-so in it. You have some say-so as to if you want flowers around, or we need a fence for this, which those are the kinds of things that we did. Versus a separate owner coming in, doing different things, or not doing things that you need. So yes, I was *very* proud.

Note that I had not asked Mary whether she was proud of her ownership; rather, I asked if she had felt like an owner. But in her answer, she equates the feeling of ownership with her feeling of pride in working together with her fellow tenants to gain control over their housing. Though Mary does not speak explicitly of race, she tells me later that the reason she moved to D.C. as a young woman in the first place was because "it was Chocolate City, it was the place to be!" Part of her pride in ownership may be her pride in being able to take control of a piece of a city that was in its heyday a center of black culture and political power.

Alice is an African American in her sixties who helped found another co-op in the Brightwood neighborhood, the Dogwood, in the early 1980s. When Alice describes why the tenants were so excited to buy their building together, she speaks of ownership explicitly in terms of race:

The fact that you were going to *own* something. That you didn't have an opportunity [before]. Blacks were afraid to go to the banks. Blacks were afraid they were not gonna be able to qualify for a loan, and that sort of thing. You didn't have to go to the bank! All you had to do was fill out the paper! . . . [I]t was a nice thing, and you were able to own something without having to go through all the government paperwork, and being afraid you weren't going to get a loan, and all of that. So I think that made people more willing to act as a team. Cause they knew collectively they could get the loan.

For Alice and her fellow co-op members, collective ownership was a way to bypass the individualizing scrutiny of institutions—namely, banks— that had a history of discriminating against black people. When Alice and her fellow co-op members held a grand opening ceremony for the Dogwood Cooperative, then-mayor Marion Barry attended. Photographic evidence indicates that he and his successor, Sharon Pratt Kelly, attended many LEC opening ceremonies throughout the 1980s and 1990s.[1] The act of low-income, primarily African American tenants taking control of their housing through purchasing it collectively was seen as a politically important move in Washington, D.C., and black mayors wanted to make their support known. For Mary, Alice, and other co-op members, the limited-equity co-op provided a way to collectively gain some control over a parcel of land in Chocolate City, the place they called home.

The Crisis of Commons Creation

Collective purchase of property, as Addisu, Mary, and Alice all indicate, can be deeply satisfying. But the reclaiming of a commons often comes at a point of crisis. For low-income tenants in D.C., the point of crisis is when their landlord informs them that the building will be sold, and the tenants realize that they are in danger of losing their homes. Brian, an African American in his fifties, lives in the Juniper Cooperative, in the Adams Morgan neighborhood. Brian, who we will hear more from in the next chapter, has been in the building since the mid-1980s. He explains the feeling of many D.C. tenants upon learning their buildings were to be sold:

For a long time, when it was really bad, and the [condominium] conversions were everywhere, it was just like an *explosion* of that, and everybody knew a lot of people who had gotten something saying, okay, 60 days. The building's sold, in 60 days, you gotta get out. And you know, you're renting, what can you do? You gotta get out, find something else. But at the same time that was happening, rents were going up, so getting out meant not just getting out of the building, it meant getting out of the neighborhood, it meant getting out of the city. A lot of people of course are in [Prince George's County, Maryland], or Virginia. And I think people were very afraid. People were just afraid! People didn't have money. And they didn't know where they could go, or what they could afford. People had children, the elderly people, it was disorienting to them—what, what is this about?

The crisis that Brian describes could become a time of chaos and unraveling. But as Rebecca Solnit (2009) notes in her study of collective response to disaster, deep human bonds of caring and mutual aid are often forged in crisis among people who had previously been strangers. When tenants come together to purchase their buildings, they do so under intense pressures of time and money. The tenant purchase process can take a year or more, time which is riddled with meetings, fundraisers, worry, and excitement. During this time, some tenants may leave the building, frustrated with the process and fearing that the purchase will fail. This puts the remaining tenants in the difficult position of attracting new members to a co-op association that does not yet own its building and has not yet completed renovations. But the intensity of the process keeps a core of members going. In the co-ops I studied, tenants had to work together to form a tenants association; find a lawyer; find financing from the city and at least one bank; select a developer (in almost all cases, tenants use some of their financing to repair and remodel their severely dilapidated housing); form a cooperative association, including writing corporate bylaws; make scores of decisions about remodeling; decide on house rules; search for new members, if necessary; and many more tasks. It was this collective labor that brought them together.

Ruth was one of the early leaders of the tenant purchase effort that led to the creation of the Aspen Cooperative, described in the introduction. Ruth worked nonstop at organizing the complex and finally had to take some time off. In the fall of 1978, she went to visit her brother in Canada. While she was away, she stayed abreast of the purchase and renovation process through exchanging letters with fellow tenants, with whom she had developed close friendships. Decades later, I sit with Ruth in her living room and, in a hushed voice, she reads to me from a letter she received from a fellow tenant in November 1978:

> I would have written sooner but I've really lacked both time and energy. Right now there seems to be a lull, after a prolonged period of almost constant meetings. I am trying to relax a bit, but find it hard even when I am doing nothing. Somehow it's unreal. We are, however, plodding along, and if you were to tell me that this craziness was going to turn out fine, I guess I wouldn't have any reason to argue with you. Right now we are going through our monthly membership crunch, looking for people to populate [two former tenants'] apartments. We are also beginning to figure out what will happen during rehab, and how we will ever survive it. We are also still waiting for the [city] money. Any day now. How are things in Canada? Any idea when you'll be returning? We miss you.

The intensity of the process conveyed in the letter Ruth received is illustrative of the kind of work that starting a limited-equity co-op involves. But the intensity of the experience can also make the time deeply meaningful for participants and give them the energy to complete what can sometimes seem like a Herculean task.

Sandy, an African American in her sixties who grew up in D.C., is the president of the smallest and most recently formed co-op in my study, the Mulberry Cooperative located in D.C.'s Trinidad neighborhood. In the 1990s this area was beset with gun and drug violence and was long considered one of the city's more dangerous neighborhoods. That reputation began to change with the resurgence of economic development along nearby H Street Northeast, a major commercial corridor that was devastated during the 1968 riots, but began receiving an influx of reinvestment dollars in the first decade of the twenty-first century. The Mulberry is in an area that is on the edge of gentrification. It is a four-unit building; each unit has one bedroom, as well as a back porch that could be enclosed to create an extra room. The tenants purchased the building in 2005, and Sandy led the effort. As of our interview the purchase had been completed, but the building was still largely unrenovated, and only two of the four units were occupied. Though the co-op association owned the building, the building was yet to stabilize. In a sense, then, this was a commons still in the midst of the work of creation. Sandy describes how, while waiting for renovation money from the city, she has taken it upon herself to fix up the other units in an attempt to attract new members:

> I had renovated the apartment upstairs. I took my income tax money one year, and said, lemme start renovating. Yeah! Why not? Get somebody up in here, cause I can't be in here by myself. So I had to make it look appealing, and I did the one that [the second member is] in. I'm gonna be working on this one [points to the unit across the hall] cause that's a vacant unit, and [points upstairs] that's a vacant unit, but it's a storage—man, I gotta get all that stuff outta there. So basically I started renovating.

Sandy is currently unemployed, and she has worked most recently cleaning houses. She does not have much extra money, and it seems remarkable that she spent her tax refund one year on fixing up a unit in which she does not live, in an ownership situation that will not allow her to reap the financial rewards of increasing home values. But her entire demeanor in describing the work of getting her co-op started is one of high-octane energy. She is working to reclaim the commons.

Working with Strangers to Seize Commodified Space: Reclaiming the Urban Commons

The particular experience of reclaiming an urban commons is marked by what I am arguing are two of the particular traits of an urban commons: intensity of capital accumulation and investment, and density and heterogeneity of people (for more on this argument see Huron 2015).

First, let's address the question of the city as a center for capital accumulation. Creating a commons in a city requires reckoning directly with the ways in which capital has long been absorbed into the land. Cities are already-commodified spaces, where property lines have been drawn and ownership declared at a fine-grained scale. City space is thick with financial investment, and competition for commodified space among a dense population of urban dwellers drives up prices. A major point of pressure lies in the fact that urban commons must be wrenched from the capitalist landscape of cities. As noted earlier, in Washington, D.C., when tenants exercise their right to purchase their buildings and convert them into LECs, they must pay their former landlords what are essentially market prices for their buildings. They do this often after enduring years of slum conditions, as their landlords have systematically disinvested in their buildings. In order to reclaim a space from a capitalist urban landscape, would-be commoners must participate in capitalist processes.

The case of the Poplar Cooperative illustrates this dynamic. This twenty-seven-unit building was situated in the Shaw neighborhood, on the northern edge of downtown D.C., an area that in the 1980s was just beginning to boom. The building was a rental at the time and was in poor shape; letters of complaint show that tenants had been organizing against poor living conditions there since at least 1981. In February 1986, a pair of investor brothers bought the building for $425,000. Just three months later, the new owners informed the tenants of their intention to sell the building. Because of the TOPA law, the owners were required to give the tenants the opportunity to purchase. The owners' declared sale price was $1.6 million—nearly *four times* the amount for which they had purchased it just *three months* earlier. The tenants couldn't meet the price, but they were determined to stay in the building. For several years, the tenants fought with the owners over maintenance issues. Finally, in 1989, the tenant association was able to purchase the building for $864,300, with assistance from the city, and convert it into a limited-equity cooperative. The landlords walked away with a tidy profit—a return of over 100 percent on their initial investment after just three years—and the tenants were left with an old, undermaintained building. If tenants were seizing their own housing without regard for landlord compensation, as writers like Colin Ward describe (see Wilbert and White 2011), that would be a different matter. But tenants must take out mortgages (typically low-cost city financing is combined with market-rate private financing), and they must, of course, pay interest on those loans. This is a commons wrested from capitalist land but still beholden to capitalism.

Second, creating a commons in a city also requires reckoning with a diversity of strangers, would-be commoners who may be coming from very different places, geographically, culturally, and linguistically. Cities are defined in part by their relatively large and heterogeneous populations of people, living in dense proximity with one another, and by relative anonymity. Ostrom notes that one of the marks of successful commons is that their members "share a past, and expect to share a future" (1990, 88).

People who have lived together for generations past and believe that they and their descendants will be living together and sharing resources for generations to come may have a different attitude toward collective governance of resources than those who do not feel this long-term commonality with their neighbors. It therefore may appear that reclaiming a commons in a city would be more difficult than in a more traditional community: the necessary commonality, in the city of strangers, is weak or absent. The reality, as I discovered in my research, is more complicated. There appears to be a dialectical relationship between commons formation and community formation: one does not necessarily precede the other. As Stavrides has observed in his work on commoning in public squares, commoning forms community, and community enables commoning (Stavrides 2016).

Addisu's co-op, the Walnut, introduced at the beginning of this chapter, provides a good example of commons formation through diversity. There, tenants had to work across differences in order to reclaim their housing. In the late 1980s, their tenant association began the process of buying their building and converting it to a co-op. At the time of their purchase, their neighborhood of Columbia Heights was still reeling from the disinvestment that had followed the 1968 riots, which had devastated the neighborhood's commercial core. Yet the tenants, who had worked hard to drive drug dealing from their block, were determined to own their building. Addisu, who speaks English with a heavy accent, jokes that even though one of his early fellow tenants, Mrs. Jones, could barely understand his speech, they grew close through working together to buy the building:

> The first thing that was a beautiful thing really, that happened,
> [Mrs. Jones]—still, still, you have to live with me to understand
> me—she couldn't still understand me. "What did he say?" she says
> to [my partner], "What did he say?" [He laughs.] Still but she loves
> me, still she likes me, still she likes me.

Despite seeming barriers of language and of culture—his building was made up of Spanish-speaking Central Americans, Amharic-speaking Ethiopians, and English-speaking African Americans—the tenants association went on to successfully purchase their building. They committed to holding all of their meetings in all three languages, and, coming together as a group, they built the collective confidence to make the many decisions they needed to make in order to take control over their housing.

Diversity is not just about racial, cultural, and linguistic identity; it can also be seen in the variety of knowledge and skills that people may bring to the collective project of commoning. Also in the Columbia Heights neighborhood, a housing organizer worked with prospective members of a newly formed co-op, all low-income Latinos and African Americans, to create a "skill exchange group inventory" in order to get to know each other, and to brainstorm what they would all be bringing to their new community. They came up with the following list of skills and material goods they had to offer each other:

- Secretarial—typing, filing, arranging schedules
- Teaching—can tutor high school English grammar, edit writings
- Waitressing—can help at parties, new small restaurants
- Sales clerking—handling cash register & customers, knowledge of latest clothing styles
- Painting—inside homes and small businesses
- Carpentering—build household furnishing, decks, teach basics
- Spanish—speaking and writing
- Board member of a housing cooperative (can exchange info, helpful hints)
- Cooking—homemade, no frozen, canned or instant here!
- Three children—21, 19, 15/exchange info—I don't have any answers but I've had lots of experience
- Problem solver—good at listening to people and helping them to analyze the pros and cons of a situation in order to make a wise decision
- Childcare—I'm big on inexpensive, fun, educational field trips
- Neighborhood activist—helped start a neighborhood monthly social and newsletter, can help you plan ways to organize your neighbors
- Gardening—foods and plants
- Taking care of ill elderly mother
- Car—old, but it will get you from here to there on short errands
- Music collection—can make tapes[2]

Inventorying their skills and possessions was an exercise in community-building in the present that was also laying the groundwork for working together in the future. In learning what each was willing to offer the others, they were preparing to do the work of commoning over the long term. But the pleasure evident in this list, and in Addisu's description of tenants coming together, should not give the impression that coming together at the time of crisis is an easy ride. Co-op members describe fights they waged over all sorts of decisions on the rocky road to collective ownership. Undoubtedly many tenants associations, unstudied here, failed in their attempts to form LECs, perhaps because of problems bridging differences within the group as much as financial limitations. But, through forging relationships with erstwhile strangers, many groups of tenants have been able to reclaim some space for living from the capitalist city.

The city is a good place to study the reclamation of the commons. Urban land, I have noted, is already-enclosed; a commons that exists in the city, therefore, must be reclaimed from enclosure. And while the commons is often theorized in opposition to the state, I argue that the state may play an important—even necessary—role in the creation of a commons. Washington D.C., in the 1970s, saw the rise of the political will to create governmental policies to allow for the reclamation of a commons. This political will was generated from the concern that low-income, mostly black people were being forced out of the nation's capital just at the moment that the city's residents were gaining the power to democratically govern themselves. The commons constituted by the city's limited-equity co-ops is partial, and it is small-scale. But there has been something politically potent about low-income, mostly African American people successfully taking control over their living space in the capital of the United States.

A commons is often formed at a time of crisis. The specific nature of reclaiming a commons in the urban context, as demonstrated here, is (1) coming up with the capital necessary to remove a resource from an urban landscape saturated with financial investment; and (2) building close working relationships with strangers—people of different cultures and languages. Tenants work as hard as they do to reclaim their housing commons because of the urgent necessity of the project. In the next chapter, I theorize why the urban commons is so necessary, and what benefits it provides its members.

4

A Decent Grounds for Life

The Benefits of Limited-Equity Cooperatives

The commons supports a life less straightjacketed by the demands of capitalism. With the support of a commons, people can move toward a life that is both more autonomous and more collective, one that allows them to make choices that otherwise might be impossible. The commons allows people to experiment with how they live their lives. The LECs studied here are imperfect commons. They do, however, mark the beginning of an effort to build lives in a different relationship to capitalism.

In this chapter, I briefly describe the need for affordable housing in Washington, D.C. Washington, of course, is just one city among many throughout the world in which finding decent, affordable housing for low- and moderate-income people is increasingly impossible. I then spend the bulk of the chapter outlining the critical benefits LECs provide their members: benefits that include affordability, control, stability, and community. I end by asking the extent to which the commons, constituted by LECs, allow their members to change their relationship to capitalism.

The Need for Affordable Housing

For people without high incomes or access to significant wealth, the lack of affordable housing in many cities is an enormous challenge. For the poor and low-income, it is an absolute crisis (Bratt, Stone, and Hartman 2006). Housing is considered "affordable" when households spend no more than 30 percent of their incomes on housing costs. But in 2010, one in five of all renting households across the United States spent at least half of their income on rent. And the problem is in no way limited to the United States. Housing costs have soared in cities around the globe, including in the cities of the global South (Desmond 2016).

The problem is particularly severe in Washington, D.C. The city has one of the highest rates of income inequality among all U.S. cities, and it also has some of the nation's highest housing costs (D.C. Fiscal Policy Institute 2016). The private real estate market in D.C. has for years been impenetrable for poor people. The "fair market rent" for a one-bedroom unit in D.C. in 2010 was $1,318; for a two-bedroom unit, it was $1,494.[1] In 2010, the median income of District residents was $60,900. This figure may seem relatively high, but it masks a glaring disparity between the well-off and the poor. In 2010, one in five District residents lived below the poverty line, and one in nine lived below *half* the poverty line (D.C. Fiscal Policy Institute 2011). The poverty line for a family of four in 2010 was $22,314, meaning that one in nine District residents was living on less than about $11,000 a year (the exact figure would vary based on household size). In 2010, a minimum wage worker in D.C. would have to work 139 hours a week, every week of the year, in order to be able to afford the fair market rent for a typical two-bedroom apartment (National Low Income Housing Coalition 2010). While the city does have modest rent control provisions, it is increasingly impossible for low-income people to pay for housing on the private market. Those who are able to do so often manage by squeezing many people into small units.

But publicly subsidized housing has for some time been just as inaccessible. In 2013, 72,000 people were on the city's waiting list for either a public housing unit or a publicly subsidized voucher to help pay the rent for a privately owned unit. That constituted about 11 percent of the city's population. A person seeking a one-bedroom apartment could expect to wait twenty-eight years until one opened up. The city's response to this dysfunction was to simply close the waiting list and try to retrench (DeBonis 2014). Like many cities around the country, Washington, D.C., is in the midst of a long process of redeveloping its public housing into mixed-income housing—a process often seen by poor residents as a way to get rid of many of them (Milloy 2014; Zippel 2016). The closure of the waiting list (three years later, it remained closed), together with the closure of existing public housing for redevelopment, has coincided with a time of soaring housing prices and a record wave of family homelessness. It is not just the market that has failed poor and working people in their attempt to be housed. The state, in many ways, has failed them, too.

The Benefits of the Commons

When considering the benefits of living in LECs, it is important to note that LEC members compare their housing situations with their previous experiences as renters, and not with the experience of market-rate homeownership. Only one of my forty respondents had ever experienced market-rate homeownership as an adult. The rest had moved from rental housing, including public housing, into their co-ops, with the exception of a few young people who moved from college dormitory housing or their parents' homes directly into the co-op. A middle-class perspective might tend to compare the LEC experience with market-rate homeownership, but since market-rate homeownership has not been a possibility for the vast majority of respondents, this is not a realistic comparison to make. The appropriate comparison is rental housing (previous research on shared-equity housing also makes this point; see Diamond, 2009). The larger point is this: the commons, fundamentally, are created by people who do not have many other options under capitalism. Tenants facing the crisis of the sale of their homes are not selecting between individual, market-rate homeownership and collective, decommodified homeownership. Their options are limited. The commons is necessary.

Previous research on shared-equity homeownership, of which the LEC model is one example, concludes that such homeownership has five key benefits: it is affordable; it is stable; it allows owners to accrue some wealth; it can lead to improvement in owners' lives; and it encourages involvement in the self-governance of housing (J. E. Davis 2006b). In my research, it became clear that affordability is indeed the primary benefit provided by limited-equity co-ops. Stability of housing is also an important benefit. Wealth building, on the other hand, is not an immediate benefit of D.C. LECs. Living in an LEC in D.C. does appear to lead to improvement in members' lives, though the degree of improvement is difficult to measure. The degree to which LECs encourage involvement in self-governance in housing varies and will be taken up in the next chapter. In addition, my interviews reveal two other benefits of LEC housing that are not considered explicitly in Davis's study: control over housing, and community. When tenants seize the commons, it is to create a world of affordability, control, stability, and community. I examine each of these benefits in turn.

Affordability

Given the context of the ongoing housing crisis described above, the single most important thing limited-equity co-ops provide their members is affordable housing. Previous research on D.C. LECs shows that, as of 2003, carrying charges for one-bedroom and two-bedroom units in LECs were about half the HUD fair market rents at the time (CNHED 2004).[2] My research corroborates that monthly housing costs of LECs are typically half the rate of market rental costs. In my sample of existing limited-equity co-ops, the mean monthly carrying charge in 2011 for one-bedroom units was $672, and for two-bedroom units was $759. Carrying charges typically include any underlying mortgage on the building, heat and water, a share of the building's property tax, the cost of hiring a management company, and money for operating and replacement reserves. The only additional bill most members pay is for electricity.

Across the board, respondents emphasize that one of the main benefits of living in an LEC is its affordability. For most respondents, this is clearly *the* most important attribute of LECs. Phyllis lives in the Magnolia Cooperative, the co-op in a relatively low-income neighborhood east of the Anacostia River, introduced in chapter 1. The Magnolia is a large, ninety-unit complex that was developed in 1971 as public housing, with the intent that the tenants, within two years of moving into the building, would be able to buy their homes. But the home ownership program disintegrated, and the tenants continued living in the development for years as public housing residents. Believing they would one day be owners, they put their own work and money into fixing up their units. Finally, in 2001, the tenants were able to purchase the complex and convert it to a limited-equity cooperative. This is an extremely affordable cooperative: the units, which range in size from three to five bedrooms, have carrying charges that range from $526 to $649. Phyllis is an African American woman in her seventies who grew up in D.C. and moved into the complex with her husband in 1971; they raised eight children while living there. Phyllis echoes several respondents in emphasizing the importance of affordability for raising children, and she compares living in an LEC to living in the private market:

> I have [grown] children, my children are out on the private [housing] market. You work, work, work, to do what—to pay your bills. And then when you get through paying your bills, and you retire, you get tired, you retire, you might have a little money to do things, if you're not too sick at that time to do it, from working all your life. But I mean, to raise children in a cooperative, it's good, because—limited-equity cooperative, let me say that. Because it's affordable. . . . If everybody decided to get a limited-equity cooperative, pool our money, and live there and raise our kids, it's

gonna be much cheaper than going out there on the private market, worrying about what they need, what they don't have, working themselves half to death.

Later, Phyllis tells me that living in a limited-equity cooperative is "less stress" than trying to find affordable housing out on the open market. In this statement and others, she focuses on the stress caused by the housing market and the waged work required to afford housing on the open market—and the illness that stress and overwork can generate over the course of a life. Phyllis values a less stressful, ultimately healthier, life in which she can raise her children, even if this means she has less money to spend on material things. For her, this is why living in a limited-equity co-op is beneficial, even though it does not allow her to build up financial equity.

It should be noted that the vast majority of limited-equity cooperatives in D.C. are, in terms of how they actually operate, in fact closer to zero-equity cooperatives. Within my sample, it is only at one co-op that members pay in a significant amount of money to join the co-op, an investment that rises along with the Consumer Price Index and that can be sold for a modest return down the line. In all the other co-ops, the initial share fee is so low that any return on an investment, even after many years, is nominal—perhaps a few hundred dollars. LECs in D.C. simply do not provide members with an opportunity to build significant wealth through their housing investment. However, one argument for limited-equity co-ops and other forms of resale-restricted housing is that, while they may not provide owners with financial equity, they do, through providing them with below market-rate housing, give them the opportunity to save money they would have otherwise spent on market-rate rents. Some of my respondents make this very argument. But in my research, I have found that most working-class respondents do not earn enough money to be able to save, even with their relatively low housing costs. Joanna is an African American in her forties who also lives in the Magnolia, sharing her co-op unit with her teenage son. She notes that if she had spent less money on her son, she might have been able to save:

> I haven't really been able to save, because it's hard with a
> 15-year-old. Where if I had been out there where I had to pay
> more, then the 15-year-old wouldn't have gotten as much. So I
> just would've changed my lifestyle.

Joanna has spent the money she's saved on her housing costs on her child, instead of putting it into a savings account. Research shows that when poor families have to spend more on their housing, they spend less on their children (Desmond 2016). So if the affordability of LECs is allowing members to spend more on their children, this may be a very good thing. Claudia is a Central American immigrant in her sixties who lives in the Juniper Cooperative in the Adams Morgan neighborhood, historically a highly diverse and immigrant-rich area that over the years has steadily gentrified. Claudia worked as a hotel housekeeper before retiring. As she explains, she has not been able to save money through living in her co-op, because she's spent all her extra money on her daughters:

> No. No, because—I have my two daughters, I was raising them alone, so even though I wanted to save, I couldn't! [She laughs.] I couldn't.

Phyllis, Joanna, and Claudia are among my respondents who I classify as having a relatively narrow range of life opportunity. All are older women of color who have raised children in their co-ops and have worked relatively low-paying jobs throughout their lives. None of them has been able to save money and build wealth, despite the relative affordability of their homes. These women represent the most common experience of lower-income respondents with regards to the benefits of living in an LEC: the affordability of their housing has enabled them to live a bit more gracefully and securely, to care for their children in the way they desire, and to live in locations that they find relatively convenient and safe for family life.

For other co-op members, the affordability of their housing has enabled them to change their relationship to waged work. Daisy, a biracial woman in her thirties, is one of these. Her co-op, the Aspen, is located in Glover Park, a neighborhood that was once white and working class but that is now increasingly upper-middle class, and still predominantly white. The co-op appears to be the only affordable housing in the neighborhood. Daisy was raised, along with her twin brother, by Sherry, the single mother we met in the introduction, in a one-bedroom apartment in the co-op. Daisy bought into the Aspen as an adult after she graduated from college and needed an affordable place to live. She currently pays about $700 a month for her one-bedroom unit. She describes how living in the co-op has enabled her to downscale her work life from a job in a law firm to one in the human resources office at a local university:

I was a paralegal, I was making pretty good money, but I just wasn't happy, and it was completely stressing me out. And I was able to leave, and take a lower-paying job, without having to worry about, am I gonna be making enough? . . . At my job [now], it's like, I don't have to make a ton of money, but I'm also not as motivated by the money, so you know to me, it's like, I wanna be happy. Which is good—it's not always realistic! [She laughs.] You know, like, I'm not having fun today, I could leave! . . . But I think I could enjoy myself more. Because I'm not so stressed that I have a mortgage bill that's $2000 a month.

Daisy values the fact that, because her housing expenses are relatively low, she could quit her job if she felt like it—a freedom unimaginable for many dwellers of this high-cost city. (Her college degree and her childless status, of course, also contribute significantly to this sense of freedom.) In her current job, Daisy has an annual tradition of taking off work every Monday in April. Her softball league starts up that month and games are on Sundays. She likes to go out for dinner with her teammates on Sunday nights and relax on the following day. She spends some of each of those Mondays helping out her mother, who is the co-op's long-time resident manager, in the co-op office, and simply enjoying the beautiful spring weather. Having access to the commons allows Daisy to structure her days by the cycle of the seasons.

For a few other respondents, co-op membership has enabled a more radical break from regular working life. Maria, who lives at the Juniper Co-op, is one of these. Her grandmother immigrated to D.C. from Latin America in the 1940s and lived in a number of different apartments in the Adams Morgan neighborhood, finally settling into her home in the early 1980s, when it was still a rental building. Maria grew up in another part of the city but spent a lot of time at her grandmother's apartment, and Maria considers the building and the neighborhood home. Unlike most LEC members, Maria's life choices have been relatively broad: her parents are well educated, she attended a private girls' school, and she later received a master's degree from a university in New York City, pursuing her dream of acting. Maria's aunt, Magdalena, is the president of the co-op. When Maria's grandmother died, Magdalena encouraged Maria to relocate back to D.C. and move into her grandmother's old unit. Because her income from acting is relatively low, she has been able to participate in the co-op's federal housing subsidy, which keeps her monthly carrying charges for her one-bedroom unit extremely low. The highest monthly rate she has ever paid was in the mid $200s. Living in the co-op, as she describes, has enabled her to pursue her dream:

> Technically, I work at . . . the restaurant across the street. But I haven't been there [for a year and a half], because I've been able to work [as an actor] and save in between. So I haven't had to have extra supplemental jobs here and there to support, because I live here, and I have this amazing set-up with our subsidy and our co-op, I'm really able to live the really *life* [she laughs], like an artist life. I don't have to do all these random job-jobs that make you unhappy, and stuff, in order to live, because I can work on a show, and save enough, and kind of plan out how much I'm gonna have, and what I need to do. So living here has been, just, amazing. Because I really do get to pursue what I studied, and what I want to do. That wouldn't happen anywhere else.

For both Daisy and Maria, the affordability of the LEC gives them the opportunity to take on different kinds of work than if they lived in market-rate housing: work that is less stressful, in Daisy's case, or more meaningful, in Maria's case. Silvia Federici notes that participating in the commons should give people power to refuse wage exploitation.[3] As noted in chapter 1, Neeson argues that a life grounded in the commons gave English commoners: "time to spend doing things other than work, as well as the ability to refuse work" (1993, 178). In these cases, LECs appear to support people in making employment decisions that in other housing circumstances might be financially ruinous. Living in an LEC, for these members, gives them more control over their time, and to a certain degree, allows them to make a break from capitalist time. It is important to note, however, that although both Daisy and Maria are women of color who come from working-class origins, they are both now relatively financially comfortable: they are young, college-educated, and without dependents. They are people with relatively broad life opportunities.

It is also important to note that not all co-op members take advantage of their housing affordability to pursue less capitalist endeavors. Todd is a middle-class African American man in his midtwenties who grew up in suburban D.C. and moved into the Sycamore Co-op in 2006, right after graduating from college. Todd was familiar with the co-op because his aunt Mary, introduced in the last chapter, had helped found it, and he had spent time there as a child. Todd works as a software developer. The monthly charges for his one-bedroom unit are $610. With the money he saves, he says:

> I was able to buy a car, and recreational activities. I'm an electronics junkie, since I'm a computer software guy. You always seem to lose [money] as soon as you get it. But it's nice to have those options for the most part. I waste a lot of money eating out at lunch at work every day, that's probably something I wouldn't be doing [if I didn't have the extra money].

After our conversation, Todd emails me to note that he also spends some of his extra money playing the stock market. Todd works full-time, and he admits that a lot of the extra cash he saves on account of his low housing costs is wasted in some way. In the long run, he says, he hopes to be able to save enough money living at his co-op to buy his own home in the city—to follow the path of his aunt Mary, who ultimately moved out of the co-op to buy her own house a few blocks away. But Todd is not an LEC resident just because his affordable housing allows him to participate more fully in consumer society. For instance, at the time of our interview he was representing the co-op at community meetings in which neighbors were trying to organize against a WalMart that was slated for construction in their neighborhood. He tells me that he genuinely cares about the unique quality of his co-op and the affordability it provides his neighbors whose life chances are more restricted than his own.

Control

Previous research shows that the ability to gain control over one's housing is important for limited-equity co-op members. A survey of Nashville public housing tenants given the opportunity to convert their housing to co-op ownership found that one of the two main reasons they were most interested in co-op ownership was because it would allow them to fix up their units the way they wanted. It would give them control over their housing (Rohe and Stegman 1995). In my research I found that, after affordability, the second most important thing that LECs provide members is a sense of control. Control manifests in three forms: control over the physical space of the building, control over decision making, and social control over the people in the building. For many LEC members, having control over their housing is a welcome relief from prior experiences living in rental housing.

Gloria, an African American in her sixties, is one of the founders of the Sycamore Co-op and lives there today. She explains how the building changed after the tenants purchased it and residents were able to gain control over the space, both in terms of physical repairs and decision making:

> It [had been] a rental. [Columbia] Realty owned this place then. And they—you know, you didn't have heat during the winter, you didn't have hot water, it was just a mess. . . . I remember the first year I was here [as a tenant], and the refrigerator I had was practically—you went to open the door, you had to do it carefully, because you felt like the door was going to fall off, that's how dilapidated it was! [She laughs.] And it took me forever, constantly calling the rental office, saying I need a new refrigerator, I've got two little kids, the food's going bad. But as owners, if somebody calls us—usually, they'll call [the board president]. And say I need a new refrigerator. Well, she'll have someone come out to check it, because we can't change it just because you painted your kitchen green and you want a green refrigerator! But if someone checks it and says, yeah, they need a new one, then we just go out and get a new refrigerator, we don't have to wait and jump through hoops. Or a new stove, or whatever. And that's what makes the difference. We have a little power, I guess that's the key word. As board members, and as owners, too. Because the owners who are not on the board, we have a democratic system. . . . So that's part of the benefit of being owners. Cause you can make a lot of your own decisions, you have the governing power.

For Gloria, the democratic nature of the co-op's self-governance is what makes it a better place to live. Members can decide for themselves how to run their homes, and they don't have to "wait and jump through hoops" in order to get repairs and other changes made as they were forced to do under their landlord. They have, as she says, a little power.

Joanna, of the Magnolia Co-op, also values the self-governance of the co-op. For her, the main difference between renting and owning has been

in her ability to participate in decision making together with fellow owners. Her thoughts echo the thoughts of many respondents:

> I guess with me, it was just the knowing that, even though I know
> we don't own our units outright, just that I have a part in it. That I
> do have now a part in this, and I can help on making the decisions
> of this cooperative, and not having someone standing over us tell-
> ing us what to do. But we can sit down collectively and decide what
> we want to do. So that was the difference.

Like Gloria, Joanna values the power she and her fellow co-op members
have: that they can "sit down collectively and decide" how they want to
operate their housing. The decisions they make together regulate both the
physical space and the social environment.

The social control possible in an LEC is very attractive to most members.
As noted earlier, Katz and Meyer (1985) warn that self-help housing movements take the responsibility for social policing from the state and place it
on the shoulders of members. But nearly all LEC members who mentioned
their collectively imposed social control were grateful for it and thought
it increased their quality of life. For Eduardo, a Salvadoran immigrant in
his forties, the social control of the co-op was very important. He came to
Washington in 1980, and he moved into his building shortly thereafter, back
when it was a rental. After the tenants purchased the building, naming it
the Ironwood Cooperative, he served on the co-op board, though he was no
longer on the board when we spoke. Eduardo lives in a one-bedroom unit
with his wife and twenty-two-year-old son, who grew up in the co-op. He
has worked for the athletic department at a local university for about four-
teen years. He describes the social control residents gained over their space
after they purchased the building and created the Ironwood:

> Well, first of all, when we renting, it's a lot of mess, it's a lot of crazy
> everything. It's too many people coming over here, we don't know
> who it is, we don't know what's going on. People come and go,
> up and in, up and in, and everything, so we were lucky when we
> came into the board because everything changed. We have more
> securities. . . . Soon as the rules and everything changed, it's a lot of
> changes in the building. Now you can see, our building's quiet. You
> don't hear no people running in the hallways, or people making

music on top of you, making noise and everything. So this one part has been nice. And everybody respects everybody.

For Eduardo, the building became a much more peaceful place to live once the tenants were able to purchase it and could write and enforce their own rules for living together. Social control can take various forms, including writing house rules that prohibit noise and other disturbances, and then enforcing those rules; monitoring who enters the building through cameras, or through the work of residents who keep an eye on the front door; being selective about incoming members, which sometimes includes visiting a prospective member's current housing to see how well they maintain it; and sometimes even evicting, or threatening to evict, members who repeatedly violate rules or do not pay their carrying charges. The Juniper Co-op appears to have some of the tightest social control in my sample. Magdalena, the co-op president, is in her sixties, an immigrant from Latin America who moved into the building in 1994 and helped lead tenants through the purchase of their building, which finally took place in 2004 after years of effort. We sit for an interview in the co-op office, where she is constantly checking a bank of security monitors above her desk. Magdalena is proud of the community that has been formed in the building and the social control it has allowed them to have. She explains:

[A]nybody that's not falling in line gets a letter, or we have another meeting, and let them know, okay, you can't do this. This is our property. You can't do this. So there's more caring because we meet—in [rental] apartments, you don't meet, you come and go, whatever—because we meet, and we share the problems of the property or the problems of whatever situation we need to share—we become more neighborly, more family-like. . . . If something happens, somebody calls and says, hey [Magdalena], did you see, did you hear? Somebody came up the [stairs]! In a [rental] apartment, maybe they *might* do that, maybe they might call and ask about each other, so maybe you have a nice apartment [building], where it's not too big, but a big apartment [building], nobody's paying attention. So for us, there is that little plus. When we were getting ready to purchase, we didn't have cameras, we did have the call-up thing, it didn't work okay—but it was unbelievable how we had a chain reaction of anything that wasn't normal, phones would start ringing. So-and-so just walked in the building! So-and-so, so-and-so! [She laughs]. It was like *major, major* policing and what-not, because we had to protect the building from any situation that would not allow us to purchase the building without a hassle.

The "major, major policing" Magdalena describes was necessary, she thinks, in order to keep the building community strong. Any incursion of criminality or even misbehavior could have weakened the building community and distracted the tenants from their goal of collective purchase. Social control is clearly important for LECs—and, as will be discussed next, is directly connected to the question of who gains access to the commons.

Stability

Previous research has demonstrated that housing stability plays a key role in supporting families. Stable housing here is defined as housing in which occupants are able to remain for the long-term, without fear of displacement. With stable housing, children are more likely to succeed in school, adults are better able to take advantage of job opportunities, and people generally experience greater emotional well-being (Bratt 2002; Haveman, Wolfe, and Spaulding 1991; The National Housing Task Force 1988). In my research, I found that the stability of co-op living has been important to members regardless of degree of life opportunity. Members valued the ability to will their units to their heirs; they also valued the stability that comes with knowing that their building will not be sold out from beneath them. Stability also meant co-op members did not need to worry about being evicted or having their rents suddenly raised. Though D.C. has strong tenant protections, illegal evictions and rent raises do happen, and many tenants—particularly in gentrifying neighborhoods—worry about losing their housing (Desmond 2016; McCoy 2016).

Rachel is a single Jewish woman in her early forties who grew up in an LEC in New York City. She lives in the Hickory Cooperative, located in the rapidly gentrifying neighborhood of Columbia Heights. Unlike the other LECs in my sample, and the vast bulk of LECs in the city, the Hickory was founded not when existing tenants got together to purchase their building, but from scratch, as an intentional community for social justice activists. Rachel pays just under $700 a month for her one-bedroom unit. The co-op, she says, has been a very supportive space for herself and other members to make career changes and pursue educational goals. The support comes both from relatively low monthly payments, but also from the stability of the community, and perhaps also from a sense that other co-op members are supportive of fellow members making life changes. She explains:

> I think there's something about having a supportive space for this kind of thing here. You know, [one member] decided, I fucking hate being an engineer, and he went to get an MFA in poetry! . . . [Tina] got her masters, so did [Sheila, Patsy]. [Kristy] got her undergraduate degree, [Amaya] as well, got her masters, so. There's something about the stability of this place, and knowing that we can't get kicked out, even maybe psychologically, that I think for many people has helped them make some sort of jump.

Because Rachel's co-op is explicitly designed as affordable housing for social justice activists, it attracts people who are politically committed to the limited-equity co-op model. For these activists, while affordability is crucial, the co-op's stability and sense of support are also important factors.

Patricia, the president of the board of the Ironwood Cooperative, is another LEC member for whom the co-op's stability has been an important factor. She is an African American middle-class woman who works a relatively high-paying job as a legal assistant in a corporate law firm downtown. Patricia is single and does not have children, and she could afford to pay more than the $800-something she pays for her one-bedroom unit. But part of the reason she values her co-op is because her sister lives in the building, and over the years has raised her daughter there, Patricia's niece, who Patricia adores. Patricia describes why it was important for her to help fight to stay in the building by purchasing it and maintaining it as a co-op over time:

> I think what kept me there, was my sister, at the time, she was in school, and she got involved with this guy and got married, of course, it didn't work out, and she had a daughter. A five-month-old daughter. And I said, why don't you move here. I'd never met [my niece]. And she moved, and that's what really made me stay in the building. My sister actually got sick with sarcoidosis, which is an autoimmune disease, and so—and she's doing okay now, but

she has problems from time to time, she's hospitalized, and—I tell you, [my niece] is the most magnificent young lady you ever want. So I was so happy to have helped her. She graduated last year from Temple University, degree in chemistry, so she's going on to graduate school. So I'm working hard to help her get in. And she's just—everybody loves her. I could take ten of her! I'd squeeze them all in one bedroom. I would say, oh god this is—because she is just a delight. And everyone who meets her feels that way. That's what really kept me there, and really made me want to work hard to save the [building]—because it's her home. Just to have everybody evicted, everybody have to up and move—we were working toward that goal, I guess! [She laughs.]

Patricia values the Ironwood in large part because it has provided a stable place for her ill sister and growing niece to live. While she herself could afford to live in market-rate housing, the co-op has enabled her to support her family in ways that might not otherwise be possible. For both Rachel and Patricia, stability of housing is intertwined with both affordability and community.

Community

Earlier research on limited-equity cooperatives has highlighted the importance of community within low-income co-ops. Leavitt and Saegert, in their study of limited-equity housing co-ops in Harlem, found that co-op members came together to share resources; these members formed what Leavitt and Saegert call "community-households" that stretch beyond the bounds of a typical nuclear family or self-contained apartment (1988). The idea that a housing cooperative could itself be a kind of household on a larger scale is evident in my research. One of my respondents, for instance, refers to his co-op's basement community room as the "family room." In my research, community manifests itself in different ways. Co-op members may help each other out financially, socialize together, or provide emotional support during difficult times. Members describe doing things like the following: visiting fellow members in the hospital; sending gift baskets and cards to members in times of illness or sorrow; cooking meals together; throwing parties for one another, or for the entire building community; lending each other money; helping elderly members with technology; and spending time with each other's children. In these ways, co-op members engage in non-market practices such as those described by Pavlovskaya in her (2004) work on household economies in Moscow in the 1990s. Several interviewees said that the cooperative felt "like a family," in comparison to the more anonymous rental situations they had lived in before.

In several co-ops, community manifested in part through mutual financial support. When the Sycamore Cooperative was forming, some tenants loaned money to other tenants to help them buy into the initial purchase of the complex. The case of the Aspen illustrates a similar story of mutual aid at the time of purchase. When the tenants were in the process of buying their buildings, they went through a period of self-management while they were still owned by their landlord. The tenants realized they needed to raise their own rents in order to cover their costs. So rents, which had been in the neighborhood of $120–$140, were raised by about $100—a substantial increase. Margaret is a white woman in her sixties who has lived in the complex since 1968 and currently is the treasurer of the Aspen Co-op board. She explains how the tenants association supported their low-income members during the initial period of self-management:

> Ninety-nine percent of the time people paid us the rent. We had
> no problem with that. But we did have people who didn't have
> much money. So we asked people for extra money each month, to
> develop a fund so we could subsidize the people who didn't have
> money every month. Some people gave $50, some people gave $10.
> So people who were limited income, we supplemented them, we
> subsidized. The rent had gone up $100 a month all of a sudden, and
> we told them come to us if you have problems, and we'll work it
> out. A number of people came, not a lot. This was enough to meet
> the monthly needs. People contributed! It was great.

This is not to suggest that tenants in rental apartments might not lend each other money to help cover each other's rent at times. But the intentionality of developing a fund to help lower-income members is striking. It was because the tenants were working together to purchase the buildings that they felt moved to contribute to each other to ensure that everyone could remain in the complex. Community was important, and they wanted to keep it together.

Socializing together is part of what builds community as well. For co-op founders, socializing was a very important part of coming together to purchase the buildings. Alice, who we met in the last chapter, is the board president of the Dogwood Cooperative, which the tenants collectively purchased as an LEC in 1983 and later converted to market-rate cooperative ownership. Alice helped found the Dogwood and has served intermittently on the board over the years. For her, socializing was an important part of co-op life from the very beginning. She explains:

> We had parties *all the time* [thumping table for emphasis]. Even after we bought. If it was somebody's birthday, we had a party, if it was Christmas, Thanksgiving, New Year's, whatever, we had a party, and everybody came! It was like, okay, on Christmas day, somebody was cooking, and you went from this apartment to this apartment to this apartment eating food, people had open house. But then again, we basically were West Indians, southern blacks, you know—it's a different kind of spirit. I don't know. The younger people, I don't know, it's like we came out of that me generation.

Alice later notes that she appreciates the co-op because most of her family is in Missouri and the Caribbean; in the Dogwood, she has something of a surrogate family. A number of members describe the family-like feel of their co-ops. In some co-ops, members literally *are* family. In seven of the ten co-ops and former co-ops, members of an extended family live in different units. But Alice misses the camaraderie of the old days, back before the building became a market-rate cooperative and began attracting members who spent more of their time at work or in their units than in socializing with fellow co-op members. (In the next chapter, we will hear more about the changes to community that can arise when the limited-equity structure is lost.)

Finally, co-ops can provide a supportive emotional community for their members that may be less likely to be found in rental or condominium buildings. Brian's story is illustrative. Brian, introduced in the last chapter, is an African American in his midfifties who lives in the Juniper Co-op. He has lived in the building since the mid-1980s, and he has been part of several different tenant organizing efforts that have taken place in the building over the years, including the one that led to the tenants finally buying the building and converting it to a cooperative in 2004. Brian is an artist who has worked in theater for many years. He had been evicted from his last apartment before moving into the Juniper, because, he admits, he hadn't really been paying attention to his bills and had gotten behind on his rent. He was homeless for about two weeks, staying nights in a park and also at his place of work. That brief experience of homelessness had a profound impact on him, and having a stable home has been of keen importance to him ever since. In the mid-1980s, Brian learned he was HIV-positive. He decided to keep his day job at a nonprofit organization in order to have health insurance and financial stability, and to pursue his art on the side. He now earns about $60,000 a year and is one of the only people in his co-op who does not receive a federal housing subsidy, but pays the full HUD-determined amount for his unit, which is about $1,200. He does not have children and, as of recently, lives alone. When Brian first moved into his unit it was a studio apartment; it was later enlarged to a one-bedroom during a building renovation. Though he does not personally receive a direct housing subsidy, living in a community that is dedicated to providing affordable housing for low-income people is of deep importance to him. He describes why:

> It's been *very* important for me. [He pauses.] In terms of—for three
> reasons. It's been important—it's important to have a home. I've—
> that little teeny period of time when I was evicted, and didn't have
> a place to stay, doesn't even count as homelessness. That was maybe
> like two weeks. But because I'm an artist, I know a lot of artists,
> and I know a lot of low-income people through my work and just
> socially—I know a *lot* of people who are in the shelters. So having
> a home is important to me. And since that time, that's been the
> scariest thing to me. Maybe the only thing scarier would be getting
> caught up in the legal system and locked up. After that, my biggest
> fear would be being homeless. So it's been important to me to have
> a home. Then, for my own political feelings, it's been important to
> me to live in a situation where it's mixed economically. I like that
> it's low-income, even if I'm not low-income, and I don't benefit
> from it directly in that sense, I like the concept of that. I don't mind
> paying, if people who couldn't pay get to stay here, because it's just
> *so hard* in this city, affordable housing is so hard to find, and is dry-
> ing up faster and faster. And it's important because in a way it has
> had a family feel to it. I have a close, extended family, most of them

are in St. Louis, and I have a family of artists that I've worked with over the years. But in addition to that, this building, the tenants in it, we have a building family. And that feels very good. It feels very good. People care about each other, they watch out for each other.

Brian goes on to tell a story about how he has felt cared for in the building:

I had a roommate, a very close friend here, for almost twenty years, who passed away in December. And this is a teeny, tiny apartment, imagine, for half the time it was half this size. So that's a long time to be in a small space with someone. So it's very different now. And I'm just getting used now, to basically living here alone. And so it helped to be living in a building where I knew the people, people sort of knew what was going on with me, and were very kind about that. Even the little boy one day, downstairs, a 13-year-old boy, just came up to me and said, how *are* you? And I was so amazed that he—I didn't even know what he was talking about, because it just didn't even occur to me that he could be expressing concern because he knew my friend had died. He said, well, how are you doing? Are you okay up there? And I was so touched by that. Because this kid is 12 or 13. I wouldn't even guess that he even knew I was in the building [he laughs], or paid any attention to me whatsoever, any of that. But people *do* care about each other.

Compared to many other LEC members, Brian has a relatively broad range of life choices. His HIV-positive status, however, narrows them. Having the emotional support of the Juniper community has been deeply important for him.

D.C.'s LECs create something of a partial oasis: not just from the capitalist housing market, but also from a more general urban capitalist aura that Maria, as will be seen in the next chapter, describes as "yuppie." One long-time co-op leader, Sheila, sees the value of limited-equity cooperatives in creating affordable housing for people so that they do not have to constantly worry about their housing and can instead turn their attention to other things. Sheila is an African American in her sixties who lives in the Hickory Cooperative. As she says:

I have always seen cooperatives as being an opportunity to create housing for people—housing for people that they can afford, and don't have to worry about their housing! Then they give you the opportunity to do a whole bunch of other stuff! Cause you don't have to worry about the primary worry that people have, and that's housing.

Later, she continues:

So you've got a nice decent place and you don't have to worry about your housing. So now, you can do other things, education, whatever you need for a job, you can—that's the opportunity! And that's how I see limited-equity cooperatives, as creating that opportunity.

Just as Federici hopes, the commons as Sheila describes it provides grounds for opening up ways for members to change their relationship to waged labor, along with other aspects of life. For Sheila, the "other stuff" LECs allow her to do is social justice activism in her community. She had come to D.C. in 1978, moving into an African American women's collective, and working on issues of violence against women and women's rights, particularly black women's rights. Later, she went to work for the grassroots organization that helped the Poplar Cooperative form, and she has personally helped many tenants' associations throughout the city form LECs. At the time of our interview, she continued to work full-time as a housing organizer. The commons has, for Sheila, provided her the ability to live decently while pursuing work that she believes in.

But the contradiction here is that, even as the commons *provides* its members so much, it also *requires* quite a bit on the part of its members. It in fact requires members to "worry," as Sheila says, about their housing in significant ways. There is tremendous need for greater enactment of the urban commons: a need to reclaim more spaces of all kinds by removing them from the capitalist landscape and governing them collectively. But it is the long-term maintenance of what has been reclaimed that is the true challenge of the commons. And it may be particularly difficult to maintain a commons in the urban context. It is to the question of the maintenance of the urban commons that I now turn.

5
_____

Survival and Collapse

Keeping and Losing Housing over Time

In chapter 3, we learned about the Walnut Cooperative, which Addisu, the Ethiopian immigrant, helped found in the Columbia Heights neighborhood of D.C. Creating the co-op was a time of great excitement, energy, and unity of purpose. But once the purchase was complete—and their co-op was officially formed—things began to change. Addisu describes the challenge:

> After you become a cooperative, then it is a new problem. Then you have to maintain it. It is easy, really, to bring people [to organize the co-op], you tell them, they come, but then you have to maintain it, it is not the same.

It is relatively easy, Addisu says, to bring people together at the point of crisis: they have every incentive to work together to keep their homes. But once they have achieved the victory of collective ownership, they must switch gears to the low-level, continuous work of maintaining their commons for the long haul. For all the difficulty of reclaiming a commons, the greater challenge, it appears, is maintaining it over time. In this chapter, I discuss the challenges of maintaining the urban commons. These challenges map onto the distinctive qualities of the urban commons discussed in chapter 2. There are financial challenges, difficult questions about whom to include and exclude, challenges of working collectively, and the temptation of dissolving the commons in favor of a market-rate ownership structure. But despite the many challenges, significant numbers of co-op members are committed to maintaining their commons over the long term, because of the benefits described in the last chapter: the affordability, control, stability, and community their co-ops provide themselves, their neighbors, and even future, as-yet-unknown members.

Financial Challenges

Long-term maintenance of the commons can be particularly difficult in urban environments, saturated with financial investment, in which land and other resources, prior to their reclamation as commons, have long been treated principally as a vehicle for profit. Once people reclaim an urban commons, they turn to the task of cleaning up the wreckage of capital disinvestment left behind by the previous owners. This is true for reclamation of contemporary commons documented in various cities: the people who took over the Woodwards building in downtown Vancouver spent a large amount of energy fixing it up; the people who turned vacant lots into community gardens in New York City had to first clean the lots and in some cases remediate the soil before planting vegetables (Blomley 2008; Eizenberg 2011). Capital won't give up its grip easily, and by the time it does, it has sucked much out of the resource. Elinor Ostrom explains how this dynamic plays out with natural resources in the developing world:

> [International development agencies] frequently encourage a national government to give resources back to local people. But the resources have been taken away, degraded and then given back in a one- or two-hour meeting. I have been to some of those meetings and it is rather incredible. They bring local people into a hall. They say "now you own x"; they give them a little bit of background of what they must do now; tell the people they are responsible; and then walk away. . . . [T]hey expect the users to perform rapidly what the government agencies have not been able to do for years. So there is a very grim history out there in terms of donor-assisted handover projects of natural resource systems to local people. (2012, 81–82)

Though the actors are different, what Ostrom describes in the context of natural resources in the developing world applies in the urban, developed world as well. Often, tenants are buying buildings that have been severely degraded over time. Archival photographs of rental buildings recently purchased by tenants in D.C. throughout the 1980s and 1990s document boarded-up windows, toilets that have come loose from the floor, exposed electrical wiring, broken outdoor steps and walkways, missing or broken fences, and other signs of under-maintenance by landlords.[1] In one rental building that the tenants were trying to purchase in Columbia Heights in the early 1990s, the landlord took a number of steps to apparently try to drive the tenants out so that they would give up trying to exercise their purchase rights. The landlord removed the boiler, the washers and dryers, discontinued extermination services, and gutted several apartments. The tenants were forced to heat their apartments over the 1991–92 winter with space heaters and ovens.[2] By the time the tenants were finally able to purchase the building in 1996, it was in severe disrepair.[3] In another instance, when tenants were finally able to purchase their building in 1995, they also had to take on $500,000 of the prior landlord's debt associated with the building,[4] which included, their lawyer noted, "past real property taxes, nuisance assessments, water and sewer charges and interest, penalties, fees, and other related charges assessed against the property."[5] Tenants who purchased their buildings were often left with both structural and financial damage wreaked by their prior landlords, which the tenants then had to clean up.

Another financial challenge, rooted in the nature of the city as an investment vehicle, lies in the physical structure of the buildings—and tenants' desires to reconfigure those structures. Many LECs were originally rental buildings of one-bedroom units. Packing a building with one-bedroom units is the most efficient way to maximize return on investment for the developer/owner. But those one-bedroom apartments, particularly in poorer neighborhoods, were often filled with families. So once they have reclaimed a building, tenants often decide to reconfigure the interior of the building to create fewer, larger units to better accommodate their families. Just a few examples follow. One building in Columbia Heights was originally made up of forty-six one-bedroom units, but was reconfigured down to thirty-four one-, two-, and three-bedroom units. The new mix of unit size, the co-op's nonprofit developer noted, was based on the needs of the twenty-four families that made up the tenant association that was creating the cooperative.[6] Another building, in the Adams Morgan neighborhood, was originally made up of thirty-two one-bedroom units and was reconfigured down to just eleven units, made up of a mix of one-, two-, three-, and four-bedroom apartments, plus two efficiencies.[7] A third apartment complex, in the Congress Heights neighborhood of Southeast D.C., was originally made up of forty-four units, including three efficiencies, seventeen one-bedrooms, twenty-three two-bedrooms, and just one three-bedroom.[8] After the new co-op members had renovated the complex to meet their needs, there were only thirty-seven units, with no efficiencies, just six one-bedrooms, twenty two-bedrooms, five three-bedrooms, and six four-bedrooms.[9] These changes in the building structure are made to accommodate the specific families that are engaged in the tenant purchase and cooperative conversion process in those buildings. Members make these changes because they prioritize creating a more livable space for their families. But they do this knowing full well that reduced numbers of units will reduce the co-op's overall income from monthly fees. Reconfiguring a building built to maximize exchange value into one that is designed for use value can, in this way, have long-term financial consequences.

Maintaining a commons often requires playing catch-up while getting that resource into livable shape. This can be a long process, under which the freshly minted co-op owners take out additional loans in order to make the necessary repairs and renovations, therefore increasing their indebtedness and their long-term enmeshment in capitalist structures. At the same time, co-op members are often loathe to raise their own monthly fees, so the building's income can be relatively low. The tendency of cooperative owners to keep their fees low, potentially leading to serious financial difficulty in the long term, has been noted in other research. Noterman (2015), for example, theorizes a cooperatively-owned mobile home community as a commons. She notes that one of the challenges to the community was that co-op fees were kept so low over the years to accommodate low-income members that when members finally voted to adjust their fees substantially upwards, in order to pay for necessary improvements, a large financial hit was incurred all at once. The problem of how to keep fees low—especially given the costs incurred by the neglect of previous landlords—bedevils many co-ops.

But even if fees are relatively low, another financial challenge can be the difficulty of collecting monthly fees from people who often have little in the way of income, or have unexpected expenses that keep them from paying their fees on time. The financial health of the commons as a whole is bound up with the financial lives of its individual members. Low-income people living in expensive cities are living on the edge. Even if their housing costs are relatively affordable, they may still have trouble paying at times. An example comes from the Hickory Cooperative. Whitney, a white woman in her thirties, lived in the Hickory for seven and a half years. For much of that time, she was the treasurer of the board, a position which demanded a great deal of work—including, importantly, the emotional work of dealing with members who could not or would not pay their monthly carrying charges. As she describes:

We had a very big problem with two members who didn't pay their carrying charges. One didn't pay for a year, and one didn't pay for nine months. . . . And we had three other members who got behind and weren't paying. You [as the treasurer] have to be this confrontational figure. And you're constantly confronting people about money! And it's hard, and they sometimes get really nasty to you. Not only do you have so much work to complete, and it's on a regular basis—and then you're having to deal with people that don't pay and are angry about it and get up in your face about it. And it wears on you after a while.

Whitney is running up against one of the primary contradictions of the commons within capitalism: though these spaces may have been created as a way to try to shelter their members from the harshest demands of the housing market, they still require financial contributions from members who may often have difficulty paying the bills. Co-op members sometimes find themselves in the very uncomfortable position of demanding payment from their fellow members. Even though the money now does not go to a landlord's profit but rather to keeping the co-op alive, sometimes members still, for whatever reason, will not or cannot contribute. And other members have to do the hard, emotionally draining work of making them pay up.

If members continually refuse to pay their co-op fees—to contribute to maintaining the commons at the most basic level—then other members must take on the work of expelling them from the commons, for the sake of the overall health of the co-op. At the Juniper Co-op, people almost always pay fees on time, but occasionally someone does not. Magdalena, the co-op president, describes the hard line she had to take against one member who had not paid fees for several months running:

So I have to get really hard on them, and tell them, you need to get a lawyer, and set up the papers. And so then I had a private meeting with the member. I says, okay. You have a decision to make. If you don't think there's a good opportunity here, to live, that means you have another plan. This is what happens when you don't pay. You get notice, and if you don't adjust, everything that you have in here, goes outside on the sidewalk. So you can start packing everything that you think you want to have, make sure you have it ready to go, grab it and run, because, this is what's gonna happen. You're going to be outside on the thing. [She pauses.] Next month, everything was paid up! Isn't that a shame! [She laughs.] It's like you think you can take advantage, you're not supposed to take advantage of this kind of situation. No, no. So we don't get that often. But there's always one that you have to open their eyes and [let them know]—can't do that!

This may sound harsh. Magdalena appears to have few qualms about evicting one of her fellow low-income co-op members. But her insistence that members not "take advantage" of the unique situation of the co-op is telling. She and others have worked hard to create their co-ops and will not lightly countenance fellow members who, as she sees it, try to get away with not paying—without, that is, contributing to the ongoing maintenance of the commons. Clearly, the challenge of keeping the co-op's financial life in order can intersect with questions of access and exclusion.

Challenges of Access and Exclusion

One of the particular qualities of an urban commons, I've argued, is that it exists in the context of relatively high concentrations of people living in relatively small amounts of space. This stands in contrast to the commons studied by most CPR scholars, which tend to exist in rural areas with relatively low densities of population. Questions of access and exclusion are therefore of particular importance in urban commons. Ostrom's first principle of commons governance deals with boundaries. The boundaries of the resource must be clear: commoners must know, for example, the spatial limits of their forest. Just as importantly, the boundaries of the commons membership must also be clear: commoners need to know who is part of their collective process, and who is not, in order to effectively govern. This is the principle Ostrom considered to be the most important: it is why she put it first in her list. It is also the principle that most directly points out the flaw in Hardin's argument: commons, Ostrom is emphasizing, are not open access. They have boundaries. They are, in a word, exclusionary (Ostrom 1990).

With Ostrom, and against many alterglobalizationist scholars, I operate with the understanding that no commons is open to all. A commons is necessarily social, and therefore necessarily exclusive: it is made and maintained by a defined group of people. The question of who has access to the commons, therefore, is paramount. Under the LEC structure, prospective new members are interviewed by the board or a committee, which then decides whether to invite these individuals and families to join the co-op. In D.C. LECs, access varies. Of the seven existing LECs studied, five were filled to capacity and maintained waiting lists for units. Two, in contrast, were actively searching for members. The two that were searching for members appeared to be in that situation because, in one case, most of the available units were studios, which are too small for families; and, in both cases, the co-op carrying charges, while below market rent levels, were not substantially lower, given the less-than-central locations of the respective properties. The two co-ops that were actively searching for members did not have the luxury of being particularly picky about applicants. But for the five co-ops with waiting lists, members must make decisions about who should be given access to the commons.

Decisions about who should be admitted to the co-op can be difficult. For one thing, co-op members must balance their desire to provide affordable housing to people who truly need it with the reality that they must have members who they trust, and who can pay their monthly carrying charges on time. Rachel describes the tension at the Hickory Co-op, which was explicitly founded for low-income social justice activists:

> We obviously need to accept people who make below a certain amount, but we finally also decided that they need to make *above* a certain amount. They have to prove that they can afford to pay their carrying charges on time. . . . So there's also been this real internal debate around, what's the benefit to living here? And I think for some members of the co-op, who gets to live in here is sort of a form—almost of charity. It's like, we should really only accept members who really need this financially. And the truth of the matter is, everyone will benefit from living here. My opinion, shared by some members of the co-op, is that even if you don't make a lot of money, because you're pursuing activism or whatever, you should still have your [financial] shit in order. Or be willing to get there.

As Rachel describes, the Hickory members eventually decided that for the health of the co-op, they needed to exclude people who seemed like they might not be able to make the monthly payments. Their reality aligns with

Ben Maddison's (2010) reading of commons history: in many cases, Maddison argues, the way English commons were regulated excluded the poorest of the poor. When co-ops depend for their existence on monthly fees from members, they cannot take a risk on including the poorest. (An important exception to this is when co-ops work in conjunction with a federal housing subsidy program, to either allow some members to use federal housing vouchers to pay their monthly fees, as the Aspen Co-op does, or to use a "project-based" federal subsidy for the building, as the Juniper does. In those cases, because those members covered by the subsidy are only paying 30 percent of their income toward their housing costs, with the rest federally subsidized, the housing commons really are open to the poorest of the poor. This housing, however, can still be exclusionary, as we will see below.)

The Magnolia Co-op, in Southeast D.C., also excludes the poorest: it requires that new members earn an annual salary of at least $19,000 to qualify for a three-bedroom unit, the smallest unit available. As the co-op manager explains, "we don't like to set anybody up for failure." Phyllis, introduced in the last chapter, is an African-American in her sixties, who with her husband raised eight children in the Magnolia. As Phyllis describes, the board selects people in part based on what they feel is the degree of the applicant's need:

> [I]t was one young lady that wanted to come in at one time . . .
> she was making like $51,000 a year, and she was living by herself.
> Well, she can afford to go out and buy something, or get something, on the private market. Whereas you take a person with five,
> six children making $51,000, they can't do it. So I think it's a good
> thing to have a limited-equity co-op, where—it's good to have
> people to come in that maybe have more money or whatever, but
> I don't think it's good for the people that doesn't have money that
> you're taking units up that they could use. That they need, for their
> children, to raise their children. And that's a good thing, under the
> cooperative form, as far as buying that way, it's good. I don't have
> any children here [anymore], but a lot of people out here that have
> children, they go through a lot out there trying to raise their kids.
> They're doing very well here.

It was this young woman applicant's relatively high income, together with her childless status, that made her, for the Magnolia board, less deserving of the commons. But not all co-ops evaluate prospective new members based on their ability to pay versus their perceived need. At the Juniper and Sycamore co-ops, for example, family members and friends appear to be given priority, regardless of their particular "need" for affordable housing—and regardless, too, of any external requirements that the co-op work from a waiting list. The Juniper, as noted, receives a housing subsidy from the federal Department of Housing and Urban Development (HUD), and it is therefore supposed to maintain a list of HUD-approved applicants to use when filling vacant units. But it doesn't quite work this way. During my interview with Magdalena, the co-op president, we are interrupted by a phone call from a person inquiring about any vacancies in the co-op. Magdalena says into the receiver, "I'm sorry, we have no vacancies, for anyone at this time. You're welcome." She hangs up and rolls her eyes.

> Girl, sometimes it's twenty calls, oh my god, sometimes. Even if we were to have—having a [waiting] list. Twenty calls a day? How many a year? Why even bother?

People rarely move out of the co-op, but I ask her how they handle it when a unit does become available. She replies:

> We sort of start in the building first. The building is first. But legally, we supposed to have a list, because of HUD, but this is a *co-op*. And not because you're on a list, you're gonna get it! Cause you must qualify, one, and two, if you don't come with some support for the co-op, [we] don't take you because you're first on the list. So the list is good, but—psht. It don't mean a whole lot of anything.

Instead of working from a HUD-mandated waiting list, the board first determines whether anyone in the building has friends or relatives that they would recommend move into the co-op—and they look specifically for people who will "come with some support for the co-op." Recall Ostrom's fourth principle: "The right of community members to devise their own rules is respected by external authorities." It is not that the external authority—HUD, in this case—is respecting the rights of these co-op members to devise their own rules for admitting new members. It is likely that HUD is unaware the building is ignoring HUD rules. But the point is that the co-op has come up with its own way of doing things, regardless of external requirements, and it appears to be functioning well, in terms of the overall health of the co-op.

This appears to be how most of the people who have moved into the Juniper since the tenants bought the building arrived. This has worked well for the Juniper: they know the new members before they move in, and they trust that the new folks will contribute to the life of the co-op. In two other co-ops, both with long waiting lists, family members are given preferential treatment when openings arise. A story from the Sycamore Co-op is illustrative. Mary, who helped found the co-op in the late 1980s, moved out in 2000, but she remained socially connected with the co-op, and her son moved into the co-op in 2009. When her nephew Todd—introduced in the last chapter—needed a place to live, she suggested that he move into the Sycamore, too. She described how she helped make that happen:

> [A]fter [Todd] graduated [from college], it was time for [Todd] to get out [of his parents' house], I couldn't think of a better place. And we were just lucky that they had a vacancy. So you know, I'm like, hey. I helped start it, so I should have some kind of pull! So I called them, "[Virginia, Opal], my nephew"—. And they know that when you get someone like that, you take a chance because, he's going to pay his rent. "You don't pay your rent, I'm calling your aunt!" [She laughs.] Or, and, [my son]'s over here, and just like with [my son]. You can't stay there [if you don't pay] because it's part of *my* reputation too.

Having extended family in the building creates trust among members— not only that the new family members will be good neighbors, but also that they will pay their carrying charges on time, lest they shame their family members who worked to find them a spot in the co-op.

One of the problems with this exclusivity is that people with relatively higher incomes may end up accessing the commons, at the expense of people with relatively lower incomes. It could be argued, for instance, that Todd, the young software developer at the Sycamore Co-op, does not need the level of affordability his co-op gives him: in 2011, $610 a month for his one-bedroom apartment. It is unlikely that truly wealthy individuals would try to join a limited-equity co-op: for one, almost all of D.C.'s LECs place ceilings on the household income of members, and secondly, this housing form tends not to appeal to people with enough money to rent or purchase a home on the open market. As Sherry, of the Aspen Co-op, points out, most LECs don't have the amenities—central air conditioning, roof decks, laundry machines and dishwashers in units—that wealthier people expect in their housing. But over time, as original members die or move in with their children or into assisted living, their units may become occupied by people with more means.

LECs also enable people with *potentially* higher incomes, like Maria, who was introduced in the last chapter, to make life choices that lower their income and allow them to qualify to live in the building—when from a policy standpoint the argument could be made that Maria's unit should be reserved for someone who does not have the opportunity to earn a higher income. The larger problem is that, in a capitalist real estate market, the commons becomes a scarce commodity. In a city in which public housing is being torn down and affordable housing of all kinds is in short supply, a commons made up of about 3,100 units of limited-equity co-op hous-ing is hardly enough to meet the need. Maria and Todd occupy units that Phyllis, of the Magnolia Co-op, might argue should be allotted to poorer people or people raising children. But should Maria and Todd be excluded? Maria serves on her co-op's security committee and takes care of small co-op-related tasks that her aunt, the board president, asks of her. Todd represents his co-op at community meetings organizing against the coming of a new WalMart to the co-op's neighborhood. Both Maria and Todd ac-tively participate in the lives of their co-ops. As Magdalena emphasized, the board wants new members who "come with some support for the co-op." They want members who will participate in the life of the co-op. As Lutz notes in his study of the urban commons of homeless tent cities, "access to the tent commons is not determined by property or status, but by need and active participation, which ensure membership" (2015, 105). Access to the commons is often bound up with questions of participation.

The Challenges of "Participation"

In talking to active co-op members about the challenges their co-op faces, the question of participation always arises. In reviewing a series of studies of limited-equity housing cooperatives, Clark and Saegert seek to under-stand what it really means to "participate" in the life of a co-op. They find that participation is most commonly linked with verbal communication: members participate by sitting in meetings, talking through issues, and solving problems. Although participation can also be made up of performing particular tasks, like maintenance or record-keeping, these tasks always stem from discussion about what needs to be done. Participation, then, is based on communication among co-op members (Clark and Saegert 1994). Much of what the commons requires is communication among members: communication that takes time and patience. While some research has shown that some LECs have extremely high levels of member participation (cf Saegert 1989), my research found that co-op work tended to be skewed toward a minority of co-op members. While a few co-op leaders had devised methods of encouraging members to participate that seemed to be working, others were frustrated at the fact that so many members seemed to take their housing for granted.

Doris, who we first met in chapter 1, served on the Magnolia Co-op board for one term. She is of the opinion that all co-op members should serve at least one term on the board, so that they can gain an understanding of all the work the board does. But at the time of our interview, Doris had stopped participating in co-op affairs. She explains why:

> I shouldn't have [stopped attending] but I did, get away from
> going—because it's like every time you go, it's the same people.
> When we all are out here, and you know, we *got* to stick together.
> Because we're definitely not going to go anywhere in this city, and
> find what we have. And we've got a good location and everything.
> We've got the subway just down the street, we can't beat it. And it
> just really frustrates you that everybody wouldn't take the time,
> at least an hour to two hours. And I understand, you come home
> from work, you tired, but they got chairs, it ain't like you standing
> up, you setting there. So I would get frustrated at that, sometimes,
> at those meetings, so I did slack up, I really did, I really did.

Despite her own current lack of participation, she is adamant that participation levels need to rise:

> But it's important to all of us. Cause what affects one is gonna affect
> us all. And that's the thing about it. And I know nobody wants to
> be homeless, cause I sure don't. You know. My sister had a one-
> bedroom apartment for $725. I mean, $725. I'm like, I could pay
> my rent with that and still have some left!

Homelessness, Doris believes, is a real possibility for herself and her family. The co-op keeps her and her fellow members housed, and very affordably. Members need to participate, she thinks, in order to ensure that the co-op continues to thrive. But over time, she herself has lost patience with attending meetings due to the time it takes to work out problems and come to joint decisions, especially when it seems like others rarely participate.

Participation in the commons, as Federici (2012) and Bennholdt-Thomsen and Mies (1999) have noted, is often highly gendered. Women do much of the unseen work of the commons, and this certainly holds true for the limited-equity cooperatives I studied. In all but one of the co-ops I studied, a woman served as president of the board; women tended to be the ones who showed up for membership meetings and volunteered to serve on co-op committees. The communication that makes up participation can be formal, as illustrated by meeting attendance, as Doris discusses. But communication—and participation—can also be informal. Magdalena's work, similar to the work of most co-op presidents, runs from the major—working out management company contracts, dealing with delinquent members, organizing meetings—to the mundane. Over the course of an interview in the co-op office, we are interrupted by phone calls several times: people calling to inquire if the co-op has units available, an insurance agent calling to sell insurance plans. The last call is from a co-op member calling from elsewhere in the building. Magdalena speaks for several minutes to the woman in Spanish, and then hangs up, laughing, repeating what the woman had been concerned about:

> "[Magdalena], two machines are working—but there's no clothes in it!" Okay, what you want me to do? [She laughs.] I says use it till it runs out! She says two dryers are running, but there's no clothes in it. It's because I'm home [that she called]. But that's okay, that's fine. That's the disabled lady, anyway.

It is because Magdalena is in the building, and available, that this woman feels free to alert Magdalena to her concern that two dryers in the laundry room are running, without clothes in them—in the grand scheme of co-op maintenance, not a particularly pressing problem. Magdalena's response is generous—she's home anyway, she says, and the lady is disabled. It's fine. Responding to concerns and requests, however minor, is the constant work of co-op presidents, and often other board members as well. Alice, the president of the Dogwood Co-op, is also often bombarded by minor requests of members that add up in terms of time and headspace. She relates one instance of a co-op member who was upset that the lotto machine wasn't working in a shop that rents storefront space from the co-op:

> Like today Mr. [Carson], the older gentleman on the second floor—I was in the [basement] office and he came and he said to me, the people in the store's lotto machine was down, and they needed to get down here to fix it. I said, well, Mr. [Carson], I'm on my way out. Do you want to come and stay with them while they—[but he said] no, no, no, no, no! But he was persistent on them coming down here, cause he needed to play his numbers! [She laughs.] I'm like, well *I'm* not gonna stay down here [and wait for them]! I'm getting ready to go to Macy's!

Mr. Carson expected that Alice would wait for the lotto machine repair people to arrive, and then do the social labor of interfacing with them, even though it was Mr. Carson who wanted to play his numbers, not Alice. This is just one of many examples of time and labor required in the constant, day in and day out work of maintaining a collective living space. Saegert notes that much of the work of the LEC leaders in her Harlem study required "constant attention, both of a physical and social nature, to repetitive and unending tasks" (1989, 304). She likens it to housework. The experiences of Magdalena, Alice, and other co-op leaders indicates that this type of constant work suffuses D.C.'s LECs as well. This is work that is largely unseen and unaccounted for—and like housework, performed overwhelmingly by women. If attention is not paid to gender relations, practicing the commons can simply replicate patterns of gendered work. The commons, as I noted in the introduction, is not necessarily a liberatory space. (I will return to the question of gender in the commons in the next chapter.)

I use the term "work" here because what is called "participation" can also, I argue, be understood as the ability of people to work together. A major challenge of maintaining the urban commons is maintaining working relationships over the long term among people who, in some ways, are quite different from each other. Once the exciting but exhausting struggle to purchase and renovate their buildings is over, co-op members often find their commonality receding. If strangers have gone through the reclamation process together, they are no longer strangers. But paradoxically, once they have succeeded in reclaiming their space from the capitalist environment, they now may return to a position of having fairly little in common. Certainly they often seem to lose their common zeal and drive for engaging in the collective work of their housing.

As Addisu from the Walnut Cooperative noted at the beginning of the chapter, once the crisis was over and the residents all owned their building, then the hard work really began. This was the time when differences and conflicts among people began spilling out. Some people began to be suspicious of other members, thinking they wanted to control the co-op. People weren't as willing to work together as they had been before. Addisu believes that the fundamental challenge to keeping a collective project like a co-op going is the individualizing nature of life in a capitalist society. He explains:

> Here [in the U.S.], because of this division of labor, the alienation is further gone, really. People in my hometown [in Ethiopia], for example, we live together, we don't even have an extra room or anything, or anything, we live together, we decide things, we share everything. Because of limitations. Here [in the U.S.], people can afford to be individual, and they have their room. At the same time, when they have their rooms, they are devoid of their families, they don't share their family's interest, I mean really, they are different. So they've now grown to be individually, further, further. But, for people who are poor still, they depend on somebody. The affluent people, they are the ones that have the luxury. These people [in Ethiopia] I mean really, they might not have their own, even here, separate rooms, they might sleep together, they have contact with their families more, they get together with their families more. So they are not more alienated. Because, because, this [the U.S.] is a capitalist country.

Addisu ultimately moved out of his co-op, disillusioned with people's ability to work collectively in a capitalist society. Several years after he left, his co-op converted to a market-rate condominium ownership structure. The commons he and others had worked so hard to claim had been re-enclosed.

The Temptation of Cooptation

The final challenge of maintaining the urban commons maps onto a key trait of the urban commons: the fact that the city itself is a site of the accumulation of surplus wealth, and that the commons is therefore always potentially a site of wealth extraction. Commoners may become convinced to sell out. Goldman describes how capital can, through international development, gain access to commons using the rhetoric of improving the efficiency of the commons:

> Access for domestic and foreign capital to more remote zones of resource- and labor-rich sites is being accomplished through social experimentation and state expansionism in the name of "making the commons work." In most cases, Third World state development agencies become the guardian of a relatively large influx of foreign capital intended specifically to restructure social-natural relations in "undeveloped" areas so that the project, and the state itself, can set root and capitalist relations can grow. (1997, 21)

The commons, that is, can serve as a source of new wealth—once it becomes fully integrated into the capitalist economy and ceases to be a commons. In the case of D.C.'s co-ops, some members at some point start thinking about the potential exchange value of their homes—and start wanting to realize that potential by converting to a market-rate ownership structure. It is important to point out here that co-op members tend not to come up with this idea alone: many co-ops are approached by developers who specialize in tenant purchase broadly, and also more specifically in helping LECs convert into market-rate condominiums. These developers serve the same role as the "Third World" state development agencies that Goldman discusses, in helping restructure, or enclose, a commons to produce financial wealth.

LECs are threatened by the promise of the short-term individualized gain that can come from dissolving the commons. In being caught in this tension between maintaining the collectivity of the commons and being coopted into capitalist markets, LEC members are hardly alone; commoners from the English peasantry to the native peoples of New England have succumbed to pressures of enclosure, to individualize and monetize resources previously managed in common (Cronon 2003; Goldstein 2013). This does not make these co-op members unethical individuals, but rather it points to the difficulty of maintaining commons in highly commodified landscapes. The LECs in Washington, D.C., must retain their affordable, nonspeculative form as long as they are receiving city subsidy in the form of a low- or zero-interest loan. But if they are able to pay off the city's loan without receiving additional public subsidies, they have the option of converting to a market-rate structure. Some LECs have chosen to go this route, while others have steadfastly held onto their affordable status.

In several of the extant LECs I investigated, members were genuinely conflicted over the idea of converting to market-rate ownership. Some members were dedicated to maintaining their spaces as nonspeculative, collective housing options for working people. But other members wondered if it might not be better for themselves and their neighbors to dissolve their LECs, take the money they could make from selling their units in a hot real estate market, and use that money to make other choices. For example, the immigrant leader of a successful LEC in the gentrified Adams Morgan neighborhood led her co-op through conversion to market-rate condominium status, sold her unit, and used the substantial proceeds to buy land and a home in her native El Salvador. For someone who had worked in low-wage jobs most of her life, this was something of a personal feat. But this action, of course, destroyed this commons as a resource for others like herself in the future.

The case of the Walnut Co-op is instructive. As noted above, the tenants purchased the building in 1992, and they ran it as a limited-equity co-op for thirteen years. On the advice of their management company, the members then voted to convert to condominiums in 2005. Their management company also served as the condominium developer, and they apparently worked hard to ensure that all the LEC members who wanted to buy into the condo would be able to. Indeed, the members all bought in for either $36,000 for a one-bedroom unit or $42,000 for a two-bedroom—unbelievably low prices, considering their location in a rapidly gentrifying neighborhood, near the height of the real estate market. At the time of the conversion, thirteen of the original fifteen co-op members still lived in the building; but within five years, only five of the original members remained. According to city records, the rest had sold their units—all after first heavily refinancing—and moved out. According to interviews with former members, none of the members who sold their units went on to buy another housing unit; all returned to renting.[10] The story of one former member, Pedro, is illustrative.

Pedro came to the United States in the early 1980s from El Salvador, fleeing that country's civil war. He had lived in the Walnut for years when it was a rental, and his sister and father had been two of the leaders of the tenant purchase effort. After the purchase, Pedro owned a two-bedroom unit in the co-op, for which he paid about $450 a month for many years. But after the condo conversion, Pedro suffered a series of personal setbacks. First, he split up from his wife. Then, he lost his job—he works in demolition, which is low-paying and back-breaking work—and was unemployed for about a year. He refinanced his unit for $135,000 in 2007, and he finally sold the unit in 2008 because he could no longer make his monthly payments. He estimates he made about $8,000 or $10,000 on the sale. At the time of our interview, he was living in a rooming house a few blocks from his old co-op, a row house that had been split up into individual rooms to house Central American immigrants like himself. His room was small. It fit a bed and a dresser; a toaster balanced on a shelf, and it was clear that he did all his eating as well as sleeping in this space. Pictures of his teenage daughter, who lived with her mother, adorned the room. Pedro was paying $475 a month for the room, plus an extra $50 a month in the summer because he needed to run the air conditioner in order to sleep, and he had to pay the landlady separately for that. It is clear that, for Pedro, the dissolution of the commons has landed him in worse housing circumstances, with less control over his home space. (When I mentioned Pedro's case to the developer who led the condo conversion, he dismissed Pedro as a "drunk." What I understood as reduced life circumstances due to the loss of the commons, the developer understood as a case of individual misfortune brought on by Pedro's own poor choices. Perhaps both views have merit.)

Yafeu, like Pedro, was another longtime Walnut Co-op member, but unlike Pedro, he is one of the five original LEC members who, as of 2010, still owned their condominium units. Yafeu, an immigrant from West Africa, is happy he still has his housing, but he is not particularly pleased with how the building has changed since going market. He reminisces about the community spirit of the old co-op. When I ask whether that feeling still exists in the building, now that it has gone condo, he vacillates almost comically between his visceral disgust at the changes and an attempt at a more broadly philosophical acceptance of the fact that "things change":

> Oooooooh. Hah! *Noooo.* Well, now, let me take it back. I think—changes. I am a believer that life don't stay the same forever. . . . But do I have that same feeling as yesterday? Noooo, no. Noooo, no, no, no. No, it's not there. But I just look at it, people are people. You never gonna see the same. That's what I say. But if you ask me, do I want to go back to those days, with those—oh, yeah. It was a com-

munity. Oh, yeah! Oh yeah. It was a community. Oh yeah. I mean, it was like a family event. . . . You feel, somebody got your back. Do somebody have my back now? No! Hell, no! Hell, no! Sorry about that. Now you on your own, high and dry. I mean, I'm sorry to say—I know we're not all going to see things the same. I always see things different.

When asked why he thinks the building feel has changed, he responds:

Well. I would be vague to say it's life. But, as you know, life. There's no guarantee. It changes every day. But I think, money. I think [long pause]—I don't know, life changes. But money, the neighborhood is changing itself, all these high, big stuff going. I receive a letter, going, two months ago, from the tax property, whatever they call it. And they're telling me my property valued for some $200,000. I'm like, wait a minute. Because they tax you according to your [property value]. . . . So I think it's money. It's the city itself changing.

He further explains this by describing the difference between the original co-op members, and the people who have bought units in the building since the conversion to condominium:

Well, you look at these people who come in and say, well, they purchased their property for $100,000-something. And they expect—they expect the world out of it. So that's a big change of itself. You're not gonna sit and invest $100,000, and then you think it's chicken change. . . . They expect that people who live here, have to be upgraded. Have to be *unique*, have to be *special*.

It would be humorous to note (if it wasn't so sadly illustrative of the yawning gap between what working-class and wealthy people expect housing to cost) that Yafeu considers "$100,000-something" an outrageous sum to pay for a condominium in what was at the time one of the hottest real estate markets in the city. Yafeu is hinting at some of the conflict that can arise in buildings that have converted from LEC to market-rate, and that thus, for at least a certain period of time, are home to people of different incomes and class positions—and who consequently may have different priorities.

After buying into the new condominium structure, Yafeu's monthly housing costs jumped from the mid-$400s to the mid-$700s. This is still, he admits, a good deal, considering the building's location in Columbia Heights. But it represents a significant increase in his cost. Before, he was working only one job, at the front desk of a downtown hotel. Since going condo, he has had to take on a second, part-time job, with a towing company, where he works a few nights a week. Yafeu has been able to hang onto his unit, and presumably he is building some wealth. He may miss the community feel of the old days, but he is still benefitting from his housing, as are the few other original LEC members who remain in the building. But he has to work longer hours to keep up with the payments: the enclosure of the commons, it appears, has made him more dependent on waged labor.

Sometimes, the dissolution of the commons results in immediate loss for its members. This happened in the case of the Poplar Cooperative, in the city's Shaw neighborhood, introduced in chapter 3. In the early 2000s, some members of the co-op began to push for converting the building to a market-rate condominium ownership structure. The exact course of events is unclear, but it appears that one member in particular pushed for conversion, believing that she would be able to sell her unit, or rent it out, for a hefty sum. In 2004, the membership narrowly voted to convert to market-rate condominium ownership. But most of the co-op members were low-income people who could not, as it turned out, afford to participate in the conversion. The developer doing the conversion paid them minor amounts of money to leave; some received nothing.

Pearl was one of the low-income co-op members who had to leave. Pearl is an African American woman in her fifties who grew up in D.C. She had been living with her children in public housing in the Southeast quadrant of the city in the early 1990s when she learned about the Poplar Co-op, and she promptly applied for a unit. She describes the day she was interviewed to move into the co-op as "the happiest day of my life." She lived there for the next twelve years and voted against converting to condominium, knowing that she could never afford to buy into the new condominium ownership structure. Ultimately, Pearl was paid $4,700 to leave the Poplar. She describes the disintegration of the co-op as "devastating," and tells how it happened:

> [T]hey offered different people different amounts [to leave]. You didn't know what nobody was getting. Some people got, like I

know one neighbor, she told the—which was good—she told them that she wanted her car paid off, and the rest she'll take in money. So when she moved, she wouldn't have no car note. So that was smart. And you know, it's like, I think it's still going on today. Like they getting rid of a lot of public housing, and giving the people money. And you know, a person that hasn't had, never had anything, that's a lot of money to them. But you know, when you're not used to stuff, you just go buying, and buying, and buying, you don't think about investing and saving and stuff like that.

Pearl is pointing here to some larger problems. One, the city is closing much of its public housing, which is eroding the ability of poor people to find housing they can afford. Two, even if commoners are able to realize the (sometimes very partial) exchange value of the commons, they are poor, and whatever money they get doesn't usually go far. Even if it sounds like a lot (and often it is actually not much at all, as Pearl's case demonstrates), it is easy for the money to slip away. Pearl had lived in two different rental apartments since she left the co-op in 2004. At the time of our interview, in 2011, she was packing up to move into a third apartment. Only three of the original Poplar LEC members were able to buy into the new condominium structure. But within three years of the condo conversion, the condominium structure was terminated, and the condo owners were bought out for undisclosed amounts of money. As of 2012, the building sat empty and boarded up. It had been bought by the Marriott Corporation, which reportedly planned to turn it into a boutique hotel.

When commoners sell out, they lose the commons. What they gain—sometimes—is cash. Other times, they gain financial equity in their homes—which they can only access through refinancing, significantly raising their monthly housing costs, or through selling their units, meaning they need to look for housing elsewhere. But when poor people's housing becomes a commodity and they are able to trade it in for cash, they often receive far less than the home is really worth. Harvey notes the problem with schemes in Global South cities that award slum dwellers titles to their squatted housing in an effort to help them build long-term assets and wealth: "The problem is that the poor, beset with income insecurity and frequent financial difficulties, can easily be persuaded to trade in that asset for a relatively low cash payment" (2008, 36). A few members—like the Adams Morgan leader who sold her unit and bought land in El Salvador—may make financial gains with the dissolution of the commons. But many co-op members end up losing out. And once the commons dissolves, there are no more opportunities for future, as-yet-unknown commoners.

Commitment to the Commons

Many LEC members are committed to maintaining the commons over time, even knowing that conversion to market-rate structures might benefit them financially on an individual level. Continued affordability is important to them because they believe low-income people should be able to live in decent, affordable housing in convenient neighborhoods. The benefits of the commons discussed in the last chapter—affordability, control over place, stability, and community—trump the risk of dissolution for market exchange. Previous research has shown that middle-class people are often in the lead of efforts to convert LECs to market-rate ownership structures (Saegert et al. 2005). Indeed, this appears to be what happened at the Poplar. But when Maria, the young woman of color who has a master's degree and a relatively broad range of life opportunities, is asked whether she would be interested in seeing the Juniper Co-op convert to condo, she demurs:

> I would love to just retain what we have. Because it really does create community here. The majority of the people in the building—we have a lot of elderly people, single mothers with children, and artists. You know? So we really are people that kind of watch out for each other. And we don't have any Adams Morgan yuppie-type people coming in here, and trying to like, rule the world. It's just not the dynamic of our building at all. So as long as we can maintain this, it's beautiful. Like I said, my grandmother moved in, and I grew up in this neighborhood as much as my own, and I've *seen* the changes first-hand, and sometimes I walk down the street, and I can't even believe all the things that are here, because Adams Morgan, when I was little, was totally, like, ghetto! Nobody wanted to live over here! So now I see it. And the thing is, the buildings, the houses, everything is so beautiful and they always have been. And people, all of a sudden, *discover* these amazing buildings that have been here since the beginning of time! Yeah, as long as we can maintain what we have, that would be awesome. Not to say that yuppie people are mean or anything,

but you know, it's nice the way it's structured here, because people can really raise their families in this amazing neighborhood that has everything. Especially because people are older, and are single moms, they may not have a car, or access to other resources if they were living in another neighborhood, where, here, you can step outside your door and have everything. . . . And as long as we can maintain that for people who may not have that living in another neighborhood, that would be amazing.

The Adams Morgan neighborhood, as Maria describes, has almost thoroughly gentrified in the time since she was a child visiting her grandmother in the building. Today, her co-op is an oasis of affordable housing in a neighborhood that is defined by its large presence of "yuppie-type people" who often try to "rule the world" with their vision of urban life. The co-op, in contrast, is a place where people "watch out for each other," and value the community they have created together. Brian, also of the Juniper, describes why the limited-equity form has been so important for himself and his fellow members:

> From the beginning it was always a low-yield—it was never
> the sort of thing where you could make money off of it. I think
> people—the tenants all sort of discussed it, and everybody agreed
> that they wanted to try to keep it a building for low-income people,
> affordable housing. And a lot of the people in the building weren't
> officially activists, but were sort of politically inclined, or artists, or
> people like that. And so that was a very attractive prospect to them.
> Well, we're gonna buy a building, it's gonna be a co-op, we're all
> gonna pull together, it's not gonna go condo. Going condo was the
> big threat back then, I guess it still is.

Like Maria and Brian, Daisy, of the Aspen Co-op, has a broader range of life opportunities than many LEC members: she is college educated, works a stable job, and has no dependents. But Daisy also wants others in the future to have the same opportunity she had:

> I just think it was so ideal when I moved in, that it was some place
> that I could afford to, that I would hate to have that opportunity
> missed for someone else. Cause it's a great starter-slash-permanent

place. Whereas I'd hate to think that you could only get in if you had enough money.

But many LEC members with narrower ranges of life options are similarly committed to the limited-equity form of ownership. Sandy, introduced in chapter 3, is the board president of the Mulberry Co-op. At the time of our interview she was unemployed and had worked most recently cleaning houses. Sandy emphasizes that incoming members must understand the limited-equity nature of the housing:

> I never want to sell this for money-market. *I* wouldn't, but I'm only one person on the board, and I don't think—when they come in, that's the adamant thing that I tell them, that we're not trying to lose our limited-equity stance. It's stable as it is, just live comfortably, if you need something fixed, just fix it, or we go to the board and get it fixed and all that. So that's the kind of attitude they have to come in with. They can't sell—if you sell your share, you sell your share. But you can't change the structure of this complex, period.

What is key, Sandy believes, is that incoming members understand the limited-equity structure when they join the co-op. Sandy—like other low-income co-op members who are accustomed to living in poor-quality rental housing—emphasizes the benefits of co-op living that are not tied to market exchange: the control members have over their space, in this case in terms of getting repairs done, and the stability of the housing. Todd, the young African American software developer who lives in the Sycamore Co-op, wants to preserve his co-op's limited-equity structure because he wants to preserve its community—and what he calls the "unique" nature of his co-op:

> I *do* care about what happens to the co-op, because it's pretty unique. A lot of individuals that are real-estate-oriented, would like to see these co-ops gone. And I'd like to see it proceed so the next generation can take advantage of it. . . . It's unique in that you are instantly part of a community, and there's a cultural tie. We're all bought into the same thing. Nothing is done to benefit one person more than another. It's a community tie, if you have a problem, it's pretty much everyone's problem in the sense that if it costs money. It's kind of like you're buying into a community.

Todd's emphasis on community speaks to the argument of institutionalists that one of the requirements of commons maintenance is a membership that has a long-term approach toward their collective resource—and also toward each other. As noted earlier, members must, as Ostrom writes, have "shared a past and expect to share a future" (1990, 88). Often, a long-term approach is theorized as one in which current members are cognizant of the fact that their children and grandchildren will need access to the resource in the future in order to survive. This is an attitude that assumes lifeworlds in which children do much the same work—and in the same places—as their parents. One of the hallmarks of urban life, in contrast, is relatively rapid change. Despite the malleability of urban life, one of the reasons LECs succeed is because of long-term relationships that already exist in their buildings, and that members, like Todd, trust will continue to exist into the future. The fact that Todd is the nephew of one of the founders of his co-op, and that his cousin lives in another unit in the co-op, undoubtedly strengthens his sense of community and dedication to the co-op. Several respondents noted the importance of long-term relationships in their co-ops. Mary explains the importance of long-term relationships to the functioning of the Sycamore Co-op:

> [T]he board did a really decent job of being accountable to the [members]. And if something went wrong, not taking forever to fix things, and stuff like that. They were very good. And I think one of the advantages of that was because everybody knew practically everyone in there, and folks had been there for a while, and so there was a certain amount of trust, and respect, and you weren't gonna be doing anything to try to intentionally hurt someone that you've been living in a community with for, you know, a period of years. So that was a good thing.

Many LEC members whose adult family members live in other units in their co-ops appear to be more likely to be committed to the continued existence of the limited-equity co-op. Maria, Daisy, and Todd are all young people with broad life opportunities who may someday move out of the co-op to purchase homes on the open market, but they value retaining the limited-equity structure of their homes. Similarly, Brian, a middle-class African American, though he does not have literal family in his co-op, feels a strong sense of family there, and he wants the co-op to remain affordable for the sake of his neighbors. For many co-op members, people who were once relative strangers have become close, sometimes almost like family, and they feel committed to each other's futures. Co-op members who are committed to maintaining the commons are committed both because of the close relationships they have built in their spaces, and because of a more abstract commitment to providing housing for new members, who have yet to arrive.

The challenges of maintaining a commons in a city are significant. Members must, first, deal with financial challenges: the co-op must take in enough cash through co-op fees that it can cover its expenses, including any mortgage payments, repairs, and ongoing maintenance. Financial challenges to the commons can be particularly great in the urban context, in which land may be scarce relative to population, and the costs of real estate are high. Second, members must grapple with the challenge of access and exclusion: who gets to be part of the commons, and how does granting them access deny the commons to others? In an urban context with high densities of people, boundaries to the commons need to be clear: how are these boundaries set? Third, members must deal also with the challenge of participation—or what I am conceiving of as the challenge of working collectively, with strangers. Cities, unlike smaller, traditional communities, are filled with strangers, and an urban commons requires members to reckon with the fact that they have to work with people unlike themselves. Finally, co-ops face the challenge of the temptation of converting the co-op to a market-rate ownership structure. Conversion, while it may financially benefit a few individual co-op members, destroys the commons for future members. This is a particular temptation in the urban context, since so much wealth is generated through the city, and it is relatively easy to cash in.

Despite all these challenges, many co-op members remain committed to their form of housing. It is precisely because they recognize the ongoing need for the affordability, control, stability, and community their housing provides that they want to see it continue into the future—for themselves and for others. Together, these co-op members are practicing the urban commons. In the next chapter, I examine key elements of the practice of the urban commons.

6

Commoning in the Capitalist City

The urban commons is an ongoing practice. The commons, other scholars have emphasized, is not an a priori resource to be consumed but is rather socially constructed, constituted through commoning (De Angelis 2010; Linebaugh 2008). *Commoning* is a suggestive, even poetic, term, which conjures up a range of ways of being in community. My close examination of the experiences of ten current and former limited-equity housing cooperatives in Washington, D.C., has made clear to me that, while the urban commons can provide much to its members, it also requires much in terms of time and energy. While ultimately I am hopeful about the potential for people working in common to collectively self-manage noncommodified resources, I want to treat the practice of the commons realistically. It can be a lot of work.

In this chapter, I make several key points about the practice of the urban commons. First, I theorize the practice of the urban commons in relation to capitalism, highlighting the challenge of participating in the commons in a capitalist city. Second, I argue for a feminist perspective on the work of the commons. Doing the work of creating and maintaining commons, as seen in previous chapters, is often the work of women, and feminist theory can help explain how commons operate. Third, I emphasize that practicing the urban commons must include the work of *expansion*, along with reclamation and maintenance. The practice of the commons is a dialectical process that moves between expansion and maintenance. Fourth, I argue that it is through practicing the urban commons that people may begin to learn to self-govern. For some LEC members, participating in the life of the co-op is an unusual opportunity to learn to live democratically. Fifth, I make an argument for understanding urban commoning as an eminently pragmatic practice. Though the idea of the commons is often imbued with a certain romanticism, I find that commoning, especially for desperate people in desperate times, can be simply a pragmatic choice, one option among a limited array of options. Finally, I conclude with a discussion of the need for a practice that moves beyond the specific, bounded membership of the commons to a wider embrace of future, as-yet-unknown commoners.

Commoning in the Midst of the Capitalist City

The urban commons, I've noted, is marked by contradiction. One of the primary contradictions is how the commons works in relation to the pressures of the capitalist city. The benefit of the commons, as described in chapter 4, is that it allows its members to live lives that are not quite as bound by capitalist strictures. In this sense, the commons can be seen as something of an oasis, as many alterglobalizationists theorize. But the commons always exists in relation to capitalism, and in the hypergentrifying city, this is even more evident. Joanna, of the Magnolia Cooperative—one of the most affordable of the co-ops in my sample—discusses how she sees this contradiction playing out. Joanna is concerned that, because the co-op is *so* affordable, it attracts many people who simply need affordable housing—and that this could work against the health of the co-op in the long term. She explains:

> [S]ome people come in here because they want to be homeowners. And some people just move here because it's affordable. Oh, here's a cheap place to move, let's go. . . . Even though they have to pay [the $1000 share fee]. Because a lot of them have come from places where they were paying maybe twelve, thirteen hundred dollars a month, and they have only had two bedrooms. Well, if I can come here and get this three-bedroom for $500, that's $700 the first month I've saved, $700 the second month. So $1000 is nothing, I can give it to you.

I ask whether these members participate in the work of the co-op. Her response:

> No. No. The ones that came in with the mentality of being homeowners, they will participate. Those that came in just because it was affordable housing, they don't participate. . . . The beginning, I think we had more with the mentality of being owners. As we go along, I think [the attitude is] gonna be more—it's affordable housing, let's move in.

When asked why she thinks these attitudes are changing over time, she replies:

> Probably one main reason is the city is closing up so many of their public housing. So people are scrambling to find somewhere to go that they can afford. And then if they come here, and we don't take vouchers, then they gotta fend for themselves, so, oh this is affordable, let's stay.

When asked what this means for the co-op, she replies:

> It means that you have a small number that's out here working hard to keep this place, and the others are just sliding, saying, well, if you fight for yours, then mine's gonna be saved too, then I don't have to fight.

There's a lot going on in this brief exchange. Many new members, Joanna is arguing, come to the Magnolia precisely because it is so affordable—and not because they have a particular desire to live in a limited-equity co-op. She fears that the co-op may suffer in the end, because of a lack of participation. What Joanna is describing, of course, is a version of Hardin's tragedy of the commons: many members use the housing, and only a few work at maintaining it. The end result is possibly failure and destruction of the commons. Here is one of the primary challenges of a commons that exists within the structure of capitalism: an affordable living environment attracts people whose main concern is affordability, but who are not necessarily interested in collective responsibility for maintenance. But to castigate some people for not participating in the commons is to oversimplify the story and miss the larger context. The people who move into the Magnolia are, Joanna says, "scrambling" for housing they can afford. The city, she notes (as did Pearl, in the last chapter), is continually tearing down its stock of public housing. Affordable housing of all kinds, as noted in chapter 4, is in very short supply. There are many understandable reasons co-op members may not participate in the work of maintaining their homes. As Doris noted in the last chapter, people are often too exhausted from working all day long to then go to a co-op meeting at night. Paradoxically, the demands of a life under capitalism can make it terribly difficult to find the time and energy to participate in the commons. What this means is that the commons, enacted within capitalism, are always contingent. This doesn't mean that the commons generally, or LECs specifically, are unrealistic approaches to supporting life. But it does mean that the work required to maintain them must be taken seriously.

A Feminist Perspective on the Work of the Commons

As noted in chapter 1, one of the key ideas alterglobalizationists bring to the study of the commons is the feminist perspective on the work of the commons. Though only a handful of the alterglobalizationist commons scholars make this connection explicitly, it is, I think, a fundamental contribution to understanding how the commons operates. Mies and Bennholdt-Thomsen argue that, under capitalist wage relations, the work of the commons, like the work of women, has been rendered invisible. Women, they write, are treated like commons, while commons are treated like women: both perform such essential functions in basic survival that the roles they perform are not even noticed or acknowledged (Mies and Bennholdt-Thomsen 2001). Federici takes the argument a step further, arguing that the commons is the basis for social reproduction: the work that keeps people alive in the world. This is work that is performed disproportionately by women. And women, she argues in a related point, rely on the commons more than men do in order to take care of their families and communities (Federici 2012).

There are two interesting points to unpack here. One, Federici is arguing that women rely on the commons for survival more than men do. In the co-ops I studied, women seemed to outnumber men by significant margins. Of my forty interviews with LEC members and former members, twenty-nine were with women and eleven were with men; about three quarters of respondents, that is, were women. This sample is too small to generalize out to the entire universe of limited-equity co-op members, but it would appear that women are overrepresented in LECs. This may be because many LECs are home to elderly people, who are disproportionately female. It may be because many LECs are home to single parents raising children, and such parents are disproportionately female, and parents may be particularly attracted to living in the commons. (Phyllis, recall, thought LECs were good places to rear children.) And it may be for other reasons. But in LECs, women appear to outnumber men.

Two, Federici notes that women tend to be the caretakers of the commons. If women are more likely to be custodians of the commons generally, it follows that they would be more likely to do the work of the commons constituted by limited-equity cooperatives. Indeed, as I noted in the discussion of participation in chapter 4, previous studies of limited-equity co-ops in New York City and Los Angeles show women in leading roles (Heskin 1991; Leavitt and Saegert 1990; Saegert 1989). This was also the case in the co-ops I examined, in which women do much of the unrecognized work that Saegert compares to housework. Of the fifteen co-op leaders interviewed, twelve were women and three were men—80 percent of leaders, that is, were women. Of course, if women are disproportionately represented in co-op membership, it makes sense that they would also be disproportionately represented in co-op leadership. Whether or not women's participation is commensurate with their numerical presence in co-ops, the amount of work they do is notable.

Very few of my male or female respondents, however, brought up the gendered nature of co-op work in our interviews. (Perhaps this is because they are so accustomed to women doing the work of the home.) Patricia, the president of the Ironwood Co-op, is one of the only ones who mentioned it. She acknowledges that most LEC leaders are women, and that there is an inherent inequity in so much unpaid female labor going into supporting the continuing existence of co-ops. She frames this inequity in terms of the question of whether her co-op may someday convert to a market-rate ownership structure, which would allow members to realize financial equity gains on their housing, if they chose to sell or refinance their units. In mulling over this question, she asks:

> And plus is it fair, for people who have been there, say as long as I have, and have put in all this blood, sweat and tears, to not have any equity at all? In the end. As [famed financial advisor] Suze Orman said, women are always volunteering their services. Where men have to get paid for everything. . . . Because men will not do what we do. For nothing, for free. They just wouldn't.

Because these commons exist within the context of the high-stakes real estate market of a capitalist city, Patricia feels she must be alert to the possibility of future commodification of the commons and how that commodification may play out in uneven ways with regards to gender.

Patricia, as she notes, is not paid for her many hours of work. But several male co-op members across the LECs I examined *are* paid or otherwise compensated for the work they do in their co-ops. Mr. Green, who we will hear more from later in this chapter, is an elderly Caribbean immigrant who lives in the Ironwood; he is retired and rarely leaves the building. For some time, the co-op gave him full concession from his carrying charges in exchange for his being at home to let in contractors, for making minor repairs in the building, and generally for keeping an eye on the building. The co-op also gave him free parking, paid for his phone, gave him a paid vacation, and took him out for his birthday each year. (Ultimately, the board decided to cut back to giving him only a half concession on his monthly fees.) In some ways, the co-op's willingness to compensate this elderly man, in his eighties, to help care for the building is an indication of an economy of care that a co-op can create. They are making decisions based in part on what the co-op needs, and in part on the needs and abilities of members. But it is also telling that the co-op long gave this man a full concession on his carrying charges, yet it has never given the board president, who works long hours on the organizational and financial matters of the co-op but does not usually do the manual labor associated with the building, any compensation at all. Patricia tells me that, between the years 2005 and 2010, she racked up five thousand email exchanges related to co-op business. This kind of organizational work is almost never paid, probably because organizational work is harder to see and quantify— but perhaps also because organizational work tends to be performed by women, while manual labor may be more visually obvious and tends to be performed by men. At the Sycamore, to provide another example, a male member was paid to do basic maintenance work at the complex, while the organizational work of women went uncompensated. Only at the Aspen Co-op is a member—a woman who has lived in the complex since it was a rental—paid a full-time salary to do the management work of the co-op. Paying her is justified because the Aspen, nearly alone among LECs in the city, does not hire an external management company.

It is clear, both from my study and from previous research, that women tend to do the bulk of the (unpaid) work associated with founding and running limited-equity cooperatives. This finding squares with Mies and Bennholdt-Thomsen and Federici's assertion that the commons more broadly tends to be cared for by women. But Federici in particular is not bemoaning this fact; nor is she arguing that it is in women's *nature* to do the work of the commons. Rather, she wants women—and all people—to appreciate women's historic contribution to the care of the commons, which she hopes can lead to its further expansion. She writes:

> Arguing that women should take the lead in the collectivization of reproductive work and housing is not to naturalize housework as a female vocation. It is refusing to obliterate the collective experiences, the knowledge and the struggles that women have accumulated concerning reproductive work, whose history has been an essential part of our resistance to capitalism. Reconnecting with this history is a crucial step for women and men today both to undo the gendered architecture of our lives and to reconstruct our homes and lives as commons. (Federici 2012)

It is critical, Federici argues, to make use of women's vast experience in working the commons, moving forward. Federici's insistence on looking toward the future of the commons—to "reconstruct[ing] our homes and lives as commons"—is critical. She is not content to defend what commons exist but to move outward into a continued expansion of the commons. She is also clear that, moving forward, expanding the commons is an opportunity for both women and men to take apart the expectations of gender that have shaped their lives. Though the commons may historically have been cared for primarily by women, this need not be the case in the future. The task of working the commons, and expanding the commons, Federici suggests, can be an explicitly feminist project—for women and for men.

From Creation and Maintenance to Expansion

The work of the urban commons, I am convinced, is a dialectical affair. In chapter 3 and chapter 5, I outlined two different times in the life of the commons: the time of creation, an experience of high intensity forged in a moment of crisis; and the time of maintenance, a long-term experience that requires, though of lower intensity than the time of creation, constant attention on the part of members. If we are concerned about fundamental transformations in society—and not just in maintaining small-scale commons projects that exist on the margins (see for example A. K. Thompson 2015)—we must be concerned about how commons are constantly recreated and how they expand. One of Harvey's (2012) main concerns about the urban commons is whether it can function at larger scales. I share this concern, though I do not frame this problem as one of whether an urban commons can "jump scale" vertically; rather, I frame it as a question of how an urban commons might expand outward, horizontally, over time.

The question of the expansion of the urban commons is taken up by Han and Imamasa in their discussion of the *Bin-Zib* housing of Seoul, first mentioned in chapter 2. *Bin-Zib*, recall, means "empty house" or "guest's house;" the people who live there, no matter how long they stay, understand themselves fundamentally as temporary dwellers of an urban commons. Han and Imamasa write,

> [R]esidents of *Bin-Zib* are not only required to maintain and reproduce the resources for the group, but they are also compelled to expand the common resources for potential, future guests. (2015, 96)

What this has meant in practice is that, over the seven-year stretch examined by the authors, *Bin-Zib* dwellers opened a new house every time existing houses became too full of guests. New homes have been funded through a communal fund created by *Bin-Zib* members called the *Bin-Go*. *Bin-Zib* members also created a café, *Bin-Café*, in order to have a space to socialize and to create jobs for themselves. The housing commons, here, has been expanded over time and has also led to—and been fed by—the establishment of financial and workplace commons.

Conversations with co-op members reveal the relationship between the ongoing work of maintaining the commons and the prospect of expanding commoning outwards, beyond the brick walls of the co-op. Sheila is one of my respondents for whom the idea of the expansion of noncapitalist ways of being, moving outwards from the co-op, is critical. Sheila, introduced in chapter 4, lived in the Poplar back when it was a rental apartment building, and she helped organize her fellow tenants to found the Poplar Co-op in the late 1980s. She later went on to help found the Hickory Co-op in the early 2000s and continues to live there today. She is a strong believer in limited-equity co-ops and in the ways they can give people power over their lives. But ultimately, she views the co-op as a springboard for other work in the world, outside the home. As she describes:

> I would even like to see—and that's what I'm hoping eventually to do—is create other cooperatives out of limited-equity cooperatives. Cause to me then that would help further people's dreams,

or whatever it is they want to do. If you have cooperative buying clubs, so you don't have to pay as much. I've always had this interest in creating a laundry detergent buying club, for people who live in limited-equity cooperatives. I have this idea in plan to create a janitorial cooperative out of—from—people who live in limited-equity cooperatives. To help folks, one, feel they can begin to live the concept of working together, pooling resources together, to help better everybody. And of course I know we live in a society where we're indoctrinated on individuality and that kind of stuff. But just as we were—we are—indoctrinated—I mean we can work on educating people that that's how we can all survive, and not just survive but have a real quality of life.

Sheila has never been satisfied simply with the collective self-provisioning of housing, as difficult as that process is. Her dream is to use the co-op as a basis for other work that will give low-income people more power over their lives: to, as she says, "help further people's dreams." Sheila, in other words, wants to *expand* the commons constituted by limited-equity cooperatives. Without expansion, the commons stagnates, and may ultimately collapse.

To expand the commons is to build on what Eizenberg (2011) calls "actually existing commons" to create more spheres of common life—be it in the realms of work, play, learning, childrearing, or any number of other parts of life that have become commodified under capitalism. As theorists like Gibson-Graham imply, continued expansion of the commons can continually challenge, and even help upend, capitalist structures. But Gibson-Graham's work is relatively theoretical; it is more of an expression of a desire for the expansion of commons than an investigation of how it could actually happen. Clark hints at possibilities for expansion of the commons in her discussion of the development of nascent networks among LECs in New York City. These co-ops were beginning to turn outwards, claiming adjacent empty lots for community gardens and planning murals for empty public walls. But it is unclear to what degree these efforts at expanding into other spaces succeeded (Clark 1994). When it comes to the co-ops in my study, the work of expanding the commons is largely theoretical. Most of the time, it is all these co-ops can do to keep themselves going, given the fact that they exist in the context of the capitalist city.

Despite the challenges, members of a few of the co-ops in my study have attempted to expand their work beyond the immediate needs of their own housing. The Walnut Co-op is a case in point. Once the purchase and renovation of the Walnut was completed, Addisu arrived at the realization that the co-op needed what he called a "cause" in order to thrive. He hit on the idea of establishing a collective management company for fellow limited-equity co-ops. He explains his thinking:

> Then later [after the renovations were completed], everybody has an apartment, now everybody is satisfied. So we have the cooperative. Now comes—the cause is done! Now people start fighting [he laughs]. About everything and anything. For example, thinking [a co-op leader] wanted to have the power. This started creating some problems. . . . So I was thinking later, I said, no, this cooperative is not going to go anywhere unless we have some causes. We have money. So why not to create a management company collective? We started working with about ten cooperatives, to create this management company. Doing some questionnaires, and mobilizing people, and they came up with about ten people, ten cooperatives, under [an outside nonprofit group]. So we'll hire some people there, we'll create our maintenance people, we'll create even stores, small stores, I was thinking about that. I said, let's *create* something.

Addisu even went back to school, studying financial management, in order to pursue this idea of creating a kind of employment commons generated from the Walnut Co-op and other likeminded LECs. But he was never able to find a for-profit partner to provide capital for the project, and the idea ultimately never got off the ground. Addisu eventually moved out of the co-op. Years later, as detailed in the last chapter, the Walnut voted to convert to a market-rate condominium ownership structure—in part, perhaps, because the members no longer had a cause to keep them united. Reflecting on this, Addisu says:

> Long after the cooperative was established, there's not another cause to mobilize it. . . . And [the management collective idea is] forgotten, really. Simply a bunch of idealists, all of them.

He shakes his head as he says this, and there is a note of regret in his voice. He appears to include himself among those naive idealists. This is a story, in a sense, of possibilities lost.

But in other cases, the commons created by an LEC has successfully extended outside the cooperative and its membership, and into the surrounding community. In the early years of the Hickory Co-op, members were eager to use the co-op as a basis for larger community work. A prison abolition group met in the co-op's community room, as did a reading group critically analyzing the charter school movement. The co-op membership helped organize a citywide campaign to change how limited-equity co-ops and other forms of resale-restricted housing were assessed, so that their property taxes properly reflected their resale-restricted status. One member, Bassam, represented the co-op in supporting a nearby boys and girls club that was threatened with condominium redevelopment. Bassam is a Lebanese immigrant in his forties who has lived in the co-op since 2003. As he says of the activist groups that met in the co-op's community room, "[T]hey liked that people were meeting at this oasis from gentrification, this oasis of activists, and so on." At the Hickory, members have been able, to a certain extent, to maintain their co-op while also working to expand the commons in areas outside their own housing.

But Bassam also describes a tension within the co-op membership over putting energy inwards, into the co-op, and outwards, into the larger community. He personally values more external, political work, and he worries that the internal work of the co-op is sucking away time and energy for external work. As he says:

> [O]ur involvement in the boys and girls club and the tax issue and other issues—it wasn't a burden. It was kind of like shifting . . . a lot of us were trying to shift back away to the community, and say, this is not a burden. So there were people who wanted to say, we cannot shift outwards, until we fix our [internal co-op] problems. And I don't [agree]—I think dialectically. If we shifted away, then our problems, people would have been forced to streamline their problems, and it would have been in context of what was happening in the city. So that's the struggle there.

Here, Bassam captures the difficulty of expanding the commons. If the commons is marked by self-management, and self-management requires ongoing work, then to add to that work by attempting to take on other work might actually act against the good of the co-op itself. This was apparently the concern of some members of the Hickory Co-op, who wanted to prioritize internal co-op work over doing work in the community at large. Yet ultimately Bassam thinks, as he says, "dialectically," believing that it is only by engaging in work with the broader world that the co-op can be successful internally. Addisu thinks similarly: it is only by working to expand the commons that the co-op itself will survive.

Sheila, Addisu, and Bassam all believe that it is only through turning outward that the co-op can maintain its inner integrity. For these co-op members, efforts to maintain the commons must be twinned with efforts to expand it: one must engage in a dialectical approach that encompasses both. This, of course, is much easier said than done. But as theorists like Hardt and Negri argue, working in common can only be learned by doing the work itself. It may be that working dialectically is also something that must be learned by doing. I turn now to how co-op members are learning to work in common and may ultimately be learning collective self-governance.

Learning Self-Governance

Democracy, as Dewey, Hardt, and even Thomas Jefferson have noted, is learned by doing (Dewey 1916; Hardt 2007). For Hardt, what made Jefferson so radical was that he believed people could learn to self-govern through engaging in the act of self-governance (2007). Hardt takes Jefferson's ideas and applies them to the idea of the common. The common, he and Negri argue, is both the means and the end of democracy (2009). And it follows that it is through laboring together in creating and managing the commons that people learn how to "do" democracy.

By doing the work of the urban commons people may begin to learn to self-govern. I qualify this statement with a *may* because my research shows that the extent to which members participate in the commons is uneven, and not all members engage equally in the activities of self-governance. Still, my research indicates that the model of the urban commons provides a way to expand the ability of members to self-govern, even if this has not always happened fully in practice. Previous researchers have argued that living in LECs and community land trusts teaches people how to work together, and helps people become more politically engaged with their larger community. Through working together to keep their housing functioning, people learn how to engage in democratic processes and become empowered to take action in areas of their lives outside their homes (Clark 1994;

DeFilippis 2001; Saegert and Winkel 1996, 1998). The sense of empowerment that many co-op members develop through their work represents a
shift in consciousness. It is a double shift: both toward realizing they can
have control over their housing, and also toward the awareness that having
more control over housing requires taking responsibility for that housing.

But tenants who band together to purchase their buildings from their
landlords are not always prepared to take on the self-governance necessary
to operate their co-ops. As noted, the vast majority of D.C.'s LECs have not
been created as intentional communities, but are rather made up of tenants who just happened to be living in the same building when that building was put up for sale. At the time their buildings are put up for sale, the
tenants are desperate: they want to save their housing. As was discussed
in chapter 3, this is a time of crisis. And if they are low-income, their only
option for purchasing their building is to do so collectively, with assistance
from the city, creating a limited-equity cooperative. Tenants therefore do
not necessarily enter into the process of cooperative formation with what
Sheila, the housing organizer who lives in the Hickory Co-op, calls "a collective owner consciousness." She explains:

> [In] my experience when housing converts, and people choose,
> or go to a limited-equity co-op, it's not because of a commitment
> to the concept of cooperatives, [but] because that's the only option
> we have. And if that's the only option, without the education,
> then yeah, it gets to be a problem. And it might be sustainable
> for a while, but then if people don't have the cooperative educa-
> tion in concept, and have a consciousness, for me that's what
> education is about: to create a cooperative, a collective owner
> consciousness—then yeah, something else is gonna happen, and
> we're gonna lose that housing. . . . So that's a major challenge in
> the city that I see.

Although a few people in a given building might embrace a cooperative
vision of collective ownership and self-governance from the start, for most
new members, the cooperative way of life is very different from their previous housing situations, dominated by landlords. Whitney, of the Hickory
Co-op, explains that a number of her fellow co-op members entered into
the co-op without an understanding of how to collectively self-govern,
which can be time consuming and difficult. As she explains:

It's just us. There's no leader or organization that tells you what to do. It's just us. So if you have a problem and you want something done, we have to do it ourselves. And a lot of people came in here not used to that way of working. They came into this used to being in a position of submission. And they would complain that this is happening, and no one is doing anything! The only way this is going to happen if one of us does it. But I don't think some people could ever adjust to that.

Co-op members who, as Whitney puts it, are "used to being in a position of submission" with regards to their living spaces, may not immediately change how they think about their relationship to their housing. Magdalena, the president of the Juniper Co-op, echoes Whitney's point. She explains that co-op members are still getting used to understanding that they alone are the ones responsible for their housing. As she says:

Like I told them in the last meeting, we don't have a bigger guy to go to. Our bigger guy is us. If something goes wrong, *it is us*, you need to understand that. So basically that's the thing, a lot of people still think they're in a [rental] apartment. . . . We are the owners, we don't go to a bigger person. The only bigger person is the bank that's gonna take the property if we don't pay [she laughs]!

Sheila, Whitney, and Magdalena all worry about the lack of a commons consciousness in their co-ops because they are concerned about the ability of their co-ops to self-govern. Some members enter into a co-op with a commons consciousness. But others develop it through doing the work of the commons. Doris, of the Magnolia Co-op, is not a major leader at her co-op, but she developed an understanding and appreciation of self-governance through serving a term on the co-op board. She says:

I was the assistant secretary. And it was a good experience. I would recommend every shareholder to do it at least once. It's really a good experience, it's a learning experience. . . . [I]t wasn't a lot of work. It could have its rough moments, by me not understanding a lot of things. It made it sometimes a little challenging for me. But other than that, it was fine. But I would definitely recommend everybody, at least do one term. Just to see, and get the insight, and know what's going on. Do it at least one term, just to see. And it really was a learning experience.

Though she has five children and works full-time, Doris was able to carve out time to participate in the work of helping run her co-op. When she emphasizes how much she learned in the process, I would argue that what she was learning, writ large, was collective self-governance.

Learning to collectively self-govern means becoming comfortable with doing prefigurative work: that is, working today in ways that model a future, desired world (cf. Chatterton 2010). If, as Hardt, following Jefferson, argues, democracy is learned by doing, then the work of self-governance must be prefigurative (Hardt 2007). The supportive environment of the commons can enable members to become comfortable with prefigurative work. Whitney describes how she took on the role as the treasurer of the Hickory Co-op, and how she learned the position as she went:

> When I first joined, I wouldn't say I had any experience with finances at all. I was never trained in that kind of thing. And after I had a bunch of questions at a meeting, [another member] suggested, why don't *you* do it? It was very scary, because I don't know anything about economics or accounting. So I just sort of jumped in there. I was the treasurer for probably four years, and then I had to take a break and move home for a year when my dad passed away, and I had to take care of my mom and my dad's small business. Then I came back and was treasurer again, did it until I was completely burned out, and then I took a break, and now I'm doing it again!

Later, she follows up on this thought:

> [L]earning about the treasurer position, and feeling confident that I could do it, that's been good. When I had to go back [home] to help with my dad's business, I used those skills then. It activates a different part of my brain—it's not natural to me, but I can do it, if I concentrate. It was a matter of figuring that out, and now if I want to do it, I can.

Whitney goes on to say that the supportive environment of the co-op was part of what enabled her to volunteer for the treasurer position even though she didn't know anything about finances at the time. Taking on the position was a risk for her, personally—it was, as she says, "very scary"—and it was also a risk for the co-op as a whole. If Whitney had failed, the co-op might have failed. As it was, Whitney's financial skills have developed to the point where, as her fellow co-op member Bassam notes, "she saves our asses every time." Whitney is just one example of the many co-op members who have learned to engage in self-governance through diving into the work. And the supportive environment of the commons helps allow this to happen.

Whitney's story underscores the experiential nature of learning collective self-governance. In a similar vein, Magdalena emphasizes the need for co-op members to adapt to changes and rethink their rules for self-governance as they go. She explains:

> Anything that we see that we need to do to create a new policy, to bring something in, something simple, like a bike rack—cause all of a sudden people are riding bikes, and they just parking them under a thing, and the mud and dirt and—oh, no, no, no, we need some controls. So get a meeting, and make a policy about bringing in your bikes, where you gonna put them, and lock them up, and so on. Everything now, one person used to have a pet, now we have a few people with pets, we need a pet policy that makes sense, you can be fined if you don't follow. Parking, there's a parking policy. But it's all additional to what we started out with. So as you go— it's a work in progress, it just never stops.

Magdalena's description of the co-op as a "work in progress" that "never stops" speaks to the consistent work required of maintaining the commons, and also to the need for a commons to adapt to changes over time. It is clear that the Juniper Co-op membership is learning as they go: they are engaged in experiential learning. Writing from a psychology perspective, Borkman theorizes collective self-help/mutual aid groups as a commons, and she emphasizes the need for experiential learning to maintain these commons (1999). Successful LECs engage in experiential learning, adapting to new circumstances, figuring out which approaches work best, and constantly working to create a better system for living.

Finally, it is critical to note that collective self-governance appears to happen best when people create a humane setting in which to work, that attends to human needs, and that may even generate real pleasure and enjoyment. Margaret describes the early meetings of the board of directors at the Aspen Co-op:

> The board of directors would get together Sunday mornings once a month, and somebody would always make breakfast. With lots of coffee and cigarettes, and we always found solutions. In those first couple of years we would even pray, at times. We had Jewish and Christian and Muslim people, and we'd sit there and say this prayer. And we *needed* prayer!

The work of self-governance, for these co-op members, was fortified with breakfast, coffee, cigarettes, and prayer across disparate faiths. There was, Margaret emphasizes, a thrill to this organizing work, even as the challenges were so great.

Similarly, Bassam describes the pleasures of working in the community garden that sits in the collective backyard of the Hickory Co-op. The garden, he says, is a place where members can relax and talk informally about co-op matters. He says:

> [O]ne sign of the health of the co-op is participation in a community garden. . . . To me it means more than just the garden. It means, you wanna do something collaboratively. I truly believe, that the more people that work on the community garden, and feel invested, the easier that our meetings will get. It's just that kind of thing. The people who used to work in the garden, we used to talk about, informally, and not in a room, about a lot of things about the co-op. And you're kind of taking care of the co-op. There's something magical that happens in taking care of the co-op physically, that you're not caught up with procedure and bureaucracy. It's more of a holistic approach.

The Hickory's community garden is an example of learning collective self-governance through working together in a relaxed manner. The garden is also an example of how the expansion of the commons may support the maintenance of an existing commons. Research indicates that working together in community gardens can open up safe spaces for people to engage in informal dialogue that leads to greater understanding (Shinew, Glover, and Parry 2004). Community gardens, Shinew et al. argue (following Linn 1999), are a form of "neighborhood commons." In this case, the community garden is an expansion of the commons—an expansion that, as already noted, was also attempted by LECs in New York City (Clark 1994). It may be that people can learn to work in common by building other commons together. The work of the commons is iterative and doubles back on itself constantly. It is not a linear progression, but a constant doing and redoing, a constant applying of new knowledge. Learning collective self-governance, and in prefigurative ways, is part of the dialectical process of commons maintenance and expansion.

Commoning: A Pragmatic Approach

I'm sitting with Mr. and Mrs. Green, an elderly Caribbean couple, in the living room of their one-bedroom apartment in the Ironwood Cooperative. And I'm hoping that they will say something—anything—that indicates they have some sort of perspective on their housing that includes a critique of capitalism. Like most LEC members, the Greens bought into their co-op for a relatively low amount—$1,700—back in 1999, and they pay a relatively low monthly co-op fee—it started at $525 and has risen a bit over the years. The Greens' living room is carefully furnished, and the walls have been painted a brilliant teal. The Greens are working-class people. Mrs. Green immigrated to D.C. in 1971 from Trinidad, and she worked as a babysitter all her life before retiring; pictures of her white children clients adorn the table where we sit. Mr. Green is from St. Vincent and the Grenadines, but worked jobs in Guyana, for a mining company and a construction company, among others, until retiring and moving to D.C. in the mid-1990s. Describing their financial situation, Mr. Green says, "I'm just hanging on. We get our little pension." Before moving into the co-op, the couple had lived in a basement apartment in a nearby house. Mr. Green says of their former landlady, with outrage in his voice, "[S]he raised our rent when she wanted to! She used our apartment to get more money!" As for the co-op, he says, "Moving in here was uplifting. An improvement in our lifestyle, living standard." The Greens appreciate the affordability of their home, and they relish the control they have over their living space. They are proud that, when prospective new members come visit the co-op, it is the Greens' apartment that they are shown, as a model of how nice the co-op's modest units can be.

My interview with the Greens is pleasant, and informative. But try as I might, I can't get them to reveal anything about their politics of living in a limited-equity co-op. Either I'm asking the wrong questions, or they just don't see their living situation in a way that is explicitly critical of capitalism. But, I have found, the Greens are not unusual. In fact, they seem to be representative of a large swath of limited-equity co-op members, for whom the LEC model is an "uplifting" (as Mr. Green puts it) alternative to the shoddy rental housing they had lived in before, either on the private market, in the Greens' case, or in public housing, as is the case for a number of other co-op members. Participating in the commons, for the Greens and for many others, is simply what makes sense. They may not have an explicit critique of capitalism. But the capitalist housing market has not worked for them. The housing commons does.

Commoning, my research shows, is a rational choice often made by people with a relatively narrow range of choices: people without access to capital, for whom capitalism is not working. Ultimately, if we understand the commons for what I argue it really is—a pragmatic practice to be pursued, within and between and against capitalist practices—then we can be quite hopeful about building postcapitalist worlds. Because these worlds are already being built all around us right now, out of necessity.

Scholars and activists sometimes strain to see people who are just making everyday decisions as "political." They—we—may have a tendency at times to ascribe a certain politics to people we may call commoners, who really "just" need stuff—food, water, land, housing—in order to live. The flip side of this tendency to want to see politics everywhere is to write off people who are seen as "nonpolitical," even though they may be participating in the commons, if they are participating for what are seen as purely "economic" reasons. Some scholars explicitly exclude "nonpolitical" commoners from their analysis. Cattaneo and Martinez (2014), for example, theorize squatting as a form of commoning. They focus on Europe and divide squatters into two camps: those who squat with a political, anticapitalist perspective, and those who squat simply because they need housing. These nonpolitical squatters, they explain, are comprised of a range of people—immigrants, Roma, and people who have lost their housing for all sorts of reasons. "Behind this type of squatting," they write, "there is often no other motivation than to remedy a desperate situation, secretly and in silence. Such a reason for action has little to do with what is usually called 'political squatting.'" In contrast, they write, "The aim of political squatters is to prefigure ways of living beyond capitalist society, implying the need to loudly express this message" (Cattaneo and Martinez 2014, 3). Cattaneo and Martinez state clearly that they have no interest in squatters they think of as nonpolitical; the bulk of the volume they have edited, together with the Squatting Europe Kollective, focuses on political squatters. But the exclusion of nonpolitical squatters, or commoners, from the analysis is, I think, a grave mistake.

It is a mistake because it assumes a separation between "economic" decisions and "political" decisions. But economic decisions *are* political decisions. Individual choices about participating in the commons cannot be divorced from the larger political-economic context within which those choices are made. For most people in the world, economic choices are very limited—and they have been limited through acts of power that have kept a minority very wealthy. What I am interested in is commoning enacted by people out of necessity, not out of a preconceived politics. This is commoning entered into as a rational, pragmatic choice. But this doesn't mean it is not also political. When I discuss the history of the Aspen Cooperative with a longtime tenant lawyer who knows their story well, he disputes that the tenants chose the LEC option because of some idealistic vision. Though Sherry insists that their mission was to preserve affordable housing in Glover Park, the lawyer says they took the limited-equity route because it was the only way they could buy the buildings. But that is exactly the point. The commons are often generated in desperate times and are pragmatic responses to life under capitalism. They don't need to be idealistic choices in order to be more life-sustaining places for people.

Theorists of the commons often characterize "homo economicus"—"economic man"—as a bogeyman, or as a fiction (see for example De Angelis and Harvie 2014). People don't always, this argument goes, make decisions based purely on economic rationality. The commons, according to this argument, are an example of other kinds of "value practices" (as De Angelis and Harvie 2014 write) coming into play. But my research shows that LEC members *are* behaving in their own economic self-interest. It is just that commoning is an act of economic self-interest in which the interest of the "self" is bound up in the interest of the "community," or collection of selves, that makes up the commons. The most important aspect of the commons, as the co-op members I interviewed explained, was its affordability. Control, stability, and community are all very important elements as well, and are intertwined with the affordability of the commons—one aspect cannot be separated out from the rest. But without affordability—without this economic component that can be measured in dollars—the commons, at least within the capitalist context, loses any broad relevance. Commoners are rational economic actors. The commons is what makes the most economic sense for them as people trying to live decently in an expensive city. LEC members consistently compare their co-op experience to their previous experiences renting, either from private landlords or from the city, in public housing. "Traditional" homeownership, as noted earlier, has not been an option for them. Typically, they are not choosing the commons out of some sort of political commitment: it is a pragmatic choice.

The point is that, for people without access to capital, commoning is rational economic behavior. It is rational economic behavior even when "the economic" is understood in the most narrow sense, as something of immediate financial benefit. But it is rational economic behavior even more so when the field of "the economic" is widened, so that diverse practices that don't immediately involve the exchange of dollars can be understood as "economic." The supportive atmosphere Brian experienced when his long-time roommate died can be seen as an instance of diverse economic practices. This is not support that he pays a professional to provide, but rather support generated through years of close co-existence with his neighbors. The stability that is so important to Patricia—and that enables her to help raise her niece, despite her sister's illness—is closely connected to the fact that her co-op payments are low. Because of the co-op's affordability, her sister—who at times is so debilitated by her illness that she cannot engage in waged labor—can live there. Patricia can care for her, and for her niece, in a way that surely makes economic sense. Physical and social control of the space, too, are economic. Co-op members having the ability to replace their refrigerators so that their food does not spoil, as Gloria describes, is surely of economic benefit; and the ability to live in a quiet, peaceful environment, as Eduardo describes, may have longer-term economic benefits in terms of getting a good night's sleep and peace of mind.

In his discussion of the word "common," Raymond Williams (1983) notes the relationship between the word "common" and the word "ordinary." At some point the term "common" took on a derogatory connotation, though Williams tells us it is difficult to date this turn in meaning. I am struck by this equation of common and ordinary—a linguistic relationship that is therefore cultural as well. The commons is not necessarily a special thing, and commoning is not necessarily a special practice. Rather, it is totally everyday, and almost unremarkable. What this implies is that to live and work in noncapitalist ways does not necessarily require a huge sea change in how we see and experience the world. It is all quite ordinary—quite common. But, especially for people raised in an environment saturated with capitalist practices, commoning may not come naturally. It takes practice.

Practicing in the Present, Practicing for the Future

Urban commoning, I believe, is best understood as a practice. The *Oxford English Dictionary* defines "practice" as follows:

> The habitual doing or carrying on of something; usual, customary, or constant action; action as distinguished from profession, theory, knowledge, etc.; conduct. . . . The doing of something repeatedly or continuously by way of study; exercise in any art, handicraft, etc., for the purpose, or with the result, of attaining proficiency; hence the practical acquaintance with or experience in a subject or process, so gained. (1971, 2264)

The word "practice" is rich in meaning: it can be either a verb or a noun. Practice is ongoing and in the present: it connotes habitual, constant action. But it also contains a sense of preparing for the future: one practices in order to attain proficiency at some future time. "Practice" can also contain a hint of discipline, of an intention in one's actions. It makes sense to think of practicing the urban commons, because the commons must both be cared for in the present moment, at specific scales (like the scale of a single apartment building), but to practice this commoning also implies to practice for a new, future society, in which commoning works on expanded scales.

A critical piece of practicing the urban commons, therefore, is to maintain awareness of their temporality. Bruun (2015) and Han and Imamasa (2015) shed light on the time frame of the commons. For these researchers, who focus on housing, an urban commons might be exclusionary at one spatial and temporal scale (the apartment building, in the present), but inclusionary at another scale (the city, over time). Bruun emphasizes that commoners—in her case, members of housing co-ops in Copenhagen—are just "caretakers" of the commons. To participate in the commons is an exercise in impermanence. Members help create this thing—this resource—but it doesn't belong exactly to them. They are merely the caretakers for the present. As the *Bin-Zib* group in Seoul writes:

> This house of guests is an empty place. Since it is empty, anyone can come at any time. Regardless of how many people are here,

Bin-Zib should be vacated for others to come. Therefore, living in
Bin-Zib means to expand it. (quoted in Han and Imamasa 2015, 96)

The *Bin-Zib* philosophy may sound radical, but it is reflected in the attitudes of some D.C. limited-equity co-op members. Sandy, of the Mulberry
Co-op, vigorously explains what limited-equity ownership means for co-
op members:

> Now you can always leave this co-op, but you come in with the full
> knowledge and agreement that this is not for profit! And I can live
> comfortably and still do what I want with my property! I paint,
> I did everything I wanted to do! I cannot argue with that. As op-
> posed to, if I paint this stuff in an apartment, I have to fix this stuff
> back up when I have to leave . . . but this is mine! That's enough! I
> don't need no financial gain, and then the next person who comes
> in, they can have the same opportunity!

For Sandy, what's important is having control over her housing, and keeping it affordable so that the next person who comes in can have the same
opportunity she did, to own a nice one-bedroom-plus-den apartment in a
rapidly gentrifying part of the city. She is aware of the value of her housing
for future co-op members, even though they are, as yet, abstract strangers.

Sherry, who we met in the introduction, is another working-class
woman who raised several children in her apartment at the Aspen Co-op.
She was one of the original tenants, and she has worked as the co-op's on-
site manager for decades. When asked why her co-op has never converted
to condo, she says:

> It's been a lot of work over the years, and I don't think anybody
> wants it to kind of end up like—we want to stay special. That's
> how I see it. We want to be for people who would like to own,
> and maybe don't even think it's possible.

Sherry notes that she wants the co-op to "stay special"—that is, she does
not want all the work that has gone in to creating this unique living situation lost to rote commodification. And she wants the co-op to be available to future, as-yet-unknown "people who would like to own, and maybe
don't even think it's possible." As we saw in the last chapter, her daughter
Daisy similarly noted that she valued the idea of the co-op being affordable

for future members, too, who could have the same opportunity she had to live in an affordable, stable place. As another early D.C. tenant leader told the Washington *Afro-American* in 1986, of her tenant association's struggle to create a cooperative: "We intend to renovate the building to keep housing costs much lower so that the people of our neighborhood will not be displaced" (N.a. 1986). The housing this leader was working so hard to save was not just for herself and her fellow tenants—in fact, most of her fellow tenants had left the building out of frustration with poor living conditions in the building and on the drug-plagued block. She was working with the small band of tenants who remained to save the housing for themselves—and to create an opportunity for "the people of our neighborhood" more broadly. The women across Washington, D.C., who worked to turn their rental apartment buildings into limited-equity cooperatives in the late 1970s and early 1980s, too, as described in glowing terms in the *Washington Post* article cited in chapter 3, were working to create affordable communities that members controlled. They did this for themselves and their families and neighbors, and for others they did not yet know. They were practicing in the present, and for the future.

To practice the urban commons is to engage directly with the contradictions of life under capitalism. It is to recognize that the commons requires real work—work that, because it is the work of social reproduction, and often performed by women, often goes unrecognized and uncompensated. Practicing the urban commons means engaging in a dialectical movement: of maintaining the commons through expanding them, and expanding them through maintaining them. It requires learning as one goes, and learning to live together democratically. It is above all a pragmatic practice, entered into out of need—and a practice that must be sustained out of this collective need. It is about creating spaces not just for the people members know and love—though, as seen, this is certainly an important part of it—but for people they don't yet know, perfect strangers tossed their way by the currents of urban life. For those of us raised in a capitalist society, commoning may not come naturally. Urban commoning is something one learns through repeated practice. In the conclusion, I emphasize the importance of the urban commons, both in thought and in practice. And I suggest how we might learn to common, in the city, here and now.

Conclusion

Keep Practicing

In the summer of 1975, Dave Clarke, a member of the Washington, D.C., city council, rose to speak at a council hearing. The D.C. city council, as described in chapter 3, was in 1975 a brand-new entity; the residents of the nation's capital had not been allowed to elect their own local leaders for one hundred years. In 1973 they finally won the right to local self-representation, electing a slate of leaders in November 1974. As soon as they took office in January 1975, the newly elected city council immediately turned its attention to one of the most pressing issues of the day: gentrification and displacement of low- and moderate-income residents. Residents were worried that, just as this majority-black city was finally gaining voting rights, low- and moderate-income people—most of them African American—would be driven out by high housing costs. David A. Clarke had been elected to represent Ward One, the city's centrally located and most densely populated and diverse ward. In his statement before the council, Clarke addressed himself to his fellow councilmember Marion Barry, then the chairman of the committee on finance and revenue, which was considering legislation that would protect low- and moderate-income people from displacement. This was legislation Clarke supported ardently. He began with a rhetorical flourish:

> Mr. Chairman, it has been my good fortune during the past ten
> years to live in an area where all of America's dreams of the ability
> of its many different people to live together have come to frui-
> tion. This area lays mostly in the first or second concentric circle
> of residential areas [of Washington, D.C.]. But over the years, by
> the sweat and toil and concentrated efforts of its neighbors, it has
> been able to become a place where black people and white people
> and brown people and old people and young people and rich

people and poor people and male people and female people and
gay people and straight people and yes even tall people and short
people have been able to find unity in their diversity.

This has not been easy for there have always been those agents
of discord who have desired to have us destroy one another but we
now face an even more perilous enemy—those who would, without having been part of its creation and therefore unaware of its
depth, advertise this diversity and capitalize upon its appeal with
the end result of its destruction.

He continued:

If you come to our area Mr. Chairman as you have done on many
occasions, you will see that much of what our neighborhoods are
has been built by their own people. An example of this exists in
Community Park West. An isolated tract of vacant land, held for
appreciation and disposition purposes, the people have transformed
it into a recreational center of such quality and with a program such
as few other communities in our city enjoy. (Clarke 1975)

The park Clarke refers to, Community Park West, was located on a 4.2-
acre tract of land in the Adams Morgan neighborhood that for years had
been vacant. In 1964, a neighborhood youth group, the Ontario Lakers,
under the leadership of community activist Walter Pierce, had taken it
upon themselves to start clearing the privately-owned lot, in order to create a park for young people to play. Together with other neighbors, they
installed playground equipment, maintained the grounds, and organized
youth sports events in the reclaimed space, renting the land from its owner,
who was waiting for the land to appreciate, for a dollar a year. By the time
Clarke made his statement in 1975, the park had been a community-run
space for eleven years. But right around that time, the owner of the tract
had finally begun negotiating to sell the land to a real estate developer, who
planned to build 156 high-end townhouse condominiums on the space. At
the time Clarke rose to speak before the council, the future of the park was
unclear (Gately 1978a).

Community Park West was a kind of urban commons. A vacant lot held
for the purposes, as Clarke described, of "appreciation and disposition"—a
space, that is, the potential exchange value of which hinged on its proxim-

ity to the centrality of the city—was reclaimed by a diversity of neighbors to create something for everyday use, not for financial return: a much-needed park, with a much-needed youth program. The urban commons exists in close relationship with capitalism: the land on which this park was built, after all, was privately owned by a speculator. It exists in relationship with the state: neighbors petitioned the city for help in securing owner-ship over the space. And it was reclaimed and maintained by a diversity of people, many of whom were strangers when commoning began. The limited-equity co-ops I have detailed in this book are just one manifesta-tion of the urban commons; parks like Community Park West may be an-other, as may schools, workplaces, food co-ops, even energy grids (Becker, Beveridge, and Naumann 2015; Bockman 2016).

But Clarke's point in his 1975 statement was that the commons was in danger. He feared for the fate of this community that had collectively built itself through "the sweat and toil and concentrated efforts of its neighbors." Community Park West, for Clarke, was just one tangible example of these efforts. Clarke soon reiterated his main point, which is underlined in the original testimony:

> The more attractive diversity becomes in the hands of those who have not labored to maintain that diversity but only to project it as an abstract value; the greater the danger of the ultimate destruction of that diversity. (Clarke 1975)

The prized diversity of his area—the lived, often messy coming together of different people to create their own community—was being turned into an abstract selling point by others—"those who [had] not labored to maintain that diversity." The hard work of commoning, that is, was in danger of be-coming commodified. The antidisplacement legislation being considered by the Council committee, Clarke hoped, would be one way to help retain the community generated through the commons.[1]

I have several reasons for beginning my conclusion with Dave Clarke's testimony. One, I want to emphasize that the urban commons can take many forms: that while the focus in this book has been on limited-equity cooperatives, we can find myriad examples of strangers coming together to claim the resources necessary for life, in the very heart of the capitalist city. Two, this story reveals the interconnectedness of commons, and the important role the state may play in supporting commons. The vibrant neighborhood commons collectively built by residents could, Clarke hoped, be supported by a commons that would be generated through the legislation he was supporting. Finally, and perhaps more grimly, Clarke's testimony emphasizes that the commons, when enacted within the capitalist context, may always be under threat.

Commoning through Limited-Equity Co-ops and Beyond

One of the important laws that came out of the antidisplacement legislation of late 1970s Washington was the Tenant Opportunity to Purchase Act, which, together with city financing, created the opportunity for low-income tenants to collectively purchase their apartment buildings and turn them into limited-equity cooperatives. Washington's LECs provide a modest amount of housing: in 2010, in a city with nearly 300,000 housing units, there were about 3,100 units of LEC housing, meaning they made up just over 1 percent of the city's total housing stock (U.S. Census Bureau 2010). The commons constituted by D.C.'s LECs represents a very partial solution to the crisis of affordable housing, because, one, commoning requires significant time and energy, and two, though many of the city's LECs make use of federal subsidies, this housing is not necessarily made to serve the poorest of the poor. Even some of the most affordable co-ops in my sample, like the Magnolia, will not accept members who earn below a certain income. For both these reasons, public housing and publicly subsidized rental housing is still urgently needed.

But it wasn't just affordability that was important to co-op members: it was also stability, community, and control. It may be possible to create publicly subsidized rental housing that is more stable than the rental housing most poor people experience. Indeed, the very purpose of creating a robust national system of publicly subsidized rental housing would be to give low-income people the stability they so desperately need in order to get and retain jobs, provide their children with consistent schooling, and live with a greater sense of peace. Research on the issue suggests that with stability may come greater community connectedness as well (Desmond 2016). But renting housing from a landlord may not engender a sense of control over one's home. And this sense of power—of being able to partake in collective decision making about how to run their spaces—was of real import to many of the people with whom I spoke about their housing. LECs create affordable and stable housing for mostly low-income tenants who had never before had an opportunity to have control over their housing. They also provide evidence that low-income people can collectively self-manage their homes, even in the midst of high-pressure housing markets. This has been particularly important ideologically in Washington, D.C., because, since the mid-twentieth century, most low-income people in the city have been African American, and black self-determination has been of paramount importance in the city's identity even before it became the nation's first majority-black city in the late 1950s. With the coming of Home Rule in the 1970s, the city of Washington achieved a modicum of democracy, but as Linebaugh's (2008) work on the Magna Carta reminds us, political rights are next to meaningless without an economic foundation that the commons can provide. The material support an urban commons provides its members is crucial, and the ideological role it can play in demonstrating possibilities for living democratically in a way that challenges capitalist valuation of housing may be equally important.

Housing is a critical place to theorize a contemporary urban commons, because housing is necessary to survival in a way that other forms of life theorized as urban commons—gardens, public spaces, street life—may not be. Housing is not optional, not a side project. You can't just quit if it gets to be too much work. You are forced to keep at it, because you depend on it for your daily life. This is not to discount the importance of other kinds of urban commons, but to emphasize housing, because it is so basic to survival, may provide a particularly good prism through which to understand both the benefits and the challenges of the urban commons.

Recognizing the ongoing presence of LECs in Washington, D.C., can open up conversations about expanding the housing commons in the city more broadly. As city leaders around the world are discovering, commodified housing markets simply do not create housing for low- and increasingly even moderate-income people (King and Handelman 2016). City governments and housing organizers are increasingly interested in decommodifying land and housing through such mechanisms as the community land trust (Campbell 2016; Mattingly 2016; Simmons 2016). The community land trust, first discussed in chapter 3, takes the idea of the limited-equity cooperative—democratically-controlled space that has been removed from the market in order to keep it an affordable, stable place for generations to come—and scales it up. Under the community land trust (CLT) model, the value of the housing is separated from the value of the land on which that housing sits. As noted earlier, in urban areas, it is the cost of land that is prohibitive for most people, not the cost of the housing itself. Though land trusts can be structured in many ways, generally the CLT owns the land beneath the housing, and the members own the housing in which they live. The CLT structure ensures that the housing is kept affordable and stable over the long term. Community land trusts are run jointly by representatives of the people who live in land trust housing and by other community members with an interest in preserving nonspeculative, community-controlled housing. A land trust can potentially encompass whole sections of a neighborhood or city (J. E. Davis 2010b). In turning to the community land trust model, city officials and activists are working to help create new commons—spaces that have been removed from the market, and are collectively controlled by the people who live in them, along with other community members dedicated to the idea of affordable housing and self-regulation over time. Community land trusts represent an instantiation of the urban commons that can provide affordability, stability, community, and control on a larger scale than the individual limited-equity co-op. Witnessing the successes, failures, and challenges of LECs may help city officials and organizers think through the best ways to organize community land trusts—a commons at a larger scale.

Recognizing the ongoing work of LECs can also help open up conversations about commoning more broadly, beyond housing. If people who have suffered under capitalist housing can create their own forms of housing, can they not also create their own forms of work, childcare, food?

The Creative Possibilities of Contradiction

The limited-equity co-ops of D.C., I have noted, are an imperfect commons. But there is no such thing as a perfectly calibrated commons. Commons are always in flux, and members are always experimenting, in ways big and small. Gibson-Graham warns us that experimental efforts like this risk being pooh-poohed. "[E]xperimental forays into building new economies," she writes, "are likely to be dismissed as capitalism in another guise or as always already coopted; they are often judged as inadequate before they are explored in all their complexity and incoherence" (Gibson-Graham 2008, 618). The attitude that experimental efforts like LECs specifically, or commons broadly, are either (a) always already coopted and/or (b) laughably pointless and puny endeavors in the face of the monster of capitalism is an attitude that infects many theorists of capitalism and social change. Capitalism must be destroyed, they say, before freedom and dignity of human life can begin. But this is a dim view. It doesn't put much stock in the ability of people to work to create structures today that will both make their everyday lives better, and potentially help lead to better worlds in the future. There is possibility in working collectively today, in spite of the enormous challenges. Gibson-Graham goes on to ask, "What if we were to accept that the goal of theory is not to extend knowledge by confirming what we already know, that the world is a place of domination and oppression? What if we asked theory instead to help us see openings, to provide a space of freedom and possibility?" (619). A theory of the urban commons, I hope, can help us see openings, and can help provide a space of freedom and possibility.

In this book, I am interested in theory and in practice. I have argued that the urban commons be taken seriously as a theoretical framework, because I think changing how we think about the world can change how we act in it. I am interested in seeing the openings that could be generated through thinking about urban life—life lived at the tense intersection of capital accumulation and state regulation, forged with a diverse, and densely packed, array of strangers—in terms of the urban commons—a practice of working together to collectively regulate the resources necessary for life. If we can think in terms of the urban commons, how might that enable us to see more of the space for which we struggle as a potential commons—a potential space of freedom and possibility?

My research has been, in part, an opportunity to explore the contradictions of the urban commons. In a recent book analyzing the contradictions of capitalism, Harvey writes:

> Contradictions are by no means all bad and I certainly don't mean to imply any automatic negative connotation. They can be a fecund source of both personal and social change from which people emerge far better off than before. We do not always succumb to and get lost in them. We can use them creatively. (2014, 3)

The contradictions of the urban commons, as outlined in chapter 2 and discussed in succeeding chapters, may in fact be a rich source of social change, if used creatively. Let us think about how that could happen.

The first contradiction is in the seemingly exclusionary nature of the urban commons. There is a tension in the commons literature between conceiving of the commons as, on the one hand, open to all, and on the other hand, open only to members. Cities, I believe, provide a particularly good context in which to examine this tension. Scholars who have closely examined the inner workings of particular commoning practices have tended to do so in relatively homogeneous environments, where population densities are relatively low and the people involved have lived and worked together for generations: in those contexts, exclusion may be a less obvious issue. But in the big, dense, diverse city, questions of exclusion come to the fore. My research shows that people of diverse backgrounds can come together to engage in commoning, which challenges the institutionalists' claim that commoning works best in homogeneous communities. But the question of exclusion remains. In the case of D.C.'s limited-equity cooperatives, or in a housing commons generally, there is only physical space enough for limited numbers of people. Some will necessarily be excluded. This isn't even taking into account those who may be excluded because they cannot afford the monthly carrying charges, no matter how low those fees may be, or those who may be excluded because their behavior causes fellow members to be concerned for their safety, or others excluded for other reasons. The question of inclusion and exclusion is a serious one, one that all commoners must wrestle with.

But the idea of exclusion breaks down in some ways when one understands commoning as taking place at an expanded temporal scale. The whole purpose of LECs, and of CLTs, too, is that they are structured in such a way that they provide access to multiple generations of people over time. As has been seen in the housing commons of Copenhagen and Seoul, the multiple-generation focus has been critical to thinking about how a housing commons can expand in space and time, continuing to provide access to future, as-yet-unknown members. In a material sense, yes, this housing may never be open to all. But commoning requires a long-term perspective, and a long-term perspective might shift how we think about "exclusion." It behooves us, too, to rethink the concept of "exclusion" from a feminist perspective of building networks of care. As seen throughout this book, some people are granted access to LECs because they are friends or relatives of co-op members and can be relied on to care for their fellow members, as well as the co-op as a whole. Or they are seen as needing this form of housing in order to raise their children more comfortably, or, in the case of at least one co-op, to support their social justice work in the world beyond the co-op walls. The practice of the urban commons must be to keep this long-term perspective, which includes the long-term project of building networks of care, always in mind, and to consistently push for more openings, more access, for more would-be commoners, however difficult and fumbling that process may sometimes be. Wrestling with the contradiction of exclusion in the urban commons can force us to consider how a long-term approach to individual commoning projects, like housing co-ops, and larger-scale commoning, like community land trusts, along with a long-term approach to organizing for support from the state, can help to expand commoning over time.

The second contradiction is the seeming impossibility of commoning in the city at all. If the city was created historically as a way to concentrate surplus wealth and the labor of people who had been kicked off their common lands through acts of enclosure, then how is it possible to speak of commoning in cities? The answer might be that the city throws commoners together in such a way that they are given the opportunity to create new forms of commons—much as the factory threw together workers in a new way, a way that opened up possibilities for new forms of worker organizing and control. There is much exciting possibility here. But as noted in these chapters, commoning in the midst of the capitalist city is a particular experience that is rife with particular challenges, and the challenges of working within and against capitalist markets must be reckoned with.

Commoning in the high-pressure environment of the city makes clear that the commons is above all a pragmatic practice. It may be relatively easy to common in the hinterland, where land is of less value and few others are around to compete for resources or contest your way of doing things. Utopian experiments have often been launched in out-of-the-way spaces for this very reason. But the urban commons is not utopian. It is not possible to be utopian smack-dab in the middle of the capitalist city, at least not for long, and that, as I see it, is a good thing. People common in cities because they have few other choices. If they had the financial resources to enable them to opt out of living in their limited-equity co-ops and buy homes on the open market, no doubt many co-op members would make that choice—indeed several of the people I interviewed did exactly that, once they had been able to save enough money to do so. Most commoners live in LECs because their choices are constricted, because of the way markets limit housing choice for low- and moderate-income people. As I emphasized in chapter 6, co-op members are not choosing to participate in the commons out of a wide array of options, but because their options are limited. It is critical to recognize commoning, especially commoning in the urban context, as a pragmatic, everyday practice for people just trying to subsist. As Federici notes, women in particular, as historic caretakers of the commons, have a wealth of experience to draw on in building commons in the here and now. This does not mean it is not important to do work to develop political consciousness among commoners, something Sheila emphasized when we spoke. But I think it is critical to do this political work grounded in the acknowledgement that commoning is a pragmatic, everyday activity of subsistence. The contradiction of trying to common in the capitalist city, I believe, points to the need to develop a pragmatic, nonromantic understanding of commoning.

The third contradiction is in the relationship between the commons and the state. Are the commons and the "public" at odds? If we push for expansion of the commons, do we neglect to push for the protection and expansion of public goods like public housing—not to mention public schools, public universities, public libraries, public utilities, public wilderness, public retirement? As noted, many alterglobalizationist theorists of the commons make substantial critiques of the state, preferring the autonomous and collectively-managed approach that they see in the commons to the top-down, often oppressive approach of the state. But in an era of increasing attacks on the state from the right, the demand from some on the left to replace the state with small autonomous community-based solutions sounds absurd, if not outright dangerous.

What my research reveals, though, is that we don't have to choose between the commons and the state: the two can work together. In Washington, D.C., as we've seen, the commons constituted by limited-equity co-ops has been enabled by the state, both through tenant rights law and through financial support. The state has enabled this commons because it has come under continuous pressure from tenants, co-op members, and activists to do so. Without this organizing work on the part of city residents, elected officials may not have passed the laws and regulations necessary for supporting limited-equity co-ops in the city. As Kratzwald (2015) notes, the idea and practice of the commons can be used to push the idea of the public in a more democratic direction. The state can play a critical role in supporting the creation, maintenance, and expansion of the commons; and the practice of the urban commons must involve continued pressure on the state to gain support for myriad forms of commoning in the city. The seeming contradiction between "the state" and "the commons" may be less relevant than it seems; in fact, the state can become an ally in commoning efforts. But only if we make it so.

Finally, as noted in chapter 2, though the city has been theorized as a site of state regulation, it has also been understood as a place of freedom, both actual and potential. The practice of the urban commons must be a practice of freedom: freedom in terms of thinking and organizing creatively, in terms of openness to broad diversities of people and perspectives, and in terms of recognizing the ways in which a commons can support emancipation on many scales.

Researching the Urban Commons: Moving Forward

My work in this book has been to bring the methods of the institutionalist scholars of the commons together with the political perspective of the alterglobalizationists. I have done this through conducting research at the granular scale of the case study, while being ever mindful of the historic and contemporary context of the capitalist city. The diverse economies approach has helped me do this: this is an approach that rejects a "capitalo-centric" way of seeing the world, forces a rethinking of what constitutes "the economy," sheds light on diverse economic practices of all kinds, and at its root is concerned with the relationship between theory and practice. A diverse economic perspective is necessarily feminist, as Derickson (2015) emphasizes, paying attention to the details of daily life while also being mindful of the connections to larger structures. Scholars of the commons need not choose between the micro and macro lens: using a feminist approach, we can bring both together. Through bringing together the institutionalist and alterglobalizationist approaches, I have been able to focus both on the time of commons creation or reclamation—which the institutionalists have tended to neglect—and the ongoing time of commons maintenance—which has often been ignored by the alterglobalizationists. These are two very different times in the life of the commons. Being able to examine both simultaneously—and marrying the two approaches to both times in the life of the commons—is critical for understanding how commons function.

My hope is that, moving forward, scholars continue to work to integrate these two approaches to studying the commons: examining both the moment of commons creation and the long-term process of commons maintenance, and theorizing commoning both through close and clear-eyed attention to the details of everyday life, and through a wide-angle perspective on larger historical and contemporary forces. Thinking, reading, writing, and talking about the commons can be part of enacting it.

It is critical to be thinking now about how to enact the urban commons. People are increasingly living lives shaped by cities: the urban is becoming the normal state of human existence. And because cities are the locus of capitalist activity, it is necessary to enact commons in that context, so that people can begin to resist or even partially escape capitalism, gain some control over their collective lives, and forge relatively stable ground from which to work to further dismantle capitalist structures of life, at the scale of the city and beyond. We need to be commoning in cities. Humanity is on the brink of a new era: an era of urbanization. If the urban commons does not yet fully exist, we must call it into existence.

Learning to Common

But calling the commons into existence, of course, can be hard, as a number of the co-op members with whom I spoke emphasized. Addisu, of the Walnut Co-op, worried that people who grew up in a capitalist country—the United States—would simply not be able to live and work together the way people could who grew up in other contexts, closely sharing space and resources. Whitney despaired that some of her fellow co-op members at the Hickory—people who were used to having landlords—could ever get used to the idea of really taking on the responsibility of collective ownership. It bothered Doris that not everyone in the Magnolia Co-op understood that more members needed to participate in order to keep what they had. Commons are built through collective work, but commoning can be an uneven process. The stress of barely getting by in an expensive city can make it hard to take the time to common.

At the same time, it is through doing—being part of the commons—that one learns "how" to common. Both the institutionalists and the alter-globalizationists see commoning as an ongoing process of learning. For Linebaugh, "Communal values must be taught, and renewed, continuously" (2014, 14). Ostrom (2005) saw participating in the commons as a process of trial-and-error learning.

Ultimately, commoning is a locally specific affair, and learning to common will reflect local circumstances and relationships. The commons, both the institutionalists and the alterglobalizationists tell us, are represented by an incredible diversity of contexts and practices. The institutionalists have worked to come up with a framework for understanding common-ing practices, and Ostrom's principles of collective governance seem to describe well a wide variety of functioning commons. Still, the enactment of those principles must be grounded in local knowledge. This means that commons can be hard to replicate. They arise in myriad ways, through so-cial connections and individual ties among particular humans. They are, to a large degree, antibureaucratic. Though they have rules, they rely more on individual real people and particular relationships than on set policy. The commons rely on people learning by doing, rather than following a set recipe. Scott theorizes this kind of practical knowledge using the Greek term *metis*. Metis, Scott writes, "represents a wide array of practical skills and acquired intelligence in responding to constantly changing natural and human environment" (1998, 313). Metis is knowledge learned over time, through experimentation. And metis cannot necessarily be widely shared, or scaled up. In another case of the urban commons—a cooperative apart-ment building in Berlin—co-op dwellers told me that they had to learn together, from the ground-up, in order to build a strong community. To just follow the blueprint of another house project would be to skip important steps in community formation, they believed. "You have to reinvent the wheel every time," one member told me (Huron 2002, 38). Reinventing the wheel took time, and from the outside seemed grossly inefficient, but co-op members thought the process of collectively building knowledge was criti-cal for the success of their commons over the long term.

Learning to common is in a sense learning to argue, in a way that is ul-timately productive. Wall believes that, though Elinor Ostrom was known for her work on the commons, her work should also be associated with "contestation." "She believed," Wall writes, "that strong argument was a technique necessary to the production of knowledge" (2014b, 21). A key element of commoning is getting into arguments—respectfully, and with an open mind, a mind willing to be changed. As Mary noted of her experi-ence at the Sycamore, "I was very proud of the fact that we as tenants took it on, and it was a lot of hard work, it was a lot of arguing, but we took it on, and we made a success out of it." These are arguments ultimately based in mutuality; at the Sycamore, remember, those same tenants lent each other money in order to help each other buy into the co-op ownership structure. In the Berlin housing cooperative, members appreciated that their necessarily close relationships with each other forced them to learn to communicate openly. When asked why he thought living in the cooperative was good for his young daughter, one member replied, half-jokingly, "So she can learn to *fight!*" (Huron 2002, 44). Growing up in the urban commons means learning to argue and figuring out how to get along with people unlike yourself. Learning to argue, of course, can also be understood as learning to do democracy.

The city has long been theorized as a place to engage in democracy. Technology has enabled democracy to happen in all sorts of ways that are not tied to particular places, but the city as a place still holds something of importance. In fact the surge of interest in "the city" as a place to live, work, and play may be related to people's need for human community, live and in person, a sort of reaction to the kind of atomized life that technology makes possible. Linebaugh, for one, insists on the importance of physical space to commoning:

> People are creating spaces in the urban environment where it becomes possible to engage in the conversation and debate that is essential to commoning. . . . [T]he first step in commoning is to find a locale, a place, and if one is not easily to hand, to create one. The emerging geography of the future requires us actively to common spaces in our factories and offices . . . how about the school?" (2014, 17)

Indeed, how about the school? I teach at a public urban university with a land-grant mission to serve the community beyond the campus. So I am particularly interested in the role the university can play in widening the field of the commons in the city and beyond. Because the university is designed as an environment for teaching and learning, it might be a place where we can all—teachers, students, and members of the public alike— teach and learn and, most importantly, practice commoning. Part of learning how to common is learning about the commons, learning about the relationships between commons and capital, and commons and the state. One of the goals of this book is to serve as a text that can help teach about the commons, as in the context of a broader agenda to teach and learn commoning.

The university, of course, is not without its own problems and contradictions. Harney and Moten (2013) reject the proscriptive nature of the university, which they see as following a certain line: you major in something, you learn the stuff you have to learn to achieve that particular major, you graduate, you get a job, you participate in the capitalist economy. Harney and Moten theorize the "undercommons" in opposition to what they see as the proscriptive university. The undercommons, they argue, is a place for real study. It is made up of people working together to learn, regardless of classes or grades or outcomes in terms of graduation rates or jobs. The undercommons, for Harney and Moten, is rehearsal, play, experiment. I think the idea of the undercommons is an exciting way to think about collective learning. But rather than encourage an underground form of subversive undercommoning, I am interested in an experience that is explicitly about commoning. Bring it up from the underground, normalize it.

If a university taught a set of skills, perhaps commoning could be one of them. To be clear, I am thinking explicitly here about the mostly urban, mostly public commuter schools throughout the United States that serve working people who are often the first in their families to attend college—though there is no reason commoning could not be studied in elite institutions as well. Learning commoning might involve learning about the history of commoning in relation to capitalism, and also the ways commoning happens all around us in the present. It would mean studying enclosure, and ways people have both succumbed to and resisted enclosure, and the complicated ways enclosure, reclamation of the commons, and reenclosure play out around the world. Learning commoning might also mean learning how to work collectively, through such seemingly mundane practices as learning how to run meetings well, and learning how to argue with a thoughtful mind and open heart—backed up with solid evidence. It could also mean learning skills for caring for ourselves and others, as well as the skills to start commoning enterprises, like community food provision and worker cooperatives. The commons is a pragmatic practice, and teaching and learning the skills of commoning can be a decidedly pragmatic affair. To teach and learn commoning would require bringing together the critical thinking skills generally attributed to a liberal arts education with the practical skills developed in programs often categorized as "workforce training." Since the university is, or should be, a place for experimentation and practice, there should be ample opportunity to engage in commoning experiments, to test out ideas, to reflect on failures, and to plan for future ways of living, in the city and beyond.

Learning to practice the urban commons—whether we study in the context of the university, or elsewhere—might also help us learn to practice commoning at larger scales, even up to the scale of the globe. This may seem paradoxical: "the urban" conjures up a specific place, a city, a neighborhood, one block. "The global" is more abstract: it is hard to fit the whole world in your head at once. Yet the forces that shape the city are, increasingly, global forces. And the challenges of commoning in the city—of working with strangers, of operating in contested environments, rife with inequality— are the same challenges that we face at the scale of the globe. Thus to tackle the problems of the global commons—the commons of the atmo- sphere, the seas, outer space—we might first begin by training ourselves in the urban commons: the tangible, the here and now. To practice the urban commons is to practice—as in, prepare for—participating in the world at a larger scale. And theorizing the urban commons can help us understand the commons more broadly. Brenner emphasizes the importance of theorizing the urban for developing a new politics of the global commons:

> Current debates on the right to the city have productively drawn
> attention to the politics of space and the struggle for the local
> commons within the world's giant cities, the densely agglomerated
> zones associated with the process of concentrated urbanization.
> However . . . such struggles must be linked to a broader politics
> of the global commons that is also being fought out elsewhere,
> by peasants, small landholders, farm workers, indigenous groups
> and their advocates, across the variegated landscapes of extended
> urbanization. (2014, 199)

The struggle for the urban commons, Brenner suggests, must be connected to the fight for the global commons. It is not exactly clear how we make this leap in scale, but I know we will have to try. We can connect struggles over particular places and particular resources—for instance, housing in Washington, D.C.—to struggles over other places and other resources. Learning to common would mean developing a global commoner con- sciousness, grounded in a particular place but aware of, and connected to, people working around the world to build spaces for life.

The purpose of this book has been to understand how the urban com- mons functions, and to think through what it means to practice the urban commons. I have strived to understand how the urban commons works through examining the experiences of commoners themselves. I have had my own interpretation of their analyses, and I don't know that the dozens of people whose words appear in this book would all agree with my interpretation. But this book is a beginning. I want people to use this book to think about the commoning going on all around them, and that they themselves participate in. I want this book to prompt people to ask questions about how commoning takes place, and how it succeeds and fails. I want it to spark argument, debate, and further investigation and experimentation into urban commoning practices.

My hope is that people—scholars, activists, commoners—can work in common to further develop a theory and practice of the urban commons, and ultimately of the global commons, too. I want us all to think more closely about the urban commons and deal realistically with the work they require. This requires listening to commoners—to the people actively engaged in claiming and maintaining the spaces they need for survival. It means grounding theory in everyday life experiences. Commoning can be joyful, but it is also work: it is figuring out how to deal with neighbors who may be coming from very different places; and it is, at least for now, dealing with the collective stress of maintaining a noncommodified space in the midst of punitive real estate markets. But ultimately, commoning is about building and continuously shoring up a steady and secure place from which to further challenge capitalist claims to life, on many fronts. To keep practicing the urban commons, and to keep learning how it works, is important for building a world in which people gain collective control over their lives so that they can, as Sheila envisions, further their dreams.

Acknowledgments

First, heartfelt thanks to the limited-equity co-op members, and everyone else, who took the time to talk to me for this research. This book exists because of your work in the world.

This book came out of research I began while studying at the City University of New York Graduate Center. I am deeply indebted to that genius, joyful, generous, noisy, occasionally quarrelsome mishmash of students I fell in with at the Graduate Center. Special thanks go to Jen Jack Gieseking, who corralled us all in the first place and forced us to start an official student group, which we named the Space-Time Research Collective, or STReaC, and to my fellow geographers. You know who you are, and I love you. For particular help thinking through the ideas in this book, and for so much more, special thanks to Christian Anderson and Jesse Goldstein.

Many people have helped inform my thinking in this book. I'm deeply grateful to my dissertation advisor, Marianna Pavlovskaya, for your sharp insight, rapid responses, and consistently buoyant attitude. And I'm thankful to the three other members of my dissertation committee: Vinay Gidwani (for your generosity of spirit and critical engagement with the urban commons), Susan Saegert (for your expertise in limited-equity cooperatives and your keen interest in my research), and David Harvey (for encouraging me to think big). I'm also grateful to Patrick Bresnihan and Mick Byrne for inviting me to participate in their symposium on the urban commons in Dublin in May 2013, and to Peter Linebaugh, whose keynote address that day inspired much thinking. Here in D.C., thanks to Katie Wells—as a team we brought together scholars of D.C. history and politics for several years, to read and learn from each other's work. Thanks also to David Kaib for spearheading the sprawling D.C. Jacobin reading group, which has spawned many discussions of writings that have informed my thinking here. And thanks to Ryan Shepherd for kick-starting our D.C. history reading group, which has helped me continue to think critically about Washington, D.C. Special thanks to Derek Gray, archivist at the

Washingtoniana Division of the Martin Luther King, Jr. Memorial Library, for his assistance on this project.

At the College of Arts and Sciences at the University of the District of Columbia, special thanks are due my chair, Shiela Harmon Martin, and my dean, April Massey, for supporting my work on this book. I'm grateful, too, for a university grant that supported the writing of this book for two summers running. I have too many wise, compassionate, committed colleagues to name everyone, but particular thanks to Mohamed El-Khawas and Wynn Yarbrough for consistently pestering me about whether I was working on the book, and a very special thanks to my good buddies Michelle Chatman, Jerome Hunt, and (for a sweet minute there!) Orisanmi Burton. Working with you has been a joy.

Many thanks to Jason Weidemann, my editor at the University of Minnesota Press, for shepherding this book to publication and being kind, generous, and thoughtful throughout the process. Special thanks to the editorial collective of the Diverse Economies and Livable Worlds series: Maliha Safri, Kevin St. Martin, Katherine Gibson, and Stephen Healy. Your guidance from the very beginning was invaluable. Particular thanks are due Louise Crabtree, who read the manuscript carefully and offered critical insight, and to several other anonymous reviewers who provided valuable comments on the book manuscript and two other related papers. Thanks to Erin Warholm-Wohlenhaus at the University of Minnesota Press for help with all the details.

To my parents, Anne Yarbrough and Doug Huron: thank you for teaching me how to think, write, and be in the world. It's amazing, isn't it?

And to Mike Andre, for keeping me honest, and for our love. I'm so grateful we are here with each other on this earth, together in space and in time.

Finally, thanks to you, the reader. I wrote this book to raise questions, inspire thinking, and promote discussion. I don't expect everyone who thinks about commons, or housing cooperatives, or capitalism, to agree with how I've framed this argument and how I've drawn my conclusions. Practicing the commons, as I note somewhere in this book, is in significant part about arguing, and that means being willing to learn from each other, and maintaining a truly open and curious stance. A book is part of a conversation, so let's talk. I mean it.

We're all in this together.

Have fun.

Notes

Introduction

1. "Alterglobalization" refers to a stance that is critical of capitalist modes of globalization, without the isolationism and nationalism that may be implied by the term "antiglobalization." The 2004 Alter-Globalization Conference, which was held in San Miguel de Allende, Mexico, and brought together scholars and activists from around the world to discuss building alternatives to capitalist forms of globalization, provides an example of how this concept has been deployed (see Caffentzis 2004).

2. This was a conservative estimate. I spent quite some time working with lawyers, developers, and tenant organizers around Washington, D.C., to put together a comprehensive list of all the city's limited-equity co-ops. (The city government had not kept careful records of LECs, and if a co-op is not in regular contact with a housing professional, it might fall off the radar of the affordable housing advocacy community.) The list originally included a number of unconfirmed LECs; in the final version of the list, I only included addresses that could be reliably confirmed as ongoing LECs. Therefore, it is possible that some of the city's LECs were left off the list, and that the number of co-op units may be higher than the figure cited here.

3. Together with library science graduate student Lauren Kenne, I created the W.I.S.H. Archives in 2009–10 under the auspices of the community organizing group Empower D.C., which had held the W.I.S.H. papers since W.I.S.H. dissolved in 2003. The W.I.S.H. Archives Project was funded by a major grant from the Humanities Council of Washington, D.C.

2. The Urban Commons

1. The names of two additional women do not appear in the table of contents but are listed in an endnote as participants in a "collaborative contribution," led by Neil Brenner.

3. Forged in Crisis

1. See, for instance, the photographs of co-op grand openings found in the WISH Papers, held in the Community Archives of the Washingtoniana Division, in the Martin Luther King Jr., Memorial Library in Washington, D.C.

2. Skill Exchange Group Inventory, Nehemiah Cooperative Estate, n.d. [WISH Papers, Properties, Nehemiah Cooperative (Board of Directors, 1995–1997), Washingtoniana Division, Martin Luther King Jr. Memorial Library].

4. A Decent Grounds for Life

1. https://www.huduser.gov/. Fair market rents, or FMRs, are calculated by the U.S. Department of Housing and Urban Development (HUD). For D.C. and other high-expense places, the FMR represents the fiftieth percentile rent for typical units occupied by recent movers. In other words, to use HUD's language, the FMR is "the dollar amount below which [50%] of the standard-quality rental housing units are rented" (U.S. Department of Housing and Urban Development 2007).

2. That research was based on a sample of thirty co-ops citywide.

3. Silvia Federici, presentation at the "Beyond Good and Evil Commons" seminar, 16 Beaver, New York City, August 2011.

5. Survival and Collapse

1. Photographs can be found in the WISH Papers, held in the Community Archives of the Washingtoniana Division, in the Martin Luther King Jr. Memorial Library in Washington, D.C.

2. Letter from Mable Braxton, president, 1327 Kenyon St. NW Tenants Association and Erik Swartzendruber, organizer, WISH, to Theresa Lewis, program manager, DCRA, January 22, 1992. [WISH Papers, Properties, 1327 Kenyon St. NW Cooperative (1992–2003), Washingtoniana Division, Martin Luther King Jr. Memorial Library].

3. Andy Waxman, "1994, Kenyon Street Tenants Suffer in Bldg.; 1996, They Own It," *W.I.S.H. Chronicle* (Winter 1997): 2 [WISH Papers, WISH Publications and Events, WISH Chronicle Newsletter (1994–2000), Washingtoniana Division, Martin Luther King Jr. Memorial Library].

4. Andy Waxman, "Victory at Last!!! The Residents of 1424 Won a Battle that began in 1991," *W.I.S.H. Chronicle* (Winter 1994): 8–9 [WISH Papers, WISH Publications and Events, WISH Chronicle Newsletter (1994–2000), Washingtoniana Division, Martin Luther King Jr. Memorial Library].

5. Letter from April Land, The Harrison Institute for Public Law, to Castina Kennedy, The Water and Sewer Authority, February 14, 1997. [WISH Papers, Properties, Archbishop Rivera y Damas Cooperative (1996–1997), Washingtoniana Division, Martin Luther King Jr. Memorial Library].

6. "Archbishop Rivera y Damas Co-op Development Plan Summary," n.d. [WISH Papers, Properties, Archbishop Rivera y Damas Cooperative (1991), Washingtoniana Division, Martin Luther King Jr. Memorial Library].

7. Robert Pohlman, Acting Director of the Department of Housing and Community Development, Washington, D.C., "Memorandum," March 29, 1988. [WISH Papers, Properties, Champlain Court Cooperative/Last Holdouts Tenants Association (1986–1994), Washingtoniana Division, Martin Luther King Jr. Memorial Library].

8. Claire Apartments Project Feasibility Report, n.d. [WISH Papers, Properties, East Side Manor Cooperative (n.d.), Washingtoniana Division, Martin Luther King Jr. Memorial Library].

9. Sources and Uses, 2nd St. S.E. Cooperative, October 7, 1991. [WISH Papers, Properties, East Side Manor Cooperative (1991), Washingtoniana Division, Martin Luther King Jr. Memorial Library].

10. Unfortunately, I was not been able to make contact with all the former members in order to verify this.

Conclusion

1. In 1978 the city finally used eminent domain to force the owner to sell the land to the city, preserving the park in perpetuity. In April of 1978, neighbors held a party in the park to celebrate their victory. Families sold homemade food to benefit the park; people gathered around a model of the park to discuss how they wanted to further make use of the space; and a neighborhood tenants association sponsored a game called "Help the People Knock the Speculators." "For 25 cents," a *Washington Post* reporter explained, "players got an opportunity to knock over a stack of beer cans that were labeled with the names of local real estate developers" (Gately 1978b). Ultimately, the park was renamed in honor of community activist Walter Pierce.

Bibliography

Agrawal, Arun. 2003. "Sustainable Governance of Common-Pool Resources: Context, Methods, and Politics." *Annual Review of Anthropology* 32:243–62.

Aligica, Paul Dragos. 2014. *Institutional Diversity and Political Economy: The Ostroms and Beyond*. New York: Oxford University Press.

Alonso, Clara Rivas. 2015. "Gezi Park: A Revindication of Public Space." In *Everywhere Taksim: Sowing the Seeds for a New Turkey at Gezi*, eds. Isabel David and Kumru Toktamis, 231–50. Amsterdam: Amsterdam University Press.

Armiero, Marco. 2011. "Enclosing the Sea: Remaking Work and Leisure Spaces on the Naples Waterfront, 1870–1900." *Radical History Review* 109:13–35.

Azozomox. 2014. "Squatting and Diversity: Gender and Patriarchy in Berlin, Madrid and Barcelona." In *The Squatters' Movement in Europe: Commons and Autonomy as Alternatives to Capitalism*, eds. Squatting Europe Kollective, Claudio Cattaneo, and Miguel A. Martinez, 189–210. London: Pluto Press.

Balmer, Ivo, and Tobias Bernet. 2015. "Housing as a Common Resource? Decommodification and Self-organization in Housing—Examples from Germany and Switzerland." In *Urban Commons: Moving Beyond State and Market*, eds. Mary Dellenbaugh, Markus Kip, Majken Bieniok, Agnes Katharina Müller, and Martin Schwegmann, 178–95. Basel: Birkhäuser.

Becker, S., R. Beveridge, and M. Naumann. 2015. "Reconfiguring Energy Provision in Berlin: Commoning between Compromise and Contestation." In *Urban Commons: Moving Beyond State and Market*, eds. Mary Dellenbaugh, Markus Kip, Majken Bieniok, Agnes Katharina Müller, and Martin Schwegmann, 196–213. Basel: Birkhäuser.

Bennholdt-Thomsen, Veronika, and Maria Mies. 1999. *The Subsistence Perspective: Beyond the Globalised Economy*. New York: Zed Books.

Besson, Jean. 2000. "The Appropriation of Lands of Law by Lands of Myth in the Caribbean Region." In *Land, Law and Environment: Mythical Land, Legal Boundaries*, eds. A. Abramson and D. Theodossopoulos, 116–35. London: Pluto Press.

Blomley, Nicholas. 2008. "Enclosure, Common Right and the Property of the Poor." *Social & Legal Studies* 17, no. 3: 311–31.

Bockman, Johanna. 2016. "Home Rule from Below: The Cooperative Movement in Washington, D.C." In *Capital Dilemma: Growth and Inequality in Washington, D.C.*, eds. Derek Hyra and Sabiyha Prince, 66–85. New York: Routledge.

Bollier, David. 2002. *Silent Theft: the Private Plunder of Our Common Wealth.* New York: Routledge.

Bookchin, Murray. 1974. *The Limits of the City.* New York: Harper Colophon Books.

Borchert, James. 1980. *Alley Life in Washington: Family, Community, Religion, and Folklife in the City, 1850–1970.* Chicago: University of Illinois Press.

Borkman, Thomasina Jo. 1999. *Understanding Self-Help/Mutual Aid: Experiential Learning in the Commons.* New Brunswick, N.J.: Rutgers University Press.

Bowman, LaBarbara. 1980. "Low-Income Tenants Buy Their Apartments." *The Washington Post.* November 9.

Bratt, Rachel G. 2002. "Housing and Family Well-Being." *Housing Studies* 17, no. 1: 13–26.

Bratt, Rachel G., Michael E. Stone, and Chester Hartman, eds. 2006. *A Right to Housing: Foundation for a New Social Agenda.* Philadelphia: Temple University Press.

Bravo, Giangiacomo, and Tine De Moor. 2008. "The Commons in Europe: From Past to Future." *International Journal of the Commons* 2, no. 2: 155–61.

Brenner, Neil, ed. 2014. *Implosions/Explosions: Towards a Study of Planetary Urbanism.* Berlin: Jovis.

Brenner, Neil, and Christian Schmid. 2011. Planetary Urbanisation. In *Urban Constellations,* ed. Matthew Gandy, 10–13. Berlin: Jovis.

Brewer, Jennifer F. 2012. "Don't Fence Me In: Boundaries, Policy, and Deliberation in Maine's Lobster Commons." *Annals of the Association of American Geographers* 102, no. 2: 383–402.

Bromley, Daniel W., ed. 1992. *Making the Commons Work: Theory, Practice, and Policy.* San Francisco: Institute for Contemporary Studies Press.

Bromley, Daniel W., and Jeffrey A. Cochrane. 1995. *A Bargaining Framework for the Global Commons.* Madison: University of Wisconsin Press.

Bruun, Maja Hojer. 2015. "Communities and the Commons: Open Access and Community Ownership of the Urban Commons." In *Urban Commons: Rethinking the City,* eds. Christian Borch and Martin Kornberger, 153–70. New York: Routledge.

Bureau of Labor Statistics. 2015. Occupational Employment and Wages, May 2014. 29–2052 Pharmacy Technicians. Retrieved from http://www.bls.gov/oes/current/oes292052.htm.

Caffentzis, George. 2004. "A Tale of Two Conferences: Globalization, the Crisis of Neoliberalism and the Question of the Commons." Paper presented at the Alter-Globalization Conference, San Miguel de Allende, Mexico, August 9.

———. 2010. "The Future of 'The Commons': Neoliberalism's 'Plan B' or the Original Disaccumulation of Capital?" *New Formations* 69:23–41.

Cameron, Jenny. 2015. "Enterprise Innovation and Economic Diversity in

Community-supported Agriculture: Sustaining the Agricultural Commons." In *Making Other Worlds Possible: Performing Diverse Economies*, eds. Gerda Roelvink, Kevin St. Martin, and J. K. Gibson-Graham, 53–71. Minneapolis: University of Minnesota Press.

Camp, Patricia. 1978. "New Housing Law Makes it Tougher on Conversions: Condominium Bill Now Awaits Mayor's Signing." *The Washington Post*. May 31.

Campbell, Caitlin. 2016. "Columbia City Council to Hear Land Trust Study Findings." *Columbia Daily Tribune*. July 17.

Castells, Manuel. 1983. *The City and the Grassroots*. Berkeley: University of California Press.

Cattaneo, Claudio, and Miguel A. Martinez. 2014. "Squatting as an Alternative to Capitalism: An Introduction." In *The Squatters' Movement in Europe: Commons and Autonomy as Alternatives to Capitalism*, eds. Squatting Europe Kollective, Claudio Cattaneo, and Miguel A. Martinez, 1–25. London: Pluto Press.

Chakrabarty, Dipesh. 2000. *Provincializing Europe: Postcolonial Thought and Historical Difference*. Princeton: Princeton University Press.

Chatterton, Paul. 2010. Introduction: Autonomy: The Struggle for Survival, Self-Management and the Common. *Antipode* 42, no. 44: 897–908.

Childe, V. Gordon. 1950. "The Urban Revolution." *Town Planning Review* 21, no. 1: 3–17.

Clapp, Tara Lynne, and Peter B. Meyer. 2000. "Managing the Urban Commons: Applying Common Property Frameworks to Urban Environmental Quality." Paper presented at Constituting the Commons, the Eighth Biennial Conference of the International Association for the Study of Common Property, Bloomington, Ind.

Clark, Heléne. 1994. "Taking up Space: Redefining Political Legitimacy in New York City." *Environment and Planning A* 26:937–55.

Clark, Heléne, and Susan Saegert. 1994. "Cooperatives as Places of Social Change." In *The Hidden History of Housing Cooperatives*, eds. Allan Heskin and Jacqueline Leavitt, 294–311. Davis: University of California Center for Cooperatives.

Clarke, David A. 1975. Statement of Councilmember David A. Clarke before Chairperson Marion Barry, Committee on Finance and Revenue, at Hearing on "Real Estate Transaction Tax of 1975." June 19. Washington, D.C.: Council of the District of Columbia.

Clay, Phillip L. 1979. *Neighborhood Renewal: Middle-class Resettlement and Incumbent Upgrading in American Neighborhoods*. Lexington, Mass.: Lexington Books.

CNHED. 2004. *A Study of Limited-Equity Cooperatives in the District of Columbia*. Washington, D.C.: Coalition for Nonprofit Housing and Economic Development.

Coase, Ronald. 1998. "The New Institutional Economics." *The American Economic Review* 88, no. 2: 72–74.

Community Economics. 1992. "Bob Swann: An Interview." *Community Economics* 25:3–5.

Compact Edition of the Oxford English Dictionary (Vol. II). 1971. Oxford: Oxford University Press.

Cronon, William. 2003. *Changes in the Land: Indians, Colonists, and the Ecology of New England.* New York: Hill and Wang.

Curl, John. 2009. *For All the People: Uncovering the Hidden History of Cooperation, Cooperative Movements, and Communalism in America.* Oakland, Calif.: PM Press.

D.C. Fiscal Policy Institute. 2011. *New Census Data Show that One in Five DC Residents Lived in Poverty in 2010.* Washington, D.C.: DCFPI.

———. 2016. *A City Breaking Apart: The Incomes of D.C.'s Poorest Residents are Falling, While Economic Growth is Benefiting Better-off Residents.* Washington, D.C.: DCFPI.

Davis, John Emmeus. 2006a. "Between Devolution and the Deep Blue Sea: What's a City or State to Do?" In *A Right to Housing: Foundation for a New Social Agenda,* eds. Rachel G. Bratt, Michael E. Stone, and Chester Hartman, 364–98. Philadelphia: Temple University Press.

———. 2006b. *Shared Equity Homeownership: The Changing Landscape of Resale-Restricted, Owner-Occupied Housing.* Montclair, N.J.: National Housing Institute.

———. 2010a. "Origins and Evolution of the Community Land Trust in the United States." In *The Community Land Trust Reader,* ed. John Emmeus Davis, 3–47. Cambridge, Mass.: Lincoln Land Institute.

———. (ed.). 1993. *The Affordable City: Toward a Third Sector Housing Policy.* Philadelphia: Temple University Press.

———. (ed.). 2010b. *The Community Land Trust Reader.* Cambridge, Mass.: The Lincoln Institute of Land Policy.

Davis, Mike. 1990. *City of Quartz: Excavating the Future in Los Angeles.* New York: Vintage Books.

———. 2006. *Planet of Slums.* New York: Verso.

De Angelis, Massimo. 2003. "Reflection on Alternatives, Commons and Communities." *The Commoner* 6:1–14.

———. 2010. "The Production of Commons and the 'Explosion' of the Middle Class." *Antipode* 42, no. 4: 954–77.

De Angelis, Massimo and David Harvie. 2014. "The Commons." In *The Routledge Companion to Alternative Organization,* eds. Martin Parker, George Cheney, Valerie Fournier, and Chris Land, 280–94. New York: Routledge.

DeBonis, Mike. 2014. "D.C. Housing Authority Says It Will Re-examine Waitlist, More Than a Year after Closing It." *The Washington Post.* May 15.

DeFilippis, James. 2001. "The Myth of Social Capital in Community Development." *Housing Policy Debate*, 12, no. 4: 781–806.

———. 2004. *Unmaking Goliath: Community Control in the Face of Global Capital.* New York: Routledge.

Derickson, Kate Driscoll. 2009. "Toward a Non-Totalizing Critique of Capitalism." *The Geographical Bulletin* 50:3–15.

———. 2015. "Urban Geography I: Locating Urban Theory in an 'Urban Age.'" *Progress in Human Geography* 39, no. 5: 647–57.

Desmond, Matthew. 2016. *Evicted: Poverty and Profit in the American City*. New York: Crown Publishers.

Dewey, John. 1916. *Democracy and Education: an Introduction to the Philosophy of Education*. Auckland: The Floating Press.

Diamond, Michael. 2009. "The Meaning and Nature of Property: Homeownership and Shared Equity in the Context of Poverty." *St. Louis University Public Law Review* 29:85–112.

Diner, Steven J. 1983. *The Regulation of Housing in the District of Columbia: An Historical Analysis of Policy Issues*. Washington, D.C.: Department of Urban Studies, University of the District of Columbia.

Eisen, Jack. 1978. "Agreement on Beecher Street." *The Washington Post*. April 6.

Eisen, Rick, Mark Looney, and Michael Williams. 1980. "Rent Control—Now More Than Ever." *The Washington Post*. January 26.

Eizenberg, Efrat. 2011. "Actually Existing Commons: Three Moments of Space of Community Gardens in New York City." *Antipode* 44, no. 3: 764–82.

Fauntroy, Michael K. 2003. *Home Rule or House Rule? Congress and the Erosion of Local Governance in the District of Columbia*. New York: University Press of America.

Federici, Silvia. 2004. *Caliban and the Witch: Women, the Body and Primitive Accumulation*. Brooklyn, N.Y.: Autonomedia.

———. 2011. "Women, Land Struggles, and the Reconstruction of the Commons." *WorkingUSA: The Journal of Labor and Society* 14, no. 1: 41–56.

———. 2012. "Feminism and the Politics of the Commons." In *The Wealth of the Commons: A World Beyond Market and State*, eds. David Bollier and Silke Helfrich, 45–54. Amherst, Mass.: Levellers Press.

Feeny, David, Fikret Berkes, Bonnie J. McCay, and James M. Acheson. 1990. "The Tragedy of the Commons: Twenty-two Years Later." *Human Ecology* 18, no. 1: 1–19.

Fine, Ben. 2010. "Beyond the Tragedy of the Commons: A Discussion of *Governing the Commons: The Evolution of Institutions for Collective Action.*" *Perspectives on Politics* 8, no. 2: 583–86.

Foster, Sheila. 2011. "Collective Action and the Urban Commons." *Notre Dame Law Review* 87: 1–63.

Fullilove, Mindy Thompson. 2004. *Root Shock: How Tearing up City Neighborhoods Hurts America, and What We Can Do About It.* New York: One World/Ballantine Books.

Gale, Dennis E. 1976. *The Back-to-the-City Movement—Or Is It? A Survey of Recent Homebuyers in the Mount Pleasant Neighborhood of Washington, D.C.* Washington, D.C.: Department of Urban and Regional Planning, George Washington University.

———. 1977. *The Back-to-the-City Movement Revisited : A Survey of Recent Homebuyers in the Capitol Hill Neighborhood of Washington, D.C.* Washington, D.C.: Department of Urban and Regional Planning, George Washington University.

Gallaher, Carolyn. 2016. *The Politics of Staying Put: Condo Conversion and Tenant Right-to-Buy in Washington, D.C.* Philadelphia: Temple University Press.

Gans, Herbert J. 1962. *The Urban Villagers: Group and Class in the Life of Italian-Americans.* New York: Free Press.

Gately, Blair. 1978a. "The 14-Year Battle for a Park in Adams Morgan." *The Washington Post.* March 23.

———. 1978b. "Cleaning, Celebrating Community Park West." *The Washington Post.* April 27.

———. 1978c. "Tenant Rebellion Fueled by Increases in Rent, Evictions." *The Washington Post.* December 21.

Ghate, Rucha, Narpat S. Jodha, and Pranab Mukhopadhyay, eds. 2008. *Promise, Trust, and Evolution: Managing the Commons of South Asia.* New York: Oxford University Press.

Gibson, Clark C., Margaret A. McKean, and Elinor Ostrom, eds. 2000. *People and Forests: Communities, Institutions, Governance.* Cambridge, Mass.: The MIT Press.

Gibson-Graham, J. K. 1996. *The End of Capitalism (as we knew it): A Feminist Critique of Political Economy.* Cambridge, Mass.: Blackwell.

———. 2006. *A Postcapitalist Politics.* Minneapolis: University of Minnesota Press.

———. 2008. "Diverse Economies: Performative Practices for 'Other Worlds.'" *Progress in Human Geography* 32, no. 5: 613–32.

Gidwani, Vinay, and Amita Baviskar. 2011. "Urban Commons." *Economic and Political Weekly* 156, no. 50: 42–43.

Gillis, Justin, and Bill Miller. 1997. "In D.C.'s Simple City, Complex Rules of Life and Death: a Bloodstained Community Reels from Crews' Violence." *The Washington Post.* April 20.

Goldman, Michael. 1997. "'Customs in Common': The Epistemic World of the Commons Scholars." *Theory and Society* 26:1–37.

Goldstein, Jesse. 2013. "Terra Economica: Waste and the Production of Enclosed Nature." *Antipode* 45, no. 2: 357–75.

Graeber, David. 2011. *Debt: The First 5000 Years.* Brooklyn: Melville House.

Green, Constance McLaughlin. 1967. *The Secret City: A History of Race Relations in the Nation's Capital*. Princeton: Princeton University Press.

Hackworth, Jason. 2007. *The Neoliberal City: Governance, Ideology, and Development in American Urbanism*. Ithaca, N.Y.: Cornell University Press.

Han, Didi K., and Hajime Imamasa. 2015. "Overcoming Privatized Housing in South Korea: Looking through the Lens of 'Commons' and 'the Common.'" In *Urban Commons: Moving Beyond State and Market*, eds. Mary Dellenbaugh, Markus Kip, Majken Bieniok, Agnes Katharina Müller, and Martin Schwegmann, 91–100. Basel: Birkhäuser.

Hansen, Karen V. 2005. *Not-so-nuclear Families: Class, Gender, and Networks of Care*. New Brunswick: Rutgers University Press.

Hardin, Garrett. 1968. "The Tragedy of the Commons." *Science* 162:1243–48.

Hardt, Michael. 2007. *Thomas Jefferson: The Declaration of Independence*. New York: Verso.

Hardt, Michael, and Antonio Negri. 2009. *Commonwealth*. Cambridge, Mass.: Harvard University Press.

Harney, Stefano, and Fred Moten. 2013. *The Undercommons: Fugitive Planning and Black Study*. New York: Minor Compositions.

Harrison Institute for Public Law. 2006. *An Analysis of the Strengths and Deficiencies of Washington, D.C.'s Tenant Opportunity to Purchase Act*. Washington, D.C.: Georgetown University Law Center.

Hartman, Chester, Dennis Keating, Richard LeGates, and Steve Turner. 1982. *Displacement: How to Fight It*. Berkeley: National Housing Law Project.

Harvey, David. 1973. *Social Justice and the City*. Baltimore: Johns Hopkins University Press.

———. 2003. *The New Imperialism*. Oxford: Oxford University Press.

———. 2008. "The Right to the City." *New Left Review* 53:23–40.

———. 2011. "The Future of the Commons." *Radical History Review* 109: 101–107.

———. 2012. *Rebel Cities: From the Right to the City to the Urban Revolution*. New York: Verso.

———. 2014. *Seventeen Contradictions and the End of Capitalism*. New York: Oxford University Press.

Haveman, R., B. Wolfe, and J. Spaulding. 1991. "Children's Events and Circumstances Influencing High School Completion." *Demography* 28, no. 1: 133–57.

Healy, Stephen. 2015. "Biofuels, Ex-felons, and Empower, a Worker-owned Cooperative: Performing Enterprises Differently." In *Making Other Worlds Possible Performing Diverse Economies*, eds. Gerda Roelvink, Kevin St. Martin, and J. K. Gibson-Graham, 98–126. Minneapolis: University of Minnesota Press.

Henig, Jeffrey R. 1982. *Gentrification in Adams Morgan: Political and Commercial Consequences of Neighborhood Change*. Washington, D.C.: Center for Washington Area Studies, George Washington University.

———. 1984. "Gentrification and Displacement of the Elderly: An Empirical Analysis." In *Gentrification, Displacement, and Neighborhood Revitalization*, eds. John J. Palen and Bruce London, 170–184. Albany: State University of New York Press.

Heskin, Allan D. 1991. *The Struggle for Community*. San Francisco: Westview Press.

Hess, Charlotte. 2000. "Is There Anything New Under the Sun?: A Discussion and Survey of Studies on New Commons and the Internet." Paper presented at Constituting the Commons, the Eighth Biennial Conference of the International Association for the Study of Common Property, Bloomington, Ind.

Hess, Charlotte, and Elinor Ostrom. 2007a. "Introduction: An Overview of the Knowledge Commons." In *Understanding Knowledge as a Commons: From Theory to Practice*, eds. Charlotte Hess and Elinor Ostrom, 3–26. Cambridge, Mass.: The MIT Press.

———. 2007b. *Understanding Knowledge as a Commons*. Cambridge, Mass.: The MIT Press.

Hopkinson, Natalie. 2012. *Go-Go Live: The Musical Life and Death of a Chocolate City*. Durham, N.C.: Duke University Press.

Howard, Ebenezer. 1965 [1898]. *Garden Cities of To-Morrow*. Cambridge, Mass.: The MIT Press.

Huron, Amanda. 2002. *Gentrification and Individualization: The Case of Fehrbelliner Strasse 6*. (Master of City and Regional Planning Thesis), University of North Carolina, Chapel Hill.

———. 2014. "Creating a Commons in the Capital: The Emergence of Limited-Equity Housing Cooperatives in Washington, D.C." *Washington History* 26, no. 2: 56–67.

———. 2015. "Working with Strangers in Saturated Space: Reclaiming and Maintaining the Urban Commons." *Antipode* 46, no. 4: 963–79.

———. 2016. "Struggling for Housing, from D.C. to Johannesburg: Washington Innercity Self Help Goes to South Africa." In *Capital Dilemma: Growth and Inequality in Washington, D.C.*, eds. Derek Hyra and Sabiyha Prince, 86–106. New York: Routledge.

Institute for Community Economics. 1982. *The Community Land Trust Handbook*. Emmaus, Pa: Rodale Press.

Jacobs, Jane. 1961. *The Death and Life of Great American Cities*. New York: Vintage Books.

Jaffe, Harry S., and Tom Sherwood. 1994. *Dream City: Race, Power, and the Decline of Washington, D.C.* New York: Simon & Schuster.

Jerram, Leif. 2015. "The False Promise of the Commons: Historical Fantasies, Sexuality and the 'Really-Existing' Urban Common of Modernity." In *Urban Commons: Rethinking the City*, eds. Christian Borch and Martin Kornberger, 47–67. New York: Routledge.

Kassa, Derese Getachew. 2008. "Tragedy of the 'Urban Commons'? A Case Study of Two Public Places in Addis Ababa." Paper presented at the Governing Shared Resources: Connecting Local Experience to Global Challenges, the Twelfth Biennial Conference of the International Association for the Study of Commons, Cheltenham, England.

Katz, Stephen, and Margit Mayer. 1985. "Gimme Shelter: Self-Help Housing Struggles Within and Against the State in New York City and West Berlin." *International Journal of Urban and Regional Research* 9, no. 1: 15–46.

King, Rebekah, and Ethan Handelman. 2016. "Technical Appendix to 'The Cost of Affordable Housing: Does it Pencil Out?'" Washington, D.C.: Urban Insitute and National Housing Conference.

Kip, Markus. 2015. "Moving Beyond the City: Conceptualizing Urban Commons from a Critical Urban Studies Perspective." In *Urban Commons: Moving Beyond State and Market*, eds. Mary Dellenbaugh, Markus Kip, Majken Bieniok, Agnes Katharina Müller, and Martin Schwegmann, 42–59. Basel: Birkhäuser.

Kip, Markus, Majken Bieniok, Mary Dellenbaugh, Agnes Katharina Müller, and Martin Schwegmann. 2015. "Seizing the (Every) Day: Welcome to the Urban Commons!" In *Urban Commons: Moving Beyond State and Market*, eds. Mary Dellenbaugh, Markus Kip, Majken Bieniok, Agnes Katharina Müller, and Martin Schwegmann, 9–25. Basel: Birkhäuser.

Klein, Hilary. 2015. *Compañeras: Zapatista Women's Stories*. New York: Seven Stories Press.

Klein, Naomi. 2001. "Reclaiming the Commons." *New Left Review*, 9 (May–June): 81–89.

Kolodny, Robert, and Marjorie Gellerman. 1973. *Self Help in the Inner City: A Study of Lower Income Cooperative Housing Conversion in New York City*. New York: United Neighborhood Houses of New York, Inc.

Kornberger, Martin, and Christian Borch. 2015. "Introduction: Urban Commons." In *Urban Commons: Rethinking the City*, eds. Christian Borch and Martin Kornberger, 1–21. New York: Routledge.

Kratzwald, Brigitte. 2015. "Urban Commons—Dissident Practices in Emancipatory Spaces." In *Urban Commons: Moving Beyond State and Market*, eds. Mary Dellenbaugh, Markus Kip, Majken Bieniok, Agnes Katharina Müller, and Martin Schwegmann, 26–41. Basel: Birkhäuser.

Leavitt, Jacqueline, and Susan Saegert. 1988. "The Community-household: Responding to Housing Abandonment in New York City." *Journal of the American Planning Association* 54, no. 4: 489–500.

———. 1990. *From Abandonment to Hope: Community-Households in Harlem*. New York: Columbia University Press.

Lee, Shin, and Chris Webster. 2006. "Enclosure of the Urban Commons." *GeoJournal* (66):27–42.

Lefebvre, Henri. 2003 [1970]. *The Urban Revolution*. Minneapolis: University of Minnesota Press.

Lesko, Kathleen M., Valerie Babb, and Carroll R. Gibbs. 1991. *Black Georgetown Remembered: A History of Its Black Community From the Founding of "The Town of George" in 1751 to the Present Day*. Washington, D.C.: Georgetown University Press.

Linebaugh, Peter. 2008. *The Magna Carta Manifesto: Liberties and Commons for All*. Berkeley: University of California Press.

———. 2014. *Stop, Thief! The Commons, Enclosures, and Resistance*. Oakland, Calif.: PM Press.

Linebaugh, Peter, and Marcus Rediker. 2013. *The Many-Headed Hydra: Sailors, Slaves, Commoners, and the Hidden History of the Revolutionary Atlantic*. Boston: Beacon Press.

Linn, Karl. 1999. "Rebuilding the Sacred Commons." *New Village* 1, no. 1: 42–49.

———. 2007. *Building Commons and Community*. Oakland, Calif.: New Village Press.

Low, Setha. 2003. *Behind the Gates: Life, Security and the Pursuit of Happiness in Fortress America*. New York: Routledge.

Lutz, Manuel. 2015. "Uncommon Claims to the Commons: Homeless Tent Cities in the U.S." In *Urban Commons: Moving Beyond State and Market*, eds. Mary Dellenbaugh, Markus Kip, Majken Bieniok, Agnes Katharina Müller, and Martin Schwegmann, 101–16. Basel: Birkhäuser.

Maddison, Ben. 2010. "Radical Commons Discourse and the Challenges of Colonialism." *Radical History Review* (108):29–48.

Mandizadza, Shingirai. 2008. "Social Movements as Agencies for Collective Action: Redefining Urban Commons in South Africa." Paper presented at the Governing Shared Resources: Connecting Local Experience to Global Challenges, the Twelfth Biennial Conference of the International Association for the Study of Commons, Cheltenham, England.

Mansfield, Stephanie. 1977. "Protest at the Ontario." *The Washington Post*. February 4.

Marx, Karl. 1973. *Capital, Vol. 1*. London: Penguin Books.

Masur, Kate. 2010. *An Example for All the Land: Emancipation and the Struggle Over Equality in Washington, D.C.* Chapel Hill, N.C.: University of North Carolina Press.

Mattingly, Justin. 2016. "Richmond Could Turn to Land Trust to Help Create Affordable Housing." *Richmond Times-Dispatch*. July 24.

McCay, Bonnie J. 2012. "Enclosing the Fishery Commons: From Individuals to Communities." In *Property in Land and Other Resources*, eds. Daniel H. Cole and Elinor Ostrom, 219–251. Cambridge, Mass.: Lincoln Institute of Land Policy.

McCay, Bonnie J., and James M. Acheson. 1987. "Human Ecology of the Commons." In *The Question of the Commons: The Culture and Ecology of Communal Resources*, eds. Bonnie J. McCay and James M. Acheson, 1–34. Tucson: University of Arizona Press.

McCay, Bonnie J., and Svein Jentoft. 1998. "Market or Community Failure? Critical Perspectives on Common Property Research." *Human Organization* 57, no. 1: 21–29.

McCoy, Terrence. 2016. "As the Nation's Capital Booms, Poor Tenants Face Eviction Over as Little as $25." *The Washington Post*. August 8.

McShane, Ian. 2010. "Trojan Horse or Adaptive Institutions? Some Reflections on Urban Commons in Australia." *Urban Policy and Research* 28, no. 1: 101–16.

Menzies, Heather. 2014. *Reclaiming the Commons for the Common Good*. Gabriola Island, B.C.: New Society Publishers.

Merrifield, Andy. 2014. *The New Urban Question*. London: Pluto Press.

Mies, Maria, and Veronika Bennholdt-Thomsen. 2001. "Defending, Reclaiming and Reinventing the Commons." *Canadian Journal of Development Studies* 22:997–1023.

Milloy, Courtland. 2014. "Initiative to Revitalize Barry Farm is Little More than an Urban Dispersal Plan." *The Washington Post*. October 28.

Mitchell, Don. 2003. *The Right to the City: Social Justice and the Fight for Public Space*. New York: The Guilford Press.

Mitchell, Timothy. 2008. "Rethinking Economy." *Geoforum* 39:1116–21.

Morçöl, Göktuğ, Lorlene Hoyt, Jack W. Meek, and Ulf Zimmerman,. eds. 2008. *Business Improvement Districts: Research, Theories, and Controversies*. New York: CRC Press.

National Low Income Housing Coalition. 2010. *Out of Reach 2010*. Washington, D.C.: NLIHC.

National Low Income Housing Coalition. 2014. *Out of Reach 2014*. Washington, D.C.: NLIHC.

National Research Council (ed.). 1986. *Proceedings of the Conference on Common Property Management*. Washington, D.C.: National Academy Press.

Neeson, J. M. 1993. *Commoners: Common Right, Enclosure and Social Change in England, 1700–1820*. Cambridge: Cambridge University Press.

Nelson, Robert H. 2005. *Private Neighborhoods and the Transformation of Local Government*. Washington, D.C.: Urban Institute Press.

Nembhard, Jessica Gordon. 2014. *Collective Courage: A History of African American Cooperative Economic Thought and Practice*. University Park, Pa.: The Pennsylvania State University Press.

Neuwirth, Robert. 2005. *Shadow Cities: A Billion Squatters, a New Urban World*. New York: Routledge.

Nonini, Donald M. 2007. "Reflections on the Intellectual Commons." In *The Global Idea of 'The Commons,'* ed. Donald M. Nonini, 66–88. New York: Berghahn Books.

North, Douglass C. 1992. "Institutions and Economic Theory." *American Economist* 36, no. 1: 3–6.

Noterman, Elsa. 2015. "Beyond Tragedy: Differential Commoning in a Manufactured Housing Cooperative." *Antipode* 48, no. 2: 433–52.

O'Toole, Aaron, and Jones, Benita. 2009. "Tenant Purchase Laws as a Tool for Affordable Housing Preservation: The D.C. Experience." *Journal of Affordable Housing and Community Development* 18, no. 4: 367–88.

Ong, Aihwa. 2011. "Introduction: The Art of Being Global." In *Worlding Cities: Asian Experiments and the Art of Being Global*, eds. Ananya Roy and Aihwa Ong, 1–26. Malden, Mass.: Wiley-Blackwell.

Organisation for Economic Co-operation and Development. 2012. *Redefining 'Urban': A New Way to Measure Metropolitan Areas*. Paris: OECD Publishing.

Ostrom, Elinor. 1990. *Governing the Commons: The Evolution of Institutions for Collective Action*. New York: Cambridge University Press.

———. 2005. *Understanding Institutional Diversity*. Princeton: Princeton University Press.

———. 2012. *The Future of the Commons: Beyond Market Failure and Government Regulation*. London: The Institute of Economic Affairs.

Paavola, Jouni. 2012. "Climate Change: the Ultimate Tragedy of the Commons?" In *Property in Land and Other Resources*, eds. Daniel H. Cole and Elinor Ostrom, 417–33. Cambridge, Mass.: Lincoln Institute of Land Policy.

Paige, Jerome S., and Margaret M. Reuss. 1983. *Safe, Decent and Affordable: Citizen Struggles to Improve Housing in the District of Columbia, 1890–1982*. Washington, D.C.: University of the District of Columbia.

Pavlovskaya, Marianna. 2004. "Other Transitions: Multiple Economies of Moscow Households in the 1990s." *Annals of the Association of American Geographers* 94, no. 2: 329–51.

Peake, Linda. 2016. "On Feminism and Feminist Allies in Knowledge Production in Urban Geography." *Urban Geography* 37, no. 6: 830–38.

Peake, Linda, and Rieker, Martina. 2013. "Rethinking Feminist Interventions into the Urban." In *Rethinking Feminist Interventions into the Urban*, eds. Linda Peake and Martina Rieker, 1–22. New York: Routledge.

Pennington, Mark. 2012. "Elinor Ostrom, Common-Pool Resources and the Classical Liberal Tradition." In *The Future of the Commons: Beyond Market Failure and Government Regulation*, Elinor Ostrom with contributing authors Christina Chang, Mark Pennington, and Vlad Tarko, 21–47. London: The Institute of Economic Affairs.

Pleyers, Geoffrey. 2010. *Alter-Globalization: Becoming Actors in a Global Age.* Malden, Mass.: Polity Press.

Poteete, Amy R., Marco A. Janssen, and Elinor Ostrom, eds. 2010. *Working Together: Collective Action, the Commons, and Multiples Methods in Practice.* Princeton: Princeton University Press.

Reed, David. 1981. *Education for Building a People's Movement.* Boston: South End Press.

Reinhold, Robert. 1977. "Middle-class Return Displaces Some Urban Poor." *The New York Times.* June 4.

Ricoveri, Giovanna. 2013. *Nature for Sale: The Commons Versus Commodities.* London: Pluto Press.

Rohe, William, and Michael Stegman. 1995. "Converting Public Housing to Cooperatives: Lessons from Nashville." In *The Hidden History of Housing Cooperatives*, eds. Allan Heskin and Jacqueline Leavitt, 105–21. Davis, Calif.: University of California Center for Cooperatives.

Rose, Carol M. 1994. *Property and Persuasion.* San Francisco: Westview Press.

Roy, Ananya. 2016. "What is Urban about Critical Urban Theory?" *Urban Geography* 37, no. 6: 810–23.

Roy, Ananya, and Aihwa Ong, eds. 2011. *Worlding Cities: Asian Experiments and the Art of Being Global.* Malden, Mass.: Wiley-Blackwell.

Ruttan, Lore M. 2006. "Sociocultural Heterogeneity and the Commons." *Current Anthropology* 47, no. 5: 843–53.

Saegert, Susan. 1989. "Unlikely Leaders, Extreme Circumstances: Older Black Women Building Community Households." *American Journal of Community Psychology* 17, no. 3: 295–316.

Saegert, Susan, and Lymari Benitez. 2005. "Limited Equity Housing Cooperatives: Defining a Niche in the Low Income Housing Market." *Journal of Planning Literature* 19, no. 4: 427–39.

Saegert, Susan, Lymari Benitez, Efrat Eizenberg, Melissa Extein, Tsai-shiou Hsieh, and Chung Chang. 2005. "The Promises and Challenges of Co-ops in a Hot Real Estate Market." *Shelterforce* 142.

Saegert, Susan, and Gary Winkel. 1996. "Paths to Community Empowerment: Organizing at Home." *American Journal of Community Psychology,* 24, no. 4: 517–50.

———. 1998. "Social Capital and the Revitalization of New York City's Distressed Inner-city Housing." *Housing Policy Debate* 9, no. 1: 17–60.

Sazama, Gerald. 2000. "Lessons from the History of Affordable Housing Cooperatives in the United States: A Case Study in American Affordable Housing Policy." *American Journal of Economics and Sociology* 59, no. 4: 573–608.

Scharper, Stephen B., and Hilary Cunningham. 2007. "The Genetic Commons:

Resisting the Neo-liberal Enclosure of Life." In *The Global Idea of 'The Commons,'* ed. Donald M. Nonini, 53–65. New York: Berghahn Books.

Schmelzkopf, Karen. 1995. "Urban Community Gardens as Contested Space." *Geographical Review* 85, no. 3: 364–81.

Scott, James C. 1998. *Seeing Like a State: How Certain Schemes to Improve the Human Condition Have Failed.* New Haven: Yale University Press.

Sennett, Richard. 1970. *The Uses of Disorder: Personal Identity and City Life.* New York: Knopf.

Sheppard, Eric, Helga Leitner, and Anant Maringanti. 2013. "Provincializing Global Urbanism: A Manifesto." *Urban Geography* 34, no. 7: 893–900.

Shinew, Kimberly J., Troy D. Glover, and Diana C. Parry. 2004. "Leisure Spaces as Potential Sites for Interracial Interaction: Community Gardens in Urban Areas." *Journal of Leisure Research,* 36, no. 3: 336–55.

Shiva, Vandana. 2013. "Foreword." In *Nature for Sale: The Commons Versus Commodities,* Giovanna Ricoveri, vii-xii. London: Pluto Press.

Simmel, Georg. 1950 [1903]. "The Metropolis and Mental Life." In *The Sociology of Georg Simmel,* ed. Kurt H. Wolff, 409–24. New York: Free Press.

Simmons, Melody. 2016. "Thousands Sign Petition to Establish an Affordable Housing Trust Fund in Baltimore." *Baltimore Business Journal.* August 12.

Smith, Sam. 1974. *Captive Capital: Colonial Life in Modern Washington.* Bloomington: Indiana University Press.

Solnit, Rebecca. 2009. *A Paradise Built in Hell: The Extraordinary Communities that Arise in Disaster.* New York: Penguin Books.

Squatting Europe Kollective, Claudio Cattaneo, and Miguel A. Martinez, eds. 2014. *The Squatters' Movement in Europe: Commons and Autonomy as Alternatives to Capitalism.* London: Pluto Press.

St. Martin, Kevin. 2009. "Toward a Cartography of the Commons: Constituting the Political and Economic Possibilities of Place." *The Professional Geographer* 61, no. 4: 493–507.

St. Martin, Kevin, Gerda Roelvink, and J. K. Gibson-Graham. 2015. "An Economic Politics for Our Times." In *Making Other Worlds Possible: Performing Diverse Economies,* eds. Gerda Roelvink, Kevin St. Martin, and J. K. Gibson-Graham, 1–25. Minneapolis: University of Minnesota Press.

Starhawk. 2004. "Reclaim the Commons." Retrieved from http://www.starhawk .org/activism/activism-writings/reclaim_commons.html

Stavrides, Stavros. 2016. *Common Space: The City as Commons.* London: Zed Books.

Sundaresan, Jayaraj. 2011. "Planning as Commoning: Transformation of a Bangalore Lake." *Economic and Political Weekly* 156, no. 50: 13–24.

The National Housing Task Force. 1988. *A Decent Place to Live.* Washington, D.C.: National Housing Task Force.

Thompson, A. K. 2015. "The Battle for Necropolis: Reclaiming the Past as Commons in the City of the Dead." In *Urban Commons: Moving Beyond State and Market*, eds. Mary Dellenbaugh, Markus Kip, Majken Bieniok, Agnes Katharina Müller, and Martin Schwegmann, 214–35. Basel: Birkhäuser.

Thompson, E. P. 1963. *The Making of the English Working Class*. New York: Pantheon Books.

Thompson, Vernon C. 1980. "Poor Tenants Learn How to Use MUSCLE to Become Homeowners." *The Washington Post*. April 30.

Turner, Margery Austin. 1998. "Moderating Market Pressures for Washington, D.C. Rental Housing." In *Rent Control: Regulation and the Rental Housing Market*, eds. W. Dennis Keating, Michael B. Teitz, and Andrejs Skaburskis, 110–24. New Brunswick, N.J.: Center for Urban and Policy Research.

U.S. Census Bureau. 2010. State & County QuickFacts: District of Columbia.

U.S. Department of Housing and Urban Development. 1974. *Housing in the Seventies: A Report of the National Housing Policy Review*. Washington, D.C.: U.S. Department of Housing and Urban Development.

U.S. Department of Housing and Urban Development. 2007. *Fair Market Rents for the Section 8 Housing Assistance Payments Program*. Washington, D.C.: U.S. Department of Housing and Urban Development.

Uchitelle, Louis. 2009. "Two Americans are Awarded Nobel in Economics." *The New York Times*. October 13.

United Nations. 2014. *Demographic Yearbook*. New York: United Nations.

United Nations Population Fund. 2007. *State of the World Population 2007: Unleashing the Potential of Urban Growth*. New York: United Nations.

Wachsmuth, David. 2014. "City as Ideology: Reconciling the Explosion of the City Form with the Tenacity of the City Concept." *Environment and Planning D* 31:75–90.

Wall, Derek. 2014a. *The Commons in History: Culture, Conflict, and Ecology*. Cambridge, Mass.: The MIT Press.

———. 2014b. *The Sustainable Economics of Elinor Ostrom: Commons, Contestation and Craft*. New York: Routledge.

Ward, Colin. 1982. *Anarchy in Action*, 2nd ed. London: Freedom Press.

Washington Afro-American. 1986. "City Officials, Candidates to Tour Chapin St. Apartments." September 2.

Washington Post. 1975. "Rental Unit Conversion Law Backed." October 9.

Washington Post. 1978. "At-Large Council Race has Bids from 11 Candidates." September 7.

Wells, Katie J. 2015. "A Housing Crisis, a Failed Law, and a Property Conflict: The U.S. Urban Speculation Tax." *Antipode* 47, no. 4: 1043–61.

Werner, Karen. 2015. "Performing Economies of Care in a New England Time

Bank and Buddhist Community." In *Making Other Worlds Possible: Performing Diverse Economies*, eds. Gerda Roelvink, Kevin St. Martin, and J. K. Gibson-Graham, 72–97. Minneapolis: University of Minnesota Press.

Wilbert, Chris, and Damian F. White, eds. 2011. *Autonomy Solidarity Possibility: The Colin Ward Reader*. Oakland, Calif.: AK Press.

Wilkerson, Isabel. 2010. *The Warmth of Other Suns: The Epic Story of America's Great Migration*. New York: Vintage Books.

Williams, Juan. 1980. "Goodbye to the Chocolate City Dream." *The Washington Post*. April 26.

Williams, Raymond. 1983. *Keywords: A Vocabulary of Culture and Society*. New York: Oxford University Press.

Williamson, Oliver E. 1998. "The Institutions of Governance." *The American Economic Review* 88, no. 2: 75–79.

Wilson, Elizabeth. 1991. *The Sphinx in the City: Urban Life, the Control of Disorder, and Women*. Berkeley: University of California Press.

Wirth, Louis. 1938. "Urbanism as a Way of Life." *American Journal of Sociology* 44, no. 1: 1–24.

Zeitz, Eileen. 1979. *Private Urban Renewal: A Different Residential Trend*. Lexington, Mass.: Lexington Books.

Zippel, Claire. 2016. *D.C.'s Public Housing: An Important Resource at Risk*. Washington, D.C.: D.C. Fiscal Policy Institute.

Zukin, Sharon. 1982. *Loft Living: Culture and Capital in Urban Change*. Baltimore: Johns Hopkins University Press.

Index

activism. *See* social justice activism

Adams Morgan neighborhood, 2, 73–74, 82–83, 96–97, 113, 127, 131–33, 162

affordable housing: commons as, 3, 9, 18, 93–99, 138–39, 156–57, 164–66; need for, 55, 56, 91–92, 93, 119, 126–27, 131, 132, 139, 156, 164

Afro-American (newspaper), 160

alterglobalizationist approach, 4–5, 13, 20, 27–29, 51, 71, 138; application of, 32–33; on commoning, 172–73; on enclosure, 29–32; gaps in, 33–34; feminist perspective, 31, 140; and institutionalist approach, 20, 34–36, 40–41, 171; on reclaiming commons, 29, 30, 40; on state, 170; theorizing commons, 53–54, 138; use of term, 27

anticapitalist commons, 33–34, 36

antidisplacement legislation, 163, 164

anti-globalization, 27

Armiero, Marco, 34

Aspen Cooperative (pseud.), 15, 75, 83–84, 96, 106, 118, 121, 133, 142, 153, 156, 159

Australia, urban commons in, 59

Baker, Ella Jo, 77

Balmer, Ivo, 8

Barry, Marion, 75, 82, 161–62

Baviskar, Amita, 53

Bennholdt-Thomsen, Veronika, 31, 35, 123, 140, 142

Benning Terrace public housing project, 17

Berlin, 27, 52, 59–60, 173–74

Bernet, Tobias, 8

Besson, Jean, 79

Bilbo, Theodore, 72

Bin-Zib housing, 56, 144, 158–59

blackness. *See* race

Blomley, Nicholas, 69, 70–71

Borch, Christian, 51–52, 54

Borchert, James, 45, 79

Borkman, Thomasina Jo, 152

Boston, 1–2, 45, 73

Bowman, LaBarbara, 77–78

Brenner, Neil, 48, 61–62, 176

Brewer, Jennifer F., 24

Brightwood neighborhood, 81

Bruun, Maja Hojer, 3, 55–56, 59, 158

Caffentzis, George, 27, 29, 35–36, 60

Canada, urbanism in, 46

capital accumulation, 6, 43, 47–49, 57–58, 63, 85–86

capitalism: and commons, 13, 18, 26–27, 33, 40–41, 43, 53, 56–59, 91, 93, 115, 121, 137, 156, 160, 163; conditions for, 57; and social change, 166–67

capitalocentrism, 36–37

Capitol Hill neighborhood, 73

Cattaneo, Claudio, 32, 155–56

Chakrabarty, Dipesh, 61

Charter of the Forest, 76

Childe, V. Gordon, 45, 47, 49

AMANDA HURON is assistant professor of interdisciplinary social sciences at the University of the District of Columbia.

Printed and bound by CPI Group (UK) Ltd, Croydon, CR0 4YY

13/04/2025